Fukuzawa Yukichi on Education

Fukuzawa Yukichi on Education

Selected Works

Translated and edited by
Eiichi Kiyooka

Introduction by
Kazuyoshi Nakayama

UNIVERSITY OF TOKYO PRESS

LB
775
.F8
1985

Publication of this volume was assisted by a grant from The Japan Foundation. The translation was supported by a grant-in-aid from the Ministry of Education, Science and Culture, Japan.

Contents

[v]

CONTENTS

Introduction

When Japan renewed its contact with the West in the mid-nineteenth century, Fukuzawa Yukichi (1835–1901) served his country as one of its most outstanding evaluators and interpreters of Western civilization. The range of his interests extended from Western philosophy to new techniques, such as bookkeeping and public speaking. And he became an effective writer and teacher in propagating the new knowledge. Besides being a successful and widely read writer of books, he founded a school, Keiō Gijuku, which grew into the present Keiō University; he also started a newspaper, *Jijishimpō*, to reach an even wider circle of people. At the root of all these activities was his strong belief in freedom and independence, concepts which were inherent in his character and reinforced by the ideas he discovered in Western philosophy.

Freedom and Independence

In his youth, Fukuzawa yearned to break away from the restraining society of his native Nakatsu in Kyūshū. Not that Nakatsu was any worse than other towns in the country; the restrictions of feudal society were such that Fukuzawa, the son of a low-ranking official, was obliged to act humbly before sons of higher-ranking families even in play. In the same way, every movement of his family and of society was regulated. His father, Hyakusuke, had been ordered to do work that he disliked but performed his duties without complaint until his premature death. His brother, Sannosuke, succeeded to the same position which he, too, accepted without complaint and died even younger. When Fukuzawa declared that "the feudal system is my father's mortal enemy," he was speaking from bitter personal experience.

Fukuzawa Yukichi was fortunate to be the second son in the family, for in a patriarchal feudal society, it was the first son who succeeded as househead and inherited the duties which went with it; the rest of the family, the mother and other siblings, were left untrammeled as mere dependents. Yukichi, therefore, was free to leave home and go to Nagasaki, then to Osaka to learn Dutch.

In 1855, when Fukuzawa entered Ogata Kōan's school in Osaka, he found himself in a new world, and for the first time he felt himself liberated. Within the school premises, family lineage, wealth, and social rank did not count. Only a student's ability and scholarship determined his position and reputation. Though it was situated in the thriving commercial city of Osaka, the school formed a world apart, a little utopia for young Fukuzawa and his fellow students.

In 1858, Fukuzawa was ordered by his clan to go to Edo (the present Tokyo) to teach Dutch to the retainers in its Edo office. This was the beginning of Fukuzawa's career in education, and the very small school he started in his home later grew into Keiō Gijuku and finally Keiō University. A few years later, Fukuzawa was to go abroad, twice to the United States (1860 and 1867) and once to Europe (1862). His personal contact with many intellectuals of the West and the knowledge he gained from reading the many books which he obtained in England, Holland, and the United States supplied him with a philosophical basis for his ideal of freedom, which had so far been a youthful longing. Thus Fukuzawa gained confidence in his own convictions, and he was an ardent admirer of the new civilization. His books proved immensely popular and made him financially independent. He was now liberated from the shackles of feudalism also because his reputation as a nationally known authority on Western civilization kept the clan superiors from ordering him around or imposing his inherited duties on him. (By this time, his brother had died, and Yukichi had inherited the headship of the Fukuzawa family.) Thus the first of his dreams of freedom and independence had been fulfilled.

As he was to later reminisce in his autobiography, a man's ambition grows according to his position. Fukuzawa had longed to extricate himself from the clutches of feudal traditions, but now that he found himself above them, he felt he would not be satisfied until he saw his fellow countrymen liberated and the country secure. He saw in his mind's eye all the people of Japan free and independent as he himself was, and Japan a free and independent country in the world. This became the ideal he was to work toward throughout the years of his adult life. His ambition had a sense of urgency in it, for he recognized the energetic and aggressive characteristics of the Western peoples. They had expanded their knowledge and control of nature through the use of science and were now extending their political influence. India, for instance, had been colonized; China, too, was in a pitiable condition. There was no time to waste or to hesitate; Japan must be awakened to the modern scientific way of thinking and build its own strength. The people must also be led to acquire the spirit of freedom and independence; they must be taught science and the scientific way of thinking—in short, liberated from feudalism and the old Confucian philosophy of resignation and blind obedience.

Learning

Fukuzawa considered learning the key to independence. Independence was the purpose and learning was the means for attaining and preserving it. He distinguished between two categories of learning: "real" learning (*jitsugaku* 実学) and "false" learning (*kyogaku* 虚学). Real learning was the kind that helped people to attain their freedom and independence. The Western type of learning belonged to this category. False learning was the kind that taught knowledge and skills but molded people into disciplined subjects or vassals, useful to the state or lord. Confucian learning belonged to this latter category. Fukuzawa regarded it more as training (*kunren* 訓練) than education (*kyōiku* 教育) in its true sense.

In the 1880s, Fukuzawa often referred to regular order (*seisoku* 正則) in education. By this he meant the correct order in which subjects should be introduced to beginning students so that they would understand and assimilate the nature of modern civilization. This order, he decided, was to begin with mathematics and physics, which he saw as basic to all modern knowledge and thinking. These were to be followed by chemistry, geography, history, social studies, ethics, literature, and other subjects. Many of the students in Fukuzawa's school were adults educated in classical Chinese and Japanese but who wished to acquire knowledge of the new civilization. Fukuzawa's plan of instruction was devised for such students. He believed that a scientific training was necessary for everyone who lived in a modern society and that the prescribed order of instruction should not be altered even for those who intended to become artists.

Higher Education

Higher education, or university education, according to Fukuzawa, was appropriate for a few gifted persons who were willing to work for the independence of the country. Simply put, general education was for the independence of each individual, while higher education was for the independence of the country.

In the first decade of Meiji, there was no institution of higher learning in Japan because there were no qualified students, although professors could have been hired from abroad. As far as modern learning was concerned, everyone was at an elementary level. The old textbooks used at Keiō Gijuku in those days, now preserved in the Keiō Library, include many elementary school textbooks published in the United States and England, some of them appropriate for first or second grade. Adult students, well versed in Japanese and Chinese learnings, were reading these books for new knowledge. By 1877, there was a sufficient number of advanced students to justify starting a university, and Tokyo Daigaku, which later grew into the Imperial University of Tokyo (Tokyo Teikoku Daigaku), was established. In the beginning, practically all the professors in this institution were foreigners. The government gave all its resources to establish and maintain this one well-equipped university in the country. Within five or six years, the establishment of a number of small private schools of higher learning specializing in one subject, such as law, were to follow.

However, Fukuzawa felt it was too early for Keiō Gijuku to launch into higher education. His policy was to consolidate the basic general education first. In other words, he was concentrat-

[x]

ing on nurturing students with common sense, or citizens conscious of where they stood in the society and what society needed from them. And although Keiō Gijuku was ranked by the Ministry of Education as a secondary school, it was generally considered to be of a very high academic level, second only to the Imperial University, and many independent minds were trained there and later went on to fill responsible positions in society.

It was in 1890 that Fukuzawa organized the university departments as a division of Keiō Gijuku. The school was not by any means financially affluent, but some 4000 alumni and the general public donated funds, and Japan's first private university was inaugurated. It had three departments: law, economics, and literature, with an American professor heading each department. At its inauguration, the university section had a total of 59 students in the three departments. The requirement of high proficiency in English to study under the American professors was the reason for this very small number, and the school was regarded as a specialized one for professionals, somewhat like the graduate schools of today. For many years, the main force of Keiō Gijuku's educational activity was its high-school section. In the present age when university education has become more common, Keiō Gijuku's university has become the largest section of the institution. But the school still maintains a complete educational system from elementary school to university.

Civilization

Outline of Civilization (*Bummeiron no Gairyaku*), published in 1875, is the most scholarly of Fukuzawa's works. This book was, in a way, Fukuzawa's attempt to treat contemporary Japanese civilization "pathologically," diagnosing its illnesses and suggesting necessary therapy. Fukuzawa thought that Japanese civilization was diseased after centuries of feudal tradition and oppression, that all the people from the administrators at the top to commoners of the lowest rank had fallen victim to old customs and traditions, and that most of them had lost their individuality and virility. They were capable, intelligent, skilled in crafts, or brave when placed in a clearly defined position of responsibility, but when left on their own, very few of them had the courage to stand and

[xi]

fight in defense of their beliefs. In other words, they were brave even to death when under orders of their master, but when the master died or when they were dismissed from the master's service, they often turned docile or helpless, or else were transformed into rogues with no ability to reason. This was the country's illness, a hangover from the feudal past.

As a cure, the only hope was to introduce a new and more powerful spirit. Even if the people seemed to lack the spirit of independence now, that was not an inborn defect. They would recover it if they made learning from Western civilization their immediate goal and studied scientific reasoning. Fukuzawa believed Western civilization was on the right path toward the ideal goal. All other civilizations in the world were, in his mind, either wrong or primitive, destined either to extinction or to evolve into the Western type. He recognized that Western civilization sometimes deviated from the correct path, but it was destined some day to reach the millennium. Fukuzawa was very optimistic because he believed in the basic goodness of human nature, and with this nature, complemented with the newly acquired knowledge and science and technology, there was no doubt that human beings were destined to a better life and society. Fukuzawa was a thoroughly scientific man of the nineteenth century.

Social Role of Scholars

In the fourth essay of the series called *Encouragement of Learning* (*Gakumon no Susume*), published in 1874, Fukuzawa expounded that the first duty of scholars in Japan was to awaken the people to a sense of independence. (See pp. 85–92 of this volume.) For a scholar, research and accumulation of knowledge or instruction thereof were not enough. It was of greater importance to awaken the power of reasoning or the sense of independence in the minds of the people. Otherwise, Japan's independence in this competitive world could not be assured. Independence cannot be instilled in the people by a government order or lectures by scholars. The only way was to have someone demonstrate a truly independent way of life for people to emulate. A candidate would not be found among farmers and merchants, nor among the scholars of classical Chinese and Japanese. The scholars of Western studies were the only hope, but most of them had been lured into lucrative government posts. In the final analysis, Fukuzawa concluded that he himself was the one to demonstrate what an independent life should be and to indicate the way of life for all the people, including the scholars in Western studies, to follow.

These bold assertions caused a great commotion among Fukuzawa's fellow scholars. Four of them, Tsuda Mamichi, Katō Hiroyuki, Mori Arinori, and Nishi Amane, all government officials, wrote rebuttals in the scholars' association magazine *Meiroku Zasshi*. They argued that with the use of government power, it was possible to educate the people and spread the influence of the West quickly, while the efforts of a private enterprise were bound to be small in scale. Japan must be modernized quickly, they insisted. Fukuzawa's point, in contrast, was the planting of a solid foundation of modern civilization in people's minds, not cursory instruction in new knowledge.

Rapid modernization was vital to Japan in those years. This all thinking people agreed upon. The government provided the most active and effective leadership in the movement, but its policy was liable to fall into standardized propagation of knowledge and technique, as seen in the uniform elementary school system throughout the country with standardized textbooks for all children regardless of background. Moral education, too, was often standardized. In contrast, there were many attempts among the people to organize private schools and some cities organized municipal educational systems. But a large percentage of these were forced to close or were absorbed into the all-powerful national system. The national policy proved very successful, but not always success in the sense of Fukuzawa's ideal. (Refer to "Announcement for Nakatsu Town School," pp. 57–63, and "The School System in Kyoto," pp. 73–78.)

Moral Education

In the early years of Meiji, people were too engrossed in the new civilization and the rush toward making progress to give much thought to examining what they were doing or to stop and think over what they were losing as they discarded elements of their traditional culture. However, in the second decade of Meiji, people began to reflect on the situation, and the scholars of traditional Japanese and Chinese learning regained their courage to speak out. The first debate of consequence between the old school and new school was that between Fukuzawa Yukichi and Nakamura Ritsuen, a noted scholar of Minakuchi near Kyoto whom Fukuzawa's father had supported while Ritsuen was still a student. In 1878, Nakamura wrote to Fukuzawa and asked him to recommend including Confucian doctrine in the elementary-school curriculum. He believed that Fukuzawa's words carried more weight with government officials and the general populace. The letter was written in Chinese, indicating that it was a very formal and serious communication to the younger Fukuzawa, whom Nakamura regarded as a close family friend. Fukuzawa responded cordially, explaining his position on moral education in schools. (See pp. 111–17 of this volume.)

Because these two letters between Nakamura and Fukuzawa touched on the fundamentals of moral education in that period, they were printed in *Minkan Zasshi*, a magazine published by Fukuzawa. This article must have caught the attention of government officials, for it was reprinted in *Kyōiku Zasshi,* the official gazette of the Ministry of Education. Before long, the entire nation was debating the moral education issue. Countless essays and refutations appeared in newspapers and magazines. Books were written on the subject. The debate continued uncontrolled for about twelve years until the Imperial Rescript on Education was proclaimed in 1890. The public discussion ended abruptly because ideas contrary to the Imperial Rescript or any argument that could be interpreted as critical of it would be regarded as treasonous. Instead, dozens of books interpreting the august words appeared, many by classical Japanese and Chinese scholars, some by Buddhists, some by Christians, each claiming that the rescript contained the essence of the doctrine that the writer believed in. Although it was Fukuzawa who sparked this national debate, he did not participate in the contest, and he refrained from discussing the Imperial Rescript in the editorials of *Jiji-shimpō,* which he had launched in 1882. He waited quietly.

The basic philosophy of the Imperial Rescript was of the old school: patriotism, filial piety, and harmony among the people. Toward the end of the rescript, the emperor said that he himself would practice them with the people. The writer of this rescript fully succeeded in presenting the emperor's personal advice to the people in beautiful prose. However, the confusion among the people on daily moral issues continued to grow, as Fukuzawa watched with concern.

In 1900, Fukuzawa made public a code generally known as "Shūshin Yōryō," Fukuzawa's Moral Code. (See pp. 269–73 of this volume.) One may surmise that this was his answer to the Imperial Rescript on Education, issued after a respectful interval of ten years. At that time, Fukuzawa was recovering from a stroke he had suffered a year earlier and was unable to do any serious work, and he had appointed his eldest son, Ichitarō, and several of his pupils to compile the code on his behalf. The resulting code was issued as a joint work by the compilers, but it is generally known as Fukuzawa's Moral Code because it was a true condensation of the thoughts he had been expounding over the years. Fukuzawa sent several groups of his pupils to many parts of the country at his own expense to propagate the ideas embodied in the code. This was his last act of service to his fellow men, for he died in 1901 before recovering enough to write and to give the speeches which he so enjoyed.

Fukuzawa did not specialize in any one field; his interest covered the whole range of civilization, and as his life work he chose to introduce the entire civilization of the modern age to the Japanese people, and that in great haste. In order to give a balanced picture of Fukuzawa's contributions, his writings on politics and economics and other fields need to be introduced. For instance, he is known to have initiated children's literature and also inspired the first movement for women's liberation in Japan. In the present volume, translations of 35 of Fukuzawa Yukichi's most representative and important works concerning education are presented in chronological order. Kazuyoshi Nakayama supervised the selection of the pieces and organization of the ideas expressed in this introduction. Eiichi Kiyooka was responsible for the translation and commentaries.

Kazuyoshi NAKAYAMA

[xv]

Fukuzawa Yukichi, taken around 1891 at about age 56. Courtesy of Fukuzawa Memorial Center for Modern Japanese Studies, Keiō University.

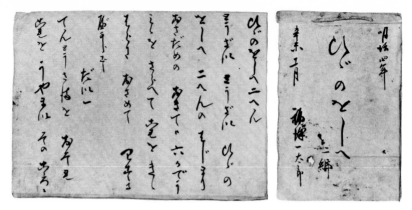

"Daily Lessons" ["Hibi no Oshie"], 1871, written in Fukuzawa's own hand. (See pp. 47–55.) Courtesy of Fukuzawa Memorial Center for Modern Japanese Studies, Keiō University.

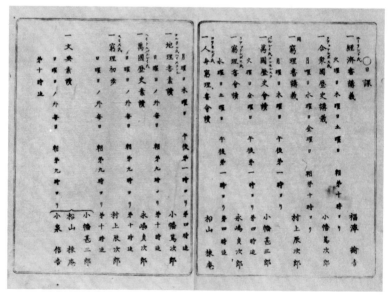

"Class Schedule" ["Nikka"], 1868. (See pp. 24–26.) Courtesy of Fukuzawa Memorial Center for Modern Japanese Studies, Keiō University.

"Methods of Bookkeeping" ["Chōai no Hō"], 1873, frontispiece. (See pp. 79–84.) Courtesy of Fukuzawa Memorial Center for Modern Japanese Studies, Keiō University.

Things Western [*Seiyō Jijō*], 1866, title page. (See pp. 3–14.) Courtesy of Fukuzawa Memorial Center for Modern Japanese Studies, Keiō University.

Outline of Civilization [*Bummeiron no Gairyaku*], 1875, six volumes. (See pp. 101–9.) Courtesy of Fukuzawa Memorial Center for Modern Japanese Studies, Keiō University.

Jijishimpō, November 19, Meiji 16th year (1883), front page. Editorial "Confucian Doctrine" starts in the second column. (See pp. 189–200.) Courtesy of Keiō University Library.

Fukuzawa Yukichi on Education

1
Things Western

Fukuzawa's first contact with the West was in 1854 when he began studying Dutch. Five years later he met a foreigner for the first time, and in 1860 went abroad to San Francisco and in 1862 to Europe. His first major book, *Seiyō Jijō* (*Things Western*), Part I, was published in 1866. As the following translation will show, it is truly amazing that Fukuzawa aquired such a vast quantity of knowledge and understanding of Western civilization within such a short time span.

Before the publication of *Things Western*, the general Japanese public had no way of learning about Western people or institutions and culture because the only knowledge that had been brought in so far had been confined to medicine and its related sciences. *Things Western* became the starting point on which all people, including government officials, built their knowledge and formed their attitudes in coping with the new age. The book was more than a best seller, Part I alone selling 150,000 copies. Including its pirated editions, some 250,000 copies were sold. Considering the size of the reading public of the time, this was a tremendous number, proving the eagerness of the people for the new civilization. This book enabled Fukuzawa to become financially independent and also provided the funds for establishing his own school.

Seiyō Jijō (西洋事情), 1866. *Fukuzawa Yukichi Zenshū*, vol. 1, pp. 302–4, 305, 308–11, 342, 349, 372–73, 547–48, 600–601.

[3]

Things Western was written in three parts. Part I contains an encyclopedic exposition of topics such as organization of governments, commercial companies, schools, public libraries, newspapers, etc., plus expositions of three countries, America, Holland, and England, with outlines of their history, government, education, army and navy, and national finance. Before taking up Part II, Fukuzawa wrote what he called an Interlude Section in 1867. It was actually a translation of a high-school textbook entitled *Political Economy*.[1] He sought to give his readers an understanding of the structure of Western society and philosophy of life before continuing with descriptions of other countries. Part II, published in 1870, contains discussions of Western political science, including definitions of rights and freedom, etc. This is followed by expositions of Russia and France. The present translation covers selections relating to education.

Schools

In no country in the West is there a place where a school cannot be found—not only in large cities but in country villages and everywhere. Some of the schools have been established by the government, which pays the teachers' salaries. Others have been established by common people who formed corporations for the purpose of opening schools and providing education. All boys and girls start school at the age of six or seven. Some of them are boarders; others live at home and commute to school every day. The schools they first enter are called elementary schools. In elementary school they are first taught to read and write. Later they are taught the history of their own country, then geography, arithmetic, astronomy, elementary sciences, poetry, painting, music, and other subjects.

---

[1] The title page of one edition of this book in Keiō University Library reads: "Chambers's Educational Course, Political Economy, for use in Schools and for Private Instruction, William and Robert Chambers, London and Edinburgh, 1873." Author unknown.

[4]

After seven or eight years when they are fairly well grounded in these subjects, they advance to college. In college, too, the same subjects are taught, but at an advanced level of instruction. Also, in college the students do not take all the subjects, but they select one or two according to their interests and specialize in them. Some of the students study in college for a while and then transfer to a military school if they wish to become military officers. Others who wish to become physicians will move on to a medical school, and there they would specialize in one field of study. Thus students begin school at the age of six or seven, and they are supposed to complete their education between the age of eighteen and twenty.

The above is the general order of studies in the elementary schools and colleges. But there are schools which combine both schools in one institution. Kings College of London (the largest school in that city) holds more than five hundred students, and the upper floor of its building contains the college, and the lower floor is devoted to the elementary school. Instruction begins at nine o'clock every day, lasting till twelve o'clock, when they stop for lunch. In the afternoon, classes begin at two o'clock and finish at five o'clock.

Every seventh day, they suspend work the whole day and the boarding students go home. Rules in the school are very strict. During lessons, students do not utter a word or indulge in pranks. Those who break rules are punished. However, between the lessons the students are allowed to play at will. For that purpose, a schoolyard is always provided, with trees and flowers planted and some pools and fountains. Also, in these yards some poles and ladders are set up or some ropes hung for the children to climb and to try some rope-walking, thus playing like beasts of nature to exercise their limbs and to dissipate the tedium of hard studies, and at the same time to preserve their health.

The annual tuition is almost the same in every country, but according to the quality of the school and also to the number of lessons a student takes, the tuition sometimes varies. When the parents are poor and unable to pay for their children's education, they can find a special school where children are taught free of charge. The expenses for this kind of school are sometimes collected from the people much like a tax; sometimes a group

[5]

of public-spirited people form themselves into a corporation and either donate their own money or solicit wealthy people throughout the country for donations and thus establish a "poor school."

In Europe, the country where the general education is most developed is Prussia. There is practically no one in the country who cannot read and write. In Berlin, the capital of Prussia, there are schools even inside the prisons, and every three or four days the convicts receive instruction. The rest may be surmised from this one example.

Public Libraries

There are libraries in the cities of the West. They are called "bibliothèques."[2] All sorts of books and pictures, from books for daily information to old and rare books from throughout the world are deposited, and anyone may come and read them at will. While people are free to read them in the library for any number of days, books may not be taken home. In the library of London, there are 800,000 volumes of books. In the library of St. Petersburg (the Russian capital), there are 900,000 volumes. In that of Paris, 1,500,000. The French boast that if those books were placed single file, they would be 7 *ri* [17 miles] long. The libraries sometimes belong to the government, sometimes to the general public. Those books published abroad are purchased, but one copy each of those published within the country are donated to the library at the time of their publication.

Schools for the Dumb

There are schools providing education for the dumb. Several hundred students are brought together for instruction in languages, arithmetic, astronomy, geography, and other subjects exactly as in any other school. The first procedure of instruction when a student enters the school is to teach the 26 letters of the alphabet using sign language. (The way they make the signs with

---

[2] This is practically the only French word found in Fukuzawa's works. He probably saw a public library for the first time in Paris, and the French word for it impressed him deeply.

their hands is somewhat like the Japanese game of *ken*.) Next, they are taught to pronounce words by watching and imitating the movements of the lips, tongue, teeth, and throat. Sometimes they will touch those organs to feel their workings. Thus, when they learn to speak, even though they are not able to hear the sounds with their ears, they are able to carry on conversations by understanding the movement of the speaker's lips, tongue, teeth, and throat. (A dumb person has the organ for producing the voice. Only because of their lack of the hearing faculty, they cannot hear voices and learn to regulate their voices according to the rule of five sounds. This can be seen in the natural sounds of their cheerful laughing and sad crying, which are not different from people with normal faculties.)

Schools for the Blind

The organization of schools for the blind is about the same as that of schools for the dumb. For teaching reading to the blind, letters are raised on paper, and for maps holes are made in the paper with a needle, and with a series of holes, seas and land are drawn, and the blind students touch them with their fingertips. For arithmetic, there is a special machine shaped like *sangi*.[3] Using this machine, it is possible to do any calculation, from addition, subtraction, multiplication, and division to difficult computations for astronomical measurements. Aside from these subjects, blind boys and girls receive instruction in music. The main manual crafts taught to boys are weaving and basket-making; for girls, knitting. Their products are sold on the market and the profits are used for school expenses.

In England, the term of education in a school for the blind is limited to six years regardless of the student's age. Generally, their studies will be completed in these six years, but those who are poor and have no way of making their living are allowed to stay on in the school. However, those staying beyond the prescribed term must engage in manual work. Schools for the blind are like other institutions in charging tuition to those

---

[3] *Sangi* was an instrument developed in China for higher mathematics beyond the usual calculations done on the abacus. Its use in Japan died out after the introduction of modern mathematics.

who can afford it, and admitting free of charge those who are poor.

Institutions for Retarded Children

This is a school for children who are naturally deficient in intelligence. In teaching the usual subjects, such as reading and arithmetic, the methods are different from those in ordinary schools. For lessons in reading, huge letters are used. Also, pictures are brought in for easier comprehension. For instance, in teaching the writing of the word "dog," a picture of a dog is drawn; for teaching the word "to buy," a scene is drawn. The children learn by writing the word next to the picture and reading it over many times.

Thus, by a slow process the children are brought to book reading. For teaching arithmetic, too, they use objects in the beginning. There are many devices, but here is an example: The teacher brings several balls, shows the children two of them, and asks them how many? The answer will be "two"; he adds two more balls and asks how many? The answer is "four"; he adds three to the four balls, and asks again how many? Or he adds three and takes away one, and asks how many? He divides this number of balls into two, then asks how many? Thus by questions and answers, the teacher leads the children on gradually until they learn the nature of numbers, and in time they will be doing arithmetic on paper.

Besides reading and arithmetic, they use devices very much like the toy puzzles that the children in Japan enjoy. These devices are for prompting the students to use their faculty of distinguishing and devising. The simplest of the toys is just a board with round and square or irregular-shaped holes. There are also small pieces shaped to fit into those holes. The idea is for the children to find the right piece to fit into the right hole. They will thus learn to distinguish between round and square and other shapes. Besides these exercises, the girls are taught singing and dancing. Boys are made to climb trees and ladders or do some imitations of military drills. This form of instruction allows them to grow healthy and strong. The countries which have this kind of school are, for the present, only France, Holland, and Prussia. All other countries have not established them yet.

[8]

Museums

A museum is established to assemble together objects—products, old things, and curios—from all over the world and to show them to the people in order to extend their knowledge. What they call a mineralogical museum is a hall that collects and exhibits mineral objects. Various metals and rocks from all over the world are gathered in one building; these are labeled and exhibited to the public. Zoological museums gather preserved beasts, birds, fish, and insects together. The skins or feathers of these beasts and birds are stuffed with something to keep their shapes; the fish are dried by the use of some chemicals, and all of them appear as if they are living. Small fish and insects are sometimes preserved in an alcohol solution.

There are also what are called zoological gardens and botanical gardens. Living beasts, birds, fish, and insects are kept in zoological gardens. Lions, rhinoceros, elephants, tigers, leopards, bears, brown bears, foxes, raccoon dogs, rabbits, ostriches, eagles, hawks, cranes, geese, swallows, sparrows, pythons, frogs, and all other strange living things of the world are gathered in this garden, without exception. To keep these animals alive, proper food according to the need of each is given, and also there are installations to regulate the temperature and humidity in the room according to the nature of the animals. Even sea fish are kept alive in glass tanks with regular supplies of fresh sea water.

In the botanical gardens, all varieties of trees, plants, and water plants from all over the world are gathered. To keep plants and trees from warm countries, a large glass room is built, iron pipes are placed in this room, and the room is kept warm by running steam through these pipes. The interior of the glass room will be thus kept higher than 80 degrees even in severe winter weather, and plants from tropical countries will thrive.

Medical museums specialize in the affairs of medical science. They dissect human bodies and preserve the skeletons or sometimes the fetuses, or when a patient has died of a rare disease, the diseased part is cut out and preserved for future studies. This kind of museum is often found within hospitals.

[9]

Education in the United States of America

The largest number of elementary schools is found in the northern part of the United States, and their organization is excellent. This may be called one of the remarkable successes of the American administration. The expenses for these schools are covered by taxes, or sometimes there are foundations attached to the schools and the interests their funds earn are used yearly. The money is distributed to different areas of the state according to the number of students. In each town, at least one school is provided, and even outside of towns, in all areas where people live, one school is provided for every 2 square *ri* [about 5 miles], thus making it convenient for the children to go to school.

In every county, twelve people are elected to supervise the school business. Any child wanting to enter a school will be admitted without regard to parentage. Books must be purchased, but there are no other expenses. The lessons taught in elementary school are elementary English, arithmetic, geography, and other such subjects. Schools in towns provide lessons in Latin and Greek as well.

The number of colleges is also numerous. Their regulations emphasize leniency. Some colleges are established by the government. Also, common people may form a corporation among themselves and establish a college. Colleges are situated all over the United States. The subjects taught are various old and contemporary languages, grammar, history, logic,[4] composition and rhetoric, physical sciences, moral philosophy, etc.

Throughout the country, the quantity of newspapers printed every year amounts to about 426 million sheets. Whenever there is a good book published in Europe, the book will be republished in the United States for the benefit of the public.

There are many who join together as corporations for the purpose of developing new arts and culture. Also, many hospitals and institutions are established for the poor.

---

[4] The Japanese word used here is *rigaku* (study of reason) which includes logic, philosophy, or any of the abstract subjects as opposed to physical sciences. The present translator chose logic as the most likely subject for the level of school in discussion. The Japanese language in this period still lacked precise words for many of the Western school subjects.

[10]

Education in Holland

Holland is an old country and should be considered the center of European civilization. The reason why Holland is not considered outstanding is that education is very prevalent in this country, and everybody studies without any distinction between high and low classes, which makes it difficult for anyone to gain fame as a pre-eminent scholar. The truth is that there are many fine scholars among the Dutch. In 1851, there were 3295 elementary schools in the country, and the number of children attending them totaled 361,015. Assuming the number of children between the ages of five and fifteen to be about 700,000 out of the whole population of 3,767,671, one may surmise that more than half of the children in the country were attending school. Besides these schools, colleges are numerous, and among them the three in Leyden, Utrecht, and Groningen are particularly outstanding. The total enrollment of the three is 1119.

Education in England

In England, the government does not enact laws on education. In most cases, religious groups establish schools and, with the donations by people who give of their free will, run the school. The amount of money gathered yearly is considerable. Most of the elementary schools were established in this way, and it is probably safe to say that this country spends greater amounts of money on the education of children than any other country in the world. Because there is no supervision by the government, sometimes those in charge of the schools go astray in the use of money. But should government supervision begin, other evils might arise; it is difficult to tell which way is better. When the annual interest on all the funds or foundations specially set aside for the schools and the annual donations are put together, the total amount is 400,000 pounds a year.

The elementary schools described above are for the children of the middle and upper classes of society. In recent years, there have been attempts to educate the children of lower classes and poorer people in order to elevate the standards of the country. Among the new attempts there is what is called "Sunday school."

[11]

In these schools, lessons are given in the late afternoons every Sunday, hence the name.

In 1851, the combined population of England and Wales was 17,927,609, and the number of children in elementary schools was 2,144,378; the number of those in Sunday schools was 2,407,642. Therefore, comparing these numbers, we see that the children in the elementary schools were in the proportion of one in every 836 of the whole population, and those in the Sunday schools were one in every 745. There are some people who believe that the school system in England lags behind those of Prussia and Holland, but it is difficult to tell the true effects of education in these countries. However, the reason why the English excel over other people in their scholarship and technical skills and other arts is not because of the prevalence of education. It comes from the leniency of the government regulations which do not restrict people but allow them to extend their natural talents freely.

Education in Russia

In Russia, education of the general public has not been extensive. It has begun improving only in the past 50 or 60 years. In 1802, Emperor Alexander promulgated an order on education which divided the whole country into districts and provided for the establishment of one college in each of the districts. The number of lesser schools was to be decided according to the population and to the size of the district. Among these schools were what they called "lyceum." They were schools designed to train young men who sought to become officials. At present, the whole country is divided into ten school districts, but only five districts have colleges.

According to an 1860 record, there were schools of various kinds totaling 8937 with 950,000 students. According to this record, we find that the proportion of students in schools is one to 77. Some time ago in Russia there were quite a number of people who operated private schools for the education of the general public, but the government made many rules controlling them. And when it ruled that unless a person is educated in a government school, he would not be eligible for government posts, the private schools began to decline.

[12]

Education in France

In France, education developed remarkably in recent years, and the general culture advanced accordingly. A publication of the Office of Education indicates that in 1832 the number of students in elementary school was 59 for every 1000 of the population. In 1847, it increased to 99.8. In 1863, it had reached 116. The number of schools is also very large. In the 16 years between 1847 to 1863, 8566 new schools were opened, providing education for 806,233 students. Averaging this number for each year, 99,000 more students were taught in these newly opened schools every year.

The whole country is divided into 37,510 districts, and they are called "communes." There are several schools in each commune. The law requires each commune to have at least one school. At present, those communes without a school number only 818 in the whole country. However, people living in these communes are able to attend schools nearby. According to a census, among children between the ages of eight and eleven, only 200,000 do not attend schools. Testing each child who had completed school in 1863, it was found that 60 out of 100 were able to read and write well and do arithmetic without difficulty. The rest of the children, 40 in number, failed the tests.

According to the public report of October, 1863, there were 82,135 elementary schools in the whole of France. This means that the number has increased by 16,136 since 1848. The number of students in these schools was 3,771,597 in 1848 and increased to 4,731,946 in 1862, which means that in the fourteen-year interval, the student population had increased by about 1,250,000. In the 36,499 districts, there are 41,426 schools which are coeducational. Of these, 37,895 are secular, and their enrollment is 2,145,420. The other 37,895 schools are parochial, and their students number 482,008.[5] Both added together will bring the number of students in schools to 2,627,428. One-third of these students are receiving education without tuition. Besides these, there are 26,592 schools

[5] Readers will notice glaring discrepancies in these numbers. Apparently the errors were made by the woodblock printers of the first edition. The proofreader missed them and in more than one hundred years since, nobody has pointed this out, and all the subsequent editions have copied the errors faithfully. Fukuzawa himself did not notice.

[13]

for girls. Of these, 13,491 are secular schools. The other 13,491 are in charge of Christian nuns. The number of girls educated in these schools is 1,601,213. Of these one-third attend secular schools and the other two-thirds go to parochial schools. One-fourth of the whole number are being taught free of charge. The salaries paid all the women teachers in a year add up to 9,169,030 francs. When this amount is divided by the number of women teachers, on the average one teacher is paid 655 francs a year.

The prevalence of education may be seen in a report of the army. In an official report of the Office of the Army for 1866, it is stated that of all the soldiers brought in from the entire country, there were only 30 out of every 100 men who could not read. However, the level of education is different by area. In general, education in southern France is not equal to the higher level of the northeastern areas.

2
Pronouncement
at the
Inauguration of Keiō Gijuku

Fukuzawa had been a school teacher for ten years but
in a clan school subject to the dictums of the clan. By
1868, because of the social unrest in connection with
the Restoration, the clan's interest in education had
waned while Fukuzawa was being inspired by a new
vision and a sense of mission to lead the Japanese people
toward a new age. At the same time, he became
financially well off with the sales of his books. Thereupon, he established a school of his own and named
it Keiō Gijuku.

In 1868 at the inauguration of the school, Fukuzawa
published the following pronouncement which may be
regarded as a declaration of education for the new age.
In contrast to the teacher-centered schools of old Japan,
Fukuzawa established Keiō Gijuku as a cooperative
school with no distinction between the teachers and
the pupils; all were comrades in search of knowledge,
everyone contributing what he could to the school.

We have gathered together as a corporation to found a school,
to collaborate with and cultivate each other in the study of
Western learning. Our purpose is not by any means private. We
have opened the doors of the school wide to the public to allow

"Keiō Gijuku no Ki" (慶応義塾之記), 1868. *Fukuzawa Yukichi Zenshū*, vol. 19, pp. 367–69.

all men, regardless of their status as samurai or commoner, to come and participate in our program.

In the initial period of Western studies in this country, in the Kyōhō era [1716–36], several interpreters in Nagasaki tendered a petition to the authorities to allow them to study written Dutch in order to expedite foreign trade, and this petition was quickly granted.[1] This, indeed, was the very beginning of our people's study of the Latin alphabet.

Later in the Hōreki [1751–64] and Meiwa [1764–72] eras, a scholar by the name of Aoki Kon'yō, on an order from above, advocated Dutch studies. Then Maeno Ranka, Katsuragawa Ho-shū, Sugita Isai, and others began devoting themselves whole-heartedly to Dutch studies, combining their knowledge, and benefiting greatly from it. But this being the primal years of Western studies, books were scarce and teachers were lacking; the best they could do was to travel the long route to Nagasaki to discuss their questions with the interpreters there, or when they happened to meet a visitor from Holland,[2] they would confirm the proper use of the language. Besides being gifted with incomparable ability, these men were fired with the conviction that they were opening a new era in the history of learning. They put their utmost efforts into the studies, for days and nights, till they were neglecting their rest and food. One of the stories records that the venerable Ranka traveled to Nagasaki and returned with the knowledge of 700 Dutch words. From this, one may surmise how ardent scholars of those days were and what difficulties they were obliged to undergo.

These men were followed by Ōtsuki Gentaku, Udagawa Kaien,

---

[1] The chief reason behind the policy of isolation of the Tokugawa regime was the fear of Catholic Christianity, which the authorities discerned as an agent of Western imperialism. But Holland, being a Protestant country, was allowed to continue trade with Japan. Even with the Dutch, however, importation of printed or written matter was prohibited for fear of religious infiltration. The professional interpreters were trained in spoken Dutch only and were not allowed to learn to read or to write. With the passage of time, however, the fear of Christian infiltration began to fade, and in the 1740s Shōgun Yoshimune eased the ban and permitted books on medicine to be imported, and he ordered Aoki Kon'yō to take up Dutch studies.

[2] Usually once a year, the chief of the Dutch post in Nagasaki made a courtesy call on the shōgun in Edo. He was accompanied by a retinue of followers often including physicians and scholars. The law prohibiting association between the Dutch and the Japanese was very strict in Nagasaki but was set aside while the party was journeying and Japanese scholars had easy access to them in their lodging in Edo.

and others. Later in the Tempō [1830–44] and Kōka [1844–48] eras, Udagawa Shinsai and his son, Tsuboi Shindō, Mitsukuri Gempo, the Sugita Seikei brothers, Ogata Kōan, and such figures appeared in rapid succession.

By this time, the arts of reading and translating had gradually developed, and a number of books translated by various scholars began appearing. However, the translations were mostly confined to books on Dutch medicine with some on such related sciences as physics, astronomy, geography, chemistry, and a few other subjects. In those days, these subjects were referred to by the general name of Dutch studies (*rangaku*), because at that time, the only Western country trading with Japan was Holland, and the one port at which their ships called was Nagasaki at the extreme west end of our country. Naturally, books from the West were scarce and the road to knowledge was so difficult and vexing as to make the students feel their efforts were for naught.

Then, in the Kaei era [1848–54], the Americans came, and for the first time concluded with our country a treaty of amity and commerce. The same was extended soon to England, France, and Russia. From that time, conditions in this country changed. All our countrymen came to feel the necessity of information on foreign countries, which led to a rapid increase in all fields of learning. Scholars promoted their schools of thought and sought to attract pupils. A new denomination of Western studies (*yōgaku*) came into being. What else could this be but a great advancement of learning?

When a new event or a new trend unfolds, its advent has to take a gradual turn, as when a person climbs an edifice, he has to climb step by step along the stairs. The origin of the rise of Dutch learning in the Tempō and Kōka eras is found in the early Hōreki and Meiwa scholars who took the first step in the field. And the present prevalence of Western learning owes itself partly to the opening of amity and trade with various countries, but more to the second rise of the learning by the Tempō and Kōka scholars. Thus, the splendor that we enjoy today is due to the bequest of those past scholars.

What places Western learning apart from all other learnings is that it is a true product of nature and it rides with reason; it teaches the ways of humankind and it moderates between an

[17]

individual and society. It contains all the truths with no vestiges of untruth, it possesses all knowledge, large or small; it is a learning that people, as long as they are people, must learn. Therefore, it may well be called a learning of the fundamental truth. Our group has pursued Western studies for many years, but we have had but a glimpse of the whole. Hundreds of subjects still untouched are so extensive that we are ever lured with the vision of the ocean of wisdom before us. It is indeed a tremendous work that we have undertaken. But to hesitate before a difficult task is not the way of a courageous person; not to volunteer labor when benefit is in sight proves lack of patriotism.

To spread this study in our society, the first requisite is a school with rules modeled on those in Western countries to guide the students. Therefore, our colleagues have conferred, and emulating the organization of those cooperative schools[3] in that distant

---

[3] It is presumed that Fukuzawa took the English public schools as the model for his Keiō Gijuku, "Gijuku" being his rendition of "public school" into Japanese. While his school was small, Fukuzawa was able to maintain his ideal of a cooperative institution. The following quotation is from his letter to a friend, Yamaguchi Ryōzō, dated 10th day, Intercalary 4th month, 1868:

"I have just opened a school in Shinsenza, and I am engaged, day and night, in studying with the students. This school is small, but when compared with others, it is the largest in Edo, except for Kaiseijo [the government school], which probably makes it the largest in Japan. In its size and appearance, the building is not much to boast about, but if it is small, it is manageable; the construction may be humble, but it is swept clean. I am not the schoolmaster, the students are not my pupils. All the members are called *shachū* [colleagues]. Among them, I hold the position of *shatō* [head colleague], and I attend to everything from reading of books to overseeing the eating and sleeping and disposal of garbage. All the rest of the colleagues have some responsibilities to discharge."

In Keiō Gijuku at this time, there was no clear distinction between the teachers and the students; all were colleagues engaged in the study of Western civilization. A new member was initiated (*nyūsha*) into the corporation rather than admitted (*nyūgaku*) into the school, and he was to share in the responsibility for the upkeep of the corporation. New members would give money toward the upkeep which they called a contribution rather than tuition, and older members would give intellectual contributions by teaching or taking part in school management. At this time, most of the members were samurai whose expenses were guaranteed by the stipends they received from their clans, and the corporation's burden of personnel expenses was small.

A year later, however, with the abolition of all the clans, the samurai were deprived of the privilege of easy living on the stipends. Thereupon, Keiō Gijuku was reorganized to make it a self-supporting institution. In other words, in order to collect salaries for the teachers it began charging substantial tuition to students who took courses. This was a startling innovation, because up to that time, teaching in Japan was not associated with the earning of money. This new arrangement made a clear distinction between teachers and students, but some acted as both, teaching some classes and

land, have established a small school and named it Keiō Gijuku[4] after the era of its establishment.

On this day in the 4th month, the construction work completed, we have issued the new rules of the school. We pray that people of similar purposes from far and near may travel here to nourish their ability, increase their knowledge, be courteous in their deportment, and faithful in all relations. And some day, if one of our graduates should stand out in society, that will be our contribution to the nation. And in the future, if our successors follow in our footsteps, build upon our groundwork, extend the activities of our corporation, and thus have for us the same respect we have for our own predecessors, would it not be gratifying? Colleagues! Join forces, give your best, and achieve your goal!

---

studying in others, receiving remuneration and paying tuition at the same time. See *A History of Keiō Gijuku Through the Writings of Fukuzawa.*
[4] This being a cooperative school, Fukuzawa did not want to call it by the founder's name.

3
Regulations

As in most other schools of the day, the administration of the clan school where Fukuzawa served as master was not systematized by any codes or rules. But at the opening of Keiō Gijuku, a set of regulations was distributed to all the resident students and prospective students, along with the "Pronouncement at the Inauguration of Keiō Gijuku."

Attention is called to the wording of the first article in the Admission Regulations. Instead of "A student admitted to the school," he wrote "A new member of the Corporation." This expresses Fukuzawa's ideal of the cooperative school, in which no clear distinction was made between teachers and students. A teacher would instruct in the beginning, but, when students advanced to the teacher's level, they would pursue their studies of Western civilization together with their erstwhile mentors.

1. In response to the common desire of the Corporation for the advancement of learning in the school, the following regulations have been set to provide an orderly and quiet atmosphere conducive to studying.

2. In all our daily activities, from sleeping to eating, care shall be taken to maintain cleanliness.

3. The lending and borrowing of money is prohibited.

"Kisoku" (規則), 1868. *Keiō Gijuku Hyakunenshi*, vol. 1, pp. 258–60, 267–68, 281–82.

4. The school gates shall be closed at *itsutsu han toki* [nine o'clock] at night.[1]

5. Reading aloud at night is prohibited.

6. Residents shall rise early every morning, put away the bedding, and sweep their own area.

7. There shall be no scribbling on the doors, walls, and also on lamp shades, even if they belong to individuals.[2]

8. Residents must not buy items through the dormitory windows facing the street or talk with people on the street through the windows.

9. The members of the Corporation make learning their life work; therefore, under no circumstance shall they draw their swords. A blade shall not be wiped even in the dormitory rooms. Residents shall first request permission from the supervisor of the dormitory, go to the lecture hall, and when there is no one nearby, remove the sheath.

10. Visitors shall be received in the reception room. There is no objection to bringing an intimate friend or fellow student into one's room, but because that is liable to cause annoyance to other residents, discretion shall be taken.

11. When there is business with a visiting merchant or such a person, residents shall meet them at the entrance to the dining room. Except for the school servants, no other workmen shall be admitted to the dormitory rooms.

12. Lectures, seminars (*kaidoku*), and reading (*sodoku*) shall all take place in the schoolrooms.[3] Such group studies shall not take place in the dormitory.

13. Cleaning of the schoolrooms shall be assigned to groups of

---

[1] Fukuzawa uses *itsutsu han toki* (9:00 P.M.) here. This is the only instance in which the old system of time is used. Keiō Gijuku emphasized its progressive spirit by adopting the Western system of time for its class schedule and dining hours; also, the seven-day week system had been adopted. However, probably to make sure that residents would not misunderstand the closing time of the gate, the old system of indicating time was employed here. A government order in 1872 abolished it in favor of the Western system of indicating time.

[2] The writing brush in general use then was the most efficient, and tempting, instrument for scribbling. The lamp in use at that time was a square frame covered with paper and burned rapeseed oil in a tray with a plant-pith wick.

[3] *Kaidoku* (seminars) was the chief method of study in all schools at that time and earlier. The procedure was to assign several pages in a book to a small group of students who would take turns in class translating and discussing the text. *Sodoku* (reading) was simple instruction in reading with some explanatory remarks.

three for one-week periods. A new group shall take over every week. This cleaning includes opening the doors and windows early every morning and dusting and sweeping the rooms, as well as closing the doors and windows in the evening. The corridors and other parts of the school buildings will be cleaned by the school servants.

14. Residents shall take turns daily at the reception room where they shall read their books while on duty.

15. When seminars, lectures, and reading classes end, the classrooms shall be cleaned at once. The commuting members shall be responsible for this work.

The above rules shall be followed, but if inconveniences are discovered, the rules shall be amended upon mutual agreement.

Dining-Room Regulations

1. Meals shall be served at eight o'clock in the morning, twelve o'clock noon, and five o'clock in the evening. However, adjustments will be made according to the length of the day.

2. Calls for the meals: at the first sound of the clappers, all residents shall assemble, and at the second clap they shall be seated. The time assigned to eating is to be one Western hour from the second clap. Those who come late to the assigned hour shall report to the dining-room supervisor, and they shall clean up after their meals. Cleaning up involves washing and drying the dishes and clearing the table they used.

3. Eating in the rooms is prohibited. No food or drinks shall be kept near one's desk.

4. If one eats in the dining room at hours other than the three regular meals, he shall without fail clean up after eating.

5. On Sundays, class schedules will be suspended, and from two o'clock in the afternoon, residents will be free to eat and drink in the dining room. However, excessive drinking and unruly and noisy behavior are strictly prohibited.

6. The dining-room furniture shall not be taken out of the dining room, nor shall they be used for other purposes. However, reading books on a dining-room chair occasionally when one is tired of sitting formally at one's desk will be tolerated.

7. After the evening meal, all residents shall climb trees, play

[23]

ball games, or engage in other sports according to the rules of gymnastics[4] and endeavor to exercise their bodies.

The above rules shall be observed, but if inconveniences are discovered, the rules shall be amended upon mutual agreement.

Admission Regulations

1. A new member of the Corporation shall pay one *ryō*.[5]

2. Upon admission to the dormitory, a member shall give 2 *shu* to the dormitory servant.[6]

3. A member of the Corporation who commutes shall pay in 2 *shu* a month.[7]

4. The guarantor of a dormitory resident shall be responsible for all the student's actions during his term of residence.

Members of Keiō Gijuku

4th month, Keiō 4th year (1868)

Class Schedule[8]

1. Lecture: Wayland's Economics   Fukuzawa Yukichi
   Tuesdays, Thursdays, Saturdays from 10 A.M.

---

[4] Fukuzawa used the English word "gymnastics" because there was no corresponding word in Japanese. The custom of including physical education in the curriculum had not yet taken root.

[5] The value of currency in Japan was fluctuating rapidly at this time. "New Order for Keiō Gijuku" (see p. 29) states that one *ryō* would buy one *to* (about half a bushel) of rice. From this the value of one *ryō* may be estimated. One *ryō* was the basic monetary unit, 4 *bu* equaled one *ryō*, and 4 *shu* equaled one *bu*, in either gold or silver coins. *Mon* was a unit of another system represented in copper coins. The exchange rate between the two systems fluctuated, but it was around 6600 *mon* to one *ryō*.

[6] According to the old custom, a student upon entrance into a new school would give a gift of money (*sokushū*) to the master, and small gifts, usually money, to the master's wife and others who were likely to care for him. Among them were the school servants. However, as these were personal gifts, there was no fixed amount for them, and each student gave what he could afford. The giving of 2 *shu* to the dormitory servant as stipulated in this regulation must be a remnant of the old custom. It disappears from the regulations one year later when Keiō Gijuku revised its regulations on tuition and fees. (See "New Order for Keiō Gijuju," p. 29.)

[7] This is the earliest mention of a fixed tuition charged in an educational institution in Japan. There was another regulation (now lost) in which the tuition was given but which was revised often according to the fluctuation of food prices.

[8] The textbooks used in Keiō Gijuku at this time had all been obtained by Fukuzawa on his trip to the United States in 1867. There were several dozen copies of each book, and each student was able to have exclusive use of a book without having to copy

2. Lecture: Quackenbos's History of the United States
Obata Tokujirō[9]
Mondays, Wednesdays, Fridays from 10 A.M.
3. Lecture: Quackenbos's Natural Philosophy
Murakami Tatsujirō
Mondays, Wednesdays from 1 P.M.

---

out the pages. This made Keiō Gijuku an outstanding school of Western studies. Some of these textbooks are preserved in the Keiō University Library.

Wayland's Economics: *The Elements of Political Economy* by Francis Wayland, D.D. (1796–1865), president of Brown University and professor of moral philosophy, Boston, Gould and Lincoln, 1866. This was the only college-level textbook used in Keiō Gijuku at this time, and it was the book that Fukuzawa was reading with his students on May 15, 1868, when the Battle of Ueno took place within sight of the school. Between lectures, he gave an impressive speech to his pupils which is recorded in his autobiography. In Keiō University today, May 15 is commemorated as Wayland Day, and a memorial lecture is held every year.

Quackenbos's History of the United States: The books used in 1868 have not been preserved, but Keiō University Library has two histories of the United States by Quackenbos. One is *Elementary History of the United States*, first copyrighted in 1860, the other is *Illustrated School History of the United States and the Adjacent Parts of America*, first copyrighted in 1857. Both are by G. P. Quackenbos, LL.D., associate principal of the Collegiate School, New York, and published by D. Appleton and Company. The *Elementary History of the United States* is a primary-school textbook of over 200 pages while the other is for high-school use with some 400 pages. The level of books being used must have been immaterial, for the students were all adults well grounded in Japanese and Chinese studies. What they needed was English-language instruction and information on the basic facts of the West. Both college textbooks and primary-school books were difficult to read and informative as well.

Quackenbos's Natural Philosophy: *Natural Philosophy: The Most Recent Discoveries in Various Branches of Physics*, by G. P. Quackenbos, published by D. Appleton and Company.

Peter Parley's Universal History: The title page reads "Peter Parley's Universal History on the Basis of Geography, a New Edition Brought Down to the Present Day, Illustrated by 20 Maps and 125 Engravings; Ivison, Blakeman, Taylor & Co., New York and Chicago. First Copyrighted in 1837 by S. G. Goodrich."

Corming's Human Physiology: This book is unavailable today, and its author unknown. "Corming" is a phonetic spelling based on the author's name given in Japanese in the Class Schedule. The title is *Jinshin Kyūrisho* [Physical Science of the Human Body].

Cornell's Geography: There is a book in Keiō University Library which is believed to be the edition used in 1868. It is a reprint made in Japan by a publisher named Watanabe and has two title pages, one in Japanese and the other in English: "Cornell's Primary Geography for the Use of Schools, First Edition, Yedo, the 2nd Year of Kei-ou." Keiō 2 was 1866. It is a book of 70 pages, or rather 35 sheets of folded Japanese paper, bound with a cord between soft paper covers. Its contents cover the whole world but is elementary, appropriate for lower primary classes.

Smith's Elementary Sciences: This book has not been preserved, and little is known about it. This title is a literal translation of *Kyūri Shoho*, listed in the Class Schedule.

Reading of English Grammar: The Class Schedule does not specify the textbook, but *First Book in English Grammar* by G. P. Quackenbos. Appleton and Company, first copyrighted in 1864, was probably used.

[9] Fukuzawa's most trusted colleague, second in command at the school.

4. Seminar: Peter Parley's Universal History

                                 Obata Jinzaburō

Tuesdays, Fridays 1–4 P.M.

5. Seminar: Quackenbos's Natural Philosophy

                               Nagashima Teijirō

Wednesdays, Saturdays 1–4 P.M.

6. Seminar: Corming's Human Physiology   Matsuyama Tōan

Mondays, Thursdays 1–4 P.M.

7. Reading: Cornell's Geography   Obata Tokujirō

Every day except Sundays 9–10 A.M.

8. Reading: Peter Parley's Universal History

Every day except Sundays 9–10 A.M.   Nagashima Teijirō

9. Smith's Elementary Sciences   Murakami Tatsujirō

Every day except Sundays 9–10 A.M.

10. Reading of English Grammar   Obata Jinzaburō,

             Matsuyama Tōan, Koizumi Nobukichi

Every day except Sundays 9–10 A.M.

[26]

4
New Order for Keiō Gijuku

After its inauguration, Keiō Gijuku quickly expanded
into a large school with an enrollment of 100 students.
Following the Restoration and with the new trend for
closer relations with the West, students swarmed to
Keiō Gijuku, and within one year the number of
students increased twofold. Buildings were built to
accommodate the new students, but soon there was no
more land, and Fukuzawa rented houses and established branch schools. The following "New Order for
Keiō Gijuku" was presented to each new applicant
along with the "Regulations" and the "Pronouncement at the Inauguration of Keiō Gijuku."

Last year when Keiō Gijuku was inaugurated, eager applicants
gathered from throughout the country, and within a few months,
the dormitory was overflowing beyond its capacity of 100. And
since the beginning of this summer, we have even been turning
down applications for day students because of the lack of space
in our classrooms.

Thereupon, the members of our Corporation discussed the
situation and decided to rent a tenement house on the estate of
Lord Okudaira [of Nakatsu Clan] at Shiodome as a temporary
school annex. It will be used chiefly for beginning students without
restriction on their number as far as we can provide effective

"Keiō Gijuku Shingi" (慶応義塾新議), 1869. *Fukuzawa Yukichi Zenshū*, vol. 19, pp.
370–73.

instruction. Students from all parts of Japan, irrespective of their being of the merchant, artisan, farmer, or samurai class, whoever has a desire to study Western learning, shall be welcome to join.

1. Three *ryō* shall be paid as entrance fee.

2. Two *bu* shall be paid every month as tuition.

3. At *Bon*[1] and at year end, 1000 *hiki*[2] shall be paid. However, when money is presented, no ceremonial cords (*mizuhiki*) and ceremonial seals (*noshi*) shall be used.

4. The school building opened on this occasion is for lectures and instruction only, and it provides no residential or dining facilities. Those students coming from distant places must find lodging nearby. Places to stay quite economically will be found easily.

5. Those wishing to join the Corporation shall come to Keiō Gijuku in Shinsenza and consult with the *jukuchō* (supervisor in charge).

6. The order of studying in this school is roughly as follows: After joining the Corporation, new members will first learn the Western alphabet; then they will take lessons in either elementary science or grammar. This stage will take about three months. After this, they will read a geography book or a physics book. This will take up the next six months. Then they will read a history book for another six months.

The above are lessons in *sodoku* (simple reading), and the students will appreciate how to read Western books. Also they will acquire the ability to select a book and read with the aid of a dictionary and some help from their seniors; also they will be able to understand difficult books when they attend lectures on them. This will introduce the students to a new stage of self-study. Besides the above lessons, the students will begin taking part in *kaidoku* (seminars) three or four months after their initiation, and this will greatly improve their skills.

Thus, the three periods of three, six, and six months will total

---

[1] A yearly festival in the 7th month when the souls of the ancestors are believed to return to their families where they are welcomed with festivities. Also, gifts were exchanged among relatives and friends on that day.

[2] A unit of money, although not an actual currency, used only in gift giving. As 400 *hiki* equaled 1 *ryō*, 1000 *hiki* equaled 2 *ryō*, 2 *bu*. This was being charged by the school as a fee, but the use of *hiki* must be a remnant of the old custom of giving gifts to teachers at *Bon*.

one year and three months. By no means will this complete their studies. Though there naturally will be differences between individuals, based on our past experience, the above indicates the time required by average students. As one acquires the ability to read without coaching, the next stage will be to translate, and then finally to teach. When one advances this far, the studies become increasingly more difficult. In fact there is not one person in Keiō Gijuku who is accomplished in his learning. There is probably not one even in the whole of Japan who considers himself perfect in Western learning. The differences will only be in the relative extent of learning.

7. School expenses cannot be fixed permanently as they depend upon the price of commodities. However, granting the price of rice to be 1 *ryō* for 1 *to*, with 6 *ryō* a month a student will be able to easily pay all expenses from tuition and fees to living expenses, including haircuts, baths, writing paper and brushes, and laundry, regardless of whether he lives in the dormitory or in private lodgings. Drinking expenses are not included as it is a very evil habit from which men of honor should abstain. On the other hand, we cannot maintain a proper balance in nutrition and health without eating some fish or meat, and their lack can influence a person for the rest of his life. Therefore, occasional fish and meat is desirable, but 6 *ryō* a month is not sufficient for a meat diet; 100 *ryō* a year will be needed.

8. After joining the Corporation, when the student's scholarship advances and he is included among the teaching staff, he will be given some remuneration from the school savings to aid his subsistence according to the level of his office and the amount of work done. The school charges tuition to the students for this purpose.

9. The prices of Western books have gone down considerably. For beginning students, the book expenses are small, as indicated below:

Elementary sciences	1 *bu*, 1 *shu*
Keiō reader and grammar	1 *bu*
Japanese-English dictionary	3 *ryō*, 2 *bu*
Geography Physics History	from 2 to 4 *ryō* each

[29]

The above books will suffice for the initial year and a half. Besides the above, it will be ideal to own an English dictionary costing 8 or 9 *ryō*.

Members of Keiō Gijuku

8th month, Meiji 2nd year (1869)

5
Agreements Among the Members of the Corporation

After about four years in the small campus of Shinsenza, Keiō Gijuku was moved to an extensive area
in Mita in the same city of Tokyo, and the school has
remained there to this day. Though at present it possesses still larger campuses in other parts of the city
and elsewhere, the Mita Campus is still the home
campus, accommodating the President's Office and
the upper classes and the Graduate School for Social
Sciences and Humanities.

Fukuzawa called the new regulations "Agreements"
in order to emphasize the cooperative spirit of the
school. They consist of 113 rules in 17 sections, only a
sample of which is translated here.

Preamble

Keiō Gijuku, situated at two-chome in Mita, Tokyo, was first established in Shinsenza, Shiba, in the Keiō era and has now
moved to this location. The school stands on land which was
leased by the government nominally to Fukuzawa Yukichi.
However, because the government allowed him the use of the
land for the explicit purpose of opening a school and teaching
students, and because the buildings on it have been built with
the money from the treasury of the school and money borrowed

"Keiō Gijuku Shachū no Yakusoku" (慶応義塾社中之約束), 1871. *Keiō Gijuku Hyakunenshi*, vol. 1, pp. 337–38.

[31]

in the school's name, the land is not to be considered Fukuzawa's personal possession. It rightly shall be the common property of the colleagues who comprise the school. It is only while a person holds the office to establish and enforce regulations that he holds the right to administer it. Therefore, the members should call this school the Center for Learning [*Gakumonjo*] of Mita, two-chome.

1) The purpose of education in this school is to read Western books widely, study their contents, and pass the knowledge on to society through translation. There is no mystery to these studies requiring tacit communion of mind with mind. Therefore, according to the ability of a person, a student who is being taught today may some day be teaching the person who is now instructing him. For this reason, in this school there is no distinction between teachers and students. They are all summarily called *shachū* (colleagues).

2) Of the colleagues, those who teach are called *kyōjukata* (teaching members) and those who are taught will be called *seito* (students). A person may be receiving instruction in one subject and at the same time teaching another subject. Such a person is a student and at the same time a teaching member.

3) Among the members of the Corporation, those who are in charge of the administration are called *shitsuji* (officers). The work of the officers does not involve learning, and those teaching members who take part in the administration will be regarded as undertaking two duties.

4) The officers may increase or decrease their numbers by the consent of more than half of the members. An officer must be above 21 years old.

5) When there is a person outside the Corporation who offers to donate money or goods, the motive for the donation must be sought, and if it is found amenable with the spirit of the Agreements by more than half of the Corporation members, the donation shall be accepted.

There are four divisions under the responsibility of the members of the Corporation:
The First Division
a. Regulations concerning the invitation of new members to the Corporation.

b. Regulations concerning admission of students into the dormitory.

c. Dormitory regulations.

d. Regulations for day students.

e. Regulations concerning admission of people through the gates.

f. Regulations for reception of guests and cleaning of rooms.

g. Regulations for lending out of books.

The proper functioning of the above seven regulations is to be the responsibility of the school headquarters (*jukukan kyoku*).

Second Division

a. Regulations concerning income and expenditure of funds.

b. Dining-room regulations.

c. Repairs and maintenance regulations.

d. Regulations for the employment of school servants.

The proper functioning of the above four items is the responsibility of the Office of Finances.

Third Division

Regulations for the Children's Division.[1]

The proper functioning of the above regulation is the responsibility of the officer in charge of the Children's Division.

Fourth Division

Regulations for instruction.

The proper functioning of the above regulation is the responsibility of the officer in charge of instructions.

For all the divisions from the first to the fourth, those in charge shall be appointed from among the officers. The officers may take turns in serving. When one conceives an idea beneficial to the school, he may express his opinion regardless of his position. Also, those officers off duty may step in to assist whenever occasion invites such an act.

---

[1] The Children's Division was open only to boys between the ages of twelve and sixteen The school for children below twelve had not been established yet.

[33]

6

Words Left Behind in Nakatsu

By 1870, Fukuzawa had become a very well known
author with his publication of *Things Western*. But his
publications had been objective descriptions of Western society and institutions with no opinions of his
own. "Words Left Behind in Nakatsu" is considered
the second revelation in which his philosophy has been
preserved, the first being *Primer on Foreigners* (c. 1862),
which was later included in the *Preface to the Collected
Works of Fukuzawa*. Neither of these two were printed
at the time of writing, though both were hand-copied
and distributed among friends.

"Words Left Behind in Nakatsu" was written and left
with a senior friend, Kuwana Hōzan, when Fukuzawa
went to Nakatsu to bring his mother to Tokyo. Fukuzawa probably felt that he was breaking ties with his
home town by taking his mother away. Perhaps this
thought induced him to write this piece as an expression of his inner self to be left behind with the people
of Nakatsu.

Human beings are the lords of creation! This saying does not
mean that anyone would deserve the title when he has a body
complete with the organs—ears, eyes, nose, mouth, hands, and
feet—and he is able to talk, eat, and sleep. One must cultivate

"Nakatsu Ryūbetsu no Sho" (中津留別之書), 1870. *Fukuzawa Yukichi Zenshū*, vol. 20,
pp. 49–53.

moral virtues by following Heaven's[1] rule, acquire knowledge and understanding worthy of a human being, associate with people and experience things, work for one's own independence and succeed in earning a living for one's family—only after these, may one be called a lord of creation.

Here is something that neither the Chinese nor the Japanese have noted in the past: the principle of freedom and independence which exists as an inborn constitution. This word "freedom" when spoken carelessly would seem to imply willfulness or selfishness, but it does not by any means. The true meaning of freedom is to act according to one's own mind without obstructing the freedom of others. Father and son, lord and vassal, man and wife, friends, each and all should be careful not to impose on the other, but each should extend his heart's desires freely, and without enslaving others with his mind, accomplish his own independence. Then, with the inborn goodness of man prevailing, no one would stray to evil ways.

Should there be a person who goes astray and oversteps the bounds of freedom to work for his own advantage by violating the interests of others, this person is clearly an enemy of his fellow men, marked by Heaven as a sinner who should not be forgiven. Therefore, without regard to his being of noble or humble birth, and whether he is young or old, he may be despised by society and he may be punished without hesitation.

Thus freedom and independence are important. When they are taken wrongly, a person will lose his moral sense, his intellect will not develop, his household will not be maintained, a clan cannot hold its own, and even a nation cannot hope to preserve its independence. Let each person accomplish his own independence, then each family will be independent. When each family is independent, the clan will be independent. When each clan is independent, the nation itself will be secure in its independence. The four classes—samurai, farmer, artisan, and merchant—must not interfere with their respective freedom and independence.

The fundamental basis of human morality is the relationship

---

[1] *Ten*, in Japanese, implying the basic principles of the universe. It is a derivation from Confucian philosophy which regarded morality, natural sciences, social sciences, government, and all subjects of learning as well as all human activities as belonging to one system of rules.

between man and wife. And following this relationship are the bonds between parents and children, brothers and sisters. When Heaven brought forth human beings, the very first must have been a man and a woman. However long a time may pass—millions or tens of millions of years—the proportion of their numbers will remain the same. Man and woman, both are individual human beings standing between Heaven and earth; there is no reason to distinguish the relative importance or dignity of the two.

According to the old customs of China and Japan, a man could keep several women as his wife and concubines and treat them as lowly servants or even as criminals, and the man would show no sign of embarrassment. Is this not a despicable custom? When the man of the house makes light of his wife, their children in imitation will slight their mother and will not obey her. When they slight their mother, it will be as though they have no mother at all; they may as well be orphans. Moreover, because the father works outside and is not at home much of the time, who in the family will look after the children's education? This state of things is pitiable—indeed much more than words can describe.

In Lun-yü, the Analects of Confucius, one passage says, "Man and wife shall be separate." This word "separate" does not mean that there should be distance between the two. There must be love and compassion between them. Suppose there were a distance between the two, like members of separate families; it would be impossible to preserve a home. Therefore, this word "separate" must be interpreted to imply "distinct" so as to clarify that a man and woman are a couple and another pair another couple; thus every couple shall be distinct from all others. This must be the true meaning of the saying. However, in a family where many concubines are kept, and the wife has her own children and each concubine has her own, the children will all be brothers and sisters with the same father but different mothers. In such a family, a man and wife cannot be recognized as distinct.

If a man has the right to take two wives, a woman should also have the right to take two husbands. Here, let me ask how a man would feel if his wife loved another husband and the two husbands and one wife were to live together. Would the master of the house tolerate this and serve his wife faithfully?

In Tso-chuan, there is a passage on temporary exchange of

[37]

wives. The venerable Confucius was so concerned about the deterioration of general morals that he took the trouble of writing *Ch'un-ch'iu*. In it, he wrote about the barbarians and China to praise the one and to deride the others. But probably as the custom of exchanging wives did not bother him much, he passed over it without a mention. To us today, his attitude appears somewhat wanting in the true sense of morality. This makes me suspect that perhaps the words in his *Analects*, "There shall be distance between husband and wife," has a different meaning from my interpretation. Scholars of Confucianism must have some opinions on this point.

Devotion to parents is a natural attitude of children. Every child should devote himself single-mindedly to his parents. There is an old saying that a child must be nursed in his parents' arms for three years, therefore he must mourn a parent's death for three years. But is this not too much of a calculating give-and-take, too mercenary a saying devoid of love?

In society, children are often blamed for their lack of filial piety, but too rarely are parents blamed for their lack of love toward children. It is very unjust of parents to say, "I brought forth this child," and treat the child as if he were a convenient tool he had made with his own hands or purchased with money. A child is a gift from Heaven. A parent must cherish the child as such. When a child is born, the father and the mother must join their forces in bringing him up and keep him close until the age of ten or more,[2] and with their love and influence, lead the child toward goodness. When the child is ready for an education, send him to school in care of a teacher, and let him grow into a person worthy of the name. Such is the parents' mission, and their dutiful service to Heaven.

When the child reaches the age of 21 or 22, he is said to have reached adulthood, and in fact he is able to care for himself. Thereupon, the parents will withdraw and let him earn his own living or let him go wherever he wishes and do whatever he likes. Yet, the bond between parents and a child will not be altered throughout their lives or even after death. A child must continue

---

[2] This is presumed to indicate the usual age when children were sent to *terakoya*, the general schools which existed before compulsory education came into being. Fukuzawa himself did not go to school until he was fourteen or fifteen.

[38]

his devotion to his parents and the parents must preserve their love for him. The statement made earlier that the parents are to withdraw simply means that they must not interfere with the independence and freedom of their children. In a Western book, it is said that after the child has reached adulthood, parents may give him advice, but not orders. This is an eternal saying that one must stop to ponder.

In educating children, calligraphy and other studies are, of course, necessary, but as has been said, learning through the body is more important than learning through the mind, and parents must therefore maintain moral conduct. They may talk of noble behavior, but if their own conduct is immoral, the child will not believe their words; he will rather imitate their behavior. How can parents hope to have their child grow into a person worthy of the name if they are wanting in both their words and in behavior! With such parents, the child would be more unfortunate than an orphan.

Some parents may be honest and love their child, but sometimes their ignorance makes them push the child blindly into the path of their own choosing. Such parents may seem innocent, but in truth they are guilty of not realizing the reasons behind their love for their child. Their attitude would lead their child into the misfortune of little knowledge and little virtue. And they are indeed criminals against the ways of Heaven and man. No parent is free from worry over a child's illness. The fact, however, is that deficiency of mind is more serious than imperfection of the body. Then, why are they concerned over the diseases of the body so much more than those of the mind? Should it be called the love of a fool? It may as well be called animal love.

The differences of people's minds are like the differences in their faces. As society developed, the number of evil-doers increased, and it became beyond the power of common people to maintain their safety and security. Thereupon, they decided to set up what may be called their representative, and after deliberating on the advantages and drawbacks from all angles, established the law, and for the first time a system of encouraging goodness and punishing evil was practiced in society. This representative has come to be called government. The head of a

[39]

government is called a sovereign who is supported by officials. These men are indispensable in preserving peace in the country and in protecting it from external disturbances.

Of the many tasks in this world, there is none more difficult than managing the government of a nation. Those who work hard are entitled to appropriate rewards, which is a law set by Heaven, and the reward will be larger for those undertaking difficult tasks. Therefore, everyone living by the benefit of the government must not complain about the salaries they receive from the sovereign and the officials. If the government is just, their salaries will be small in proportion to their benefit. People must not only envy the men in office but they must respect them. Also, the sovereign and the officials themselves must not forget the great law that man must work and earn his living, and they must always compare their work and the compensation they receive and calculate the values of both. This is perhaps what one would call the law of integrity between the sovereign and the subjects.

The above is an outline of relationships among people. To describe it minutely, two or three pages will not suffice. One must begin by reading. The books to be read should not be confined to Japanese books alone. Chinese books must be read; books from India, too, must be read; also, books from various countries of the West must be included. Today we have scholars trained in the various schools of Japanese, Chinese, and Western learning, and each school has its own theories with which they slander each other. This is a very sad state of affairs. Studying usually means simply the reading of words on paper, and it is not a very difficult task to accomplish. The argument on the merits and demerits of different schools is something that should come after one has accumulated knowledge. Therefore, it is simply a foolish waste of time to argue before concluding one's studies. With the wisdom we are equipped with, how much effort will it take to learn a few languages, such as Japanese, Chinese, English, and French? Is it not cowardly to slander a school of learning before one even masters the language, much less knows anything about it? In taking up a subject, one should first consider the advantage it will bring to our country rather than the merits and the demerits of the school itself.

[40]

Now that foreign trade has opened our country, there at times have appeared some outrageous foreigners who endeavor to make our country poor and make fools of us by reaping profits for themselves. And those among us who advocate old Japanese or Chinese studies—looking back longingly to the past and never taking to the new, nor caring to know anything of the world or the people of the world as they now are, thus remaining ignorant of their own accord—they are the easy victims of these foreigners. At such a juncture, the only way to defy these foreigners is Western studies. We should read widely in the books of all the countries and learn the true circumstances of the world and enable ourselves to discuss the public affairs of the world in the common language of the world. We must accumulate the knowledge and virtues for giving free rein to the independence and freedom of each citizen, and in international business abide by the laws of the world to exalt the independence of our nation. Such is the way to establish the true greatness of Japan. This is what I am seeking. And this is the reason I urge the pursuance of Western studies without weighing the merits and demerits of the Japanese, Chinese, and Western schools.

I pray with all my heart that the people of my old home town, Nakatsu, too will open their eyes to the new age, take up the Western studies, work themselves to earn their own living,[3] attain their freedom without encroaching on the freedom of others, strive to be virtuous, seek knowledge, cast away petty thoughts, and acquire the true means for attaining security for their family and greatness for the nation.

Who under the Heavens does not hold nostalgic thoughts toward his native town? Who in the world does not pray for the happiness of his old friends? The time of my departure is near at hand. I, in haste, took up the writing brush and wrote the general substance of what is found in the Western books which I am leaving behind with friends for their future reference.

Night of November 27, Meiji 3rd year (1870)
Under the broken window of my old house in Rusui-chō, Nakatsu

[3] The samurai, who had brought about the Meiji Restoration and who displayed strong interest in Western culture, lived on stipends from their clans. Fukuzawa was alluding here to the imminent abolition of the clans (which occurred in 1871) when all the samurai would be forced to find their own means of living.

[41]

7
Preface to
the Penmanship Copybook

In the early years following the Restoration, Fukuzawa was not entirely sure of the new government's policies. He also feared the ruthless "Expel the Foreigners" advocates, and he refrained from coming out boldly with his progressive ideas. He spent much of his energy in what may be called the groundwork, that is, writing elementary textbooks for providing basic education to children. His publications included *Penmanship Copybook, Illustrated Book of Physical Sciences (Kyūri Zukai,* 1868), and *All the Countries of the World (Sekai Kunizukushi,* 1869). In the prefaces to these textbooks, the reader is able to grasp the great schemes which were taking form in Fukuzawa's mind, and also the very revolutionary ideas in education that he was pushing forward through such traditional subjects as penmanship.

Penmanship copybooks were the chief textbooks used in *terakoya,* the one-teacher home schools in the days before the advent of the Ministry of Education and the nationwide elementary school system. *Terakoya* were private enterprises, but they did a remarkable job in educating children throughout the country. The chief subject taught was penmanship. The idea was that in practicing brush writing, the children would copy many textbooks and subconsciously learn model compositions and at the same time absorb knowledge.

"Keimō Tenarai no Fumi Jo" (啓蒙手習之文序), 1871. *Fukuzawa Yukichi Zenshū,* vol. 3, pp. 3–4.

[43]

The book entitled *A Model for a School*, a translation from a Western book by my colleague Obata, says, "Not that we are straining our efforts toward making all our countrymen into scholars and political advocates, but we do hope to provide a wide education to guide our people toward goodness, so that our government will be solid and the national power ever stronger." In keeping with this goal, our schools should be large in number, reaching out to all the people, rather than boasting high standards but being exclusive and few in number.

Among the countries of the West, education in Russia is the least widespread. The ratio of students in Russia to the whole population is only about 1 to 77. In a country like Holland, on the other hand, where education is very prevalent, the number of students is about 1 in every 8 of the general population. Now, if Japan should establish a law on education and endeavor to place itself halfway between Russia and Holland, our objective will be to have 1 student for every 42 people.

Estimating the population of Japan to be about 40 million, one-forty-second of this number will be about 940,000. To put this number of students in schools, the expense will be tremendous—in meeting the need to build large schools quickly and equip them with educational materials of high standard so that these 940,000 students may be properly accommodated. Even if the living expenses of the students are borne by the parents, the salaries for the teachers and the staff, the maintenance of the buildings, books and instruments for instruction, when added together and divided by the number of students, will be about 100 *ryō*[1] per student per year. This 100 *ryō* multiplied by 940,000 comes out to 94 million *ryō*, and this will be the annual national expenditure for education.

Will the present economic power of the country be able to meet such an expenditure? My private concern is on this very point. Therefore, following a policy of gradual progress, I am proposing a plan to begin at a low level by inviting the penmanship teachers to open the way toward this great movement. Then the purpose of widespread education will be initiated with great financial savings for the whole country.

[1] *Ryō.* The new monetary system with *yen* as its basic unit was created in 1871, but the actual currency was still the old *ryō* surviving from the Tokugawa period.

However, it has always been the way with the penmanship teachers to neglect what I consider *jitsugaku*[2] and to give all their attention to proper letter writing for conveying congratulations for coming-of-age ceremonies, weddings, and festivals, or for letters of condolence. At times they may turn attention to other subjects, but they seldom go beyond Japanese and Chinese classical poetry which are of such indirect use in this age of developing civilization.

For all these reasons, I have discussed this problem with my colleagues and decided to publish a copybook for penmanship to include the Japanese alphabet—*i, ro, ha*—names of all the provinces and such usual subjects, and adding new ideas taken from several Western books[3] but written in an easy style.

I pray that this book will help children of five or six in learning the contents while practicing writing, thus guiding them to various fields of study in later years. In this way, this book will assist penmanship teachers in providing the service of general education. If the purpose of this book should be served, my colleagues and I will be greatly pleased.

Fukuzawa Yukichi

3rd month, Meiji 4th year (1871)

---

[2] *Jitsugaku*, a term coined by Fukuzawa, implied scientific and functional learning which contributed directly to human life, in contrast to the traditional disciplines, such as classical Chinese philosophy and literature.

[3] The subject matter introduced from Western books was geography, mathematics, general sciences, world history, economics, and ethics. Fukuzawa explains briefly what each one is and why each is important.

[45]

8
Daily Lessons

Fukuzawa wrote these "Daily Lessons" for his two eldest sons when the elder was eight years old and the younger one six. He made two small notebooks by folding some sheets of paper and binding them with strings of twisted strips of paper which he made himself. On the covers he wrote "Daily Lessons" and the boys' names.

Then, every day, or every few days, he called the boys to his desk and wrote that day's lesson in both the notebooks and explained the lesson to them. The younger son, Sutejirō, recalled in later years that he thought the lessons very boring, but he sat through them patiently because his father would reward him with a piece of cake after each lesson. The "Daily Lessons" were stopped short one day, only one month after they were begun. Apparently Fukuzawa became too preoccupied with Keiō Gijuku to continue.

Though these lessons are for children of eight or younger, they contain some thoughts on religion and other ideas which Fukuzawa seldom discussed elsewhere. Some researchers have been puzzled over his true philosophy, because he seemed to take religion seriously when addressing children, while appearing purely rational and scientific when he discussed problems with adults. (Refer to the lesson of the 27th of the 10th month and the first lesson in Part II.)

"Hibi no Oshie"(ひゞのをしへ), 1871. *Fukuzawa Yukichi Zenshū*, vol. 20, pp. 67–77.

Daily Lessons Part I

10th month, Meiji 4th year   Fukuzawa Ichitarō[1]

THE RULES
1. You must not lie.
2. You must not take things that are not yours.
3. You must not accept presents without your parents' permission.
4. You must not be obstinate.
5. Quarreling between brothers is strictly prohibited.
6. Gossiping about people is strictly prohibited.
7. You must not wish to own things that belong to others.

14th day, 10th month
In reading a book, to forget its first part is like drawing water into a bucket which has no bottom. There will only be the hard work of drawing the water, and the water will not remain in the bucket. Therefore, if you, Ichi and Sute, do not go over what you have read and remember the first part of it, you will have wasted your labor in reading and you will have learned nothing.

15th day, 10th month
Anyone who calls himself a human being must not kill insects or treat animals unkindly or do anything cruel. When one goes on with such merciless acts, by and by he will be treating his fellow men in the same way. Take care to heed this warning.

16th day, 10th month
You may be children now, but you will not be children forever. You are bound to grow up, and some day you will become full-fledged adults. Therefore, from the time you are children, try not to depend on others. Wash your face yourself, clean your own mouth, dress yourself, put your socks on yourself, and do everything else that you can do by yourself. This, in the Western language is "independence." In Japanese it is *dokuritsu*, and it means to stand up by yourself and not look for assistance from others.

---

[1] Fukuzawa Yukichi's eldest son (1863–1938). Later in his life, he was appointed *shatō*, honorary head of Keiō Gijuku.

[48]

17th day, 10th month

People's minds, like their faces, are different. There is no one person who is the same as another. One person will have a round face, another a long one. Similarly, their minds are different, one from the other, from birth. Some are short in temper, some are patient, some are quiet, some active and noisy. And so, when you watch others act, you must not lose your temper and show that you are angry because you don't like the way they act. You should forgive and bear as much as you can and make friends.

18th day, 10th month

Those who are blind or deaf are called handicapped. Ichi and Sute, you are both fortunate not to be handicapped. But this defect does not happen to the eyes and ears alone. The mind can also be handicapped. When one hears correct reasoning yet does not understand it, he is worse than a deaf person. Those who cannot read when they look on the pages of a book are worse than a blind person. Therefore, one should not be ashamed of being blind and deaf. Those who are maimed in mind are the ones who should be really ashamed of themselves.

19th day, 10th month

A cheap cotton kimono or taffeta overgarment is nothing to be ashamed of. But when your clothes are dirty or when your face or hands or feet are filthy, you should be ashamed of yourself. Children should always remember to wash their hands and feet, and see that their clothing is not soiled.

21st day, 10th month

A person must have courage. Courage means to be strong, to have a nature that fears nothing. Whatever you have decided to do, you should persist, and without fearing hardships keep at it till you finish. For instance, when you do not understand a book, you must not give up. You should read it over and over, ten times or twenty times, until you understand and learn it. Have courage and persevere.

27th day, 10th month

In the world, there is no one more wonderful than your father and mother, nor anyone kinder than your father and mother. All children will wish that their fathers and mothers be well and live a long life, but we cannot tell if they will die tomorrow, even if they are well today.

The life and death of your father and mother is according to the mind of God.[2] God made your father and mother, God keeps them alive, but at times He will let them die. All things in the world were made by God, and there is nothing that He did not make. You should begin to learn the wonderfulness of God from the time you are still children and obey the mind of God.

Three times a day you eat your meals, you sleep at night, you get up in the morning. We live only fifty years and if you repeat the same thing day after day, you will grow old before you realize. One day you will suddenly find that you have aged and have grey hair, and before too long you will turn into dirt in the grave-yard of a temple.

After all, eating, sleeping, and waking are things that even horses and pigs do. Being a human being, can you be satisfied with doing the same things that horses and pigs do? It will be a shame if you are. Since you have been born a human being, you must accomplish things that birds and beasts cannot and prove that you are different from them. The difference will be that you can learn to reason and to keep yourselves from all that tempts you. You can learn to read and write; understand the world you live in and how it has changed from ancient times, and then make good friends. You will then have nothing to be ashamed of in your own mind. Only when you do all this, can you call yourself the lord of creation.

The old tale tells us that Momotarō[3] went to Demon's Island to bring back treasures. Wasn't that a very shameful thing to do? The treasures belonged to the demons, and the demons had been keeping them with care. And Momotarō simply went out for no

---

[2] In the original text, Fukuzawa used this English word "God," spelling it out in Japanese. There was no Japanese word to represent it. The great creator of the universe was a new concept brought in from the West.

[3] Momotarō is the hero of a folk tale; often called *Nippon Ichi*, the first in Japan in courage and power.

[50]

good reason and carried those treasures away. Momotarō is a thief and an evil child.

If, however, the demons were bad and had been menacing the people nearby, it would have been acceptable for Momotarō with his great courage to go out and punish the demons. But the story tells that he brought back treasures and gave them to the old man and the old woman, who had been like his father and mother. This shows that he was simply greedy. He was a very mean boy.

When you injure your hand or foot, tie it with a piece of paper or put some plaster on the wound, and the wound will heal in a short while. If it is a slight cut, it will not even leave a scar.

Now, a person who is worthy of being called a human being is not supposed to tell a lie, and he is not supposed to steal. If he lies or steals even once, it is like a wound on his mind. This wound on the mind is a greater concern than wounds on hands or feet. It cannot be healed with medicine or with plaster. It will cripple you for your whole lives. This being so, you boys should take more care of your mind than of your hands and feet.

Children must memorize numbers. For instance, people have five fingers on each of their hands, five toes on each of their feet. All together, they have twenty fingers and toes. Now, if someone asks you how many fingers and toes there are all together on all the hands and feet of you five brothers and sisters, what will be your answer?

We divide the time from sunrise this morning to sunrise tomorrow morning into twelve, and call each one of them one hour.[4] We call the time when the sun rises in the morning hour six, and then hour five, hour four, and hour nine. This hour nine comes at the middle of the day, which is when you eat your noon meal. Hour nine is followed by hour eight, hour seven, and hour six. This hour six is when the sun sets. And so, the hour six in the morning to hour six in the afternoon is day time, and it is made

---

[4] At this time, Japan was using the lunar calendar and a system of its own for keeping time. The calendar and the time system were modernized by an imperial order in 1872.

up of six hours. Night time hours are counted in the same manner, and there are six hours from hour six in the afternoon until hour six in the morning when the sun rises again.

Children should always be gentle and loving. In treating people outside, you should, of course, be quiet and gentle, and also at home when you order men and women servants, you should not put on airs or use rude and commanding language. For instance, when you want to have a drink of water, instead of just ordering the maid sternly, "Bring me water!" if you ask her, "Will you please bring me some water to drink?" the maid will gladly bring it to you at once. In all that you do, be kind at heart and never appear haughty.

We call people who do difficult work high and important persons and the people who do simple tasks lowly persons. To read books and to ponder things and to work for the good of society are difficult, but the mixing of mud which the plasterers do and pulling rickshaws along the streets are easy, because the work does not require mental strain. Therefore, because the difference between high and low among the people is simply the difference in the work done, you should not think too much of those lords [daimyō], courtiers [kugé], and samurai who ride horses about and wear long swords to impress others.

They may appear distinguished, but their minds are often like an empty barrel. They cannot read a book, they cannot follow difficult reasoning, and they spend their days doing nothing but loafing. You will meet many such people, and you will see that there is no reason to think of them as noble or high in society. Only because they have a great deal of money and rice, which has been handed down from their ancestors, are they able to live as splendidly as they do, but these people are of no greater value than rickshawmen. They are really very lowly indeed.

A proverb says, "Observe how others appear, and care for your own appearance." You both have come along so far without any worries over your food or clothing. But suppose you stop being nice and turn rough, stop reading books, and become an ignorant person. However well you dress, and however large a house you

[52]

may live in, you will be made light of by the people and pointed to with scorn, and you will be thought of as being as low as a beggar or even worse.

Daily Lessons   Part II

11th month, Meiji 4th year   Fukuzawa Ichitarō

Listen, boys, listen! This is the beginning of the Daily Lessons, Part II.

The rules given here are six in all. Open your ears and listen, put all the rules in your heads and never forget.

1. Fear the Sun, revere it, and obey its will. However, the Sun I am speaking of here is not the sun that shines in the sky. It is called "God" in the Western language. When translated into Japanese, it will be "Creator of All Things."

2. Revere your father and mother, be close to them, and obey their wishes.

3. Do not kill people. Do not be cruel to animals and kill not even a worm without reason.

4. Do not steal. Do not take what others have left behind.

5. Never lie. Never lie and trouble others.

6. Do not be greedy. Do not let yourself wish to have what others have.

The rules of the great Sun have never failed since long, long ago. When you sow wheat, wheat will grow; if you sow beans, beans will grow; a boat made of wood will float and a boat made of mud will sink. All these are true always and people do not stop to wonder at them. And so, when you do good, you will have good results and when you do evil, you will be rewarded with evil. All these are the rules of the Sun, and they have not changed since ancient times. But some fools who do not know the rules of the Sun will sometimes be overcome with greed and try to commit an evil deed in order to gain happiness. This is exactly like riding on a mud boat to sail across the ocean. The Sun will never be deceived by this kind of trick. When a bad seed is sown, a bad plant will grow. There are ears in the wall and eyes in the doors! Never think of escaping when you do evil.

[53]

One day is from sunrise this morning to sunrise tomorrow morning. Thirty days make one month. The long month is thirty days and the short month is twenty-nine days. But suppose we count all the months as thirty days, one year will have 360 days because a year is made up of twelve months. So, ten years will be 3600 days, fifty years will be 18,000 days. Counting from tonight, suppose you sleep 360 times; then you will be one year older, and the New Year will be here and you will be enjoying the festivities. But when you sleep many many more times, such as 18,000 times more, you both will be old men of 56 or 57 and you will no longer find much to make merry of. Waste not a day now but be diligent in learning your lessons.

In Japan, we divide a day and a night into 12 hours, but in the Western countries, they divide it into 24 hours. And their one hour is exactly the same as one-half hour of our way of measuring time:

Japanese Time: 6 6½ 5 5½ 4 4½ 9 9½ 8 8½ 7 7½
Western Time: 6 7   8 9   10 11   12 1   2 3   4 5

After five, time goes back to six again and repeats in the same way again.

One Western hour is divided into 60, and they call this shorter time unit one minute. In our language this one minute is called one *fun-ji*. They divide this one minute into 60 again and call this shorter unit one second. One second is just about the interval between your pulses.

Because one day is twelve hours in the Western way of counting, it will be 720 minutes when counted in minutes. In seconds, it will be 43,200 seconds.

The length of a *tatami* mat is 6 *shaku* and the height of a door is 5 *shaku*, 7 *sun*. One *shaku* divided by 10 is one *sun*; one *sun* divided by 10 is one *bu*, and this *bu* divided by 10 is one *rin*. Therefore, one *shaku* is 1000 *rin*, or 100 *bu*, or 10 *sun*.

Six *shaku* is called one *ken*; 60 *ken* is one *chō* and 36 *chō* is one *ri*. Therefore, one *chō* is 360 *shaku*. One *ri* is 12,960 *shaku*. In *ken* this will be 2160 *ken*.

[54]

Suppose one step of a man is 2 *shaku*, one *ri* will take 6480 steps. Therefore, a person who walks 10 *ri* in a day takes 64,800 steps.

The above is according to the measure called *kane jaku* which we use in building houses, making boxes, and other similar things. For measuring the length of cloth, there is another kind of measure called *kujira jaku*. Drapers and dressmakers use it. This *kujira jaku* is longer than *kane jaku*, and *kujira jaku's* 8 *sun* equals one *shaku* of *kane jaku*.

One *tsubo* is an area one *ken* long and one *ken* wide, which is the same as 2 *tatami* placed side by side. For measuring the size of paddy fields, in the language of the farmers, this one *tsubo* is called one *bu*. Thirty *bu* makes one *se*, and 10 *se* makes one *tan*, and 10 *tan* makes one *chō*. And so, one *chō* equals 3000 *tsubo*, one *tan* 300 *tsubo*, one *se* 30 *tsubo*, and one *bu* is one *tsubo*.

For instance, when someone says, "This field is 4 *tan*, 7 *se*, and 15 *bu*," that means that the field is 1425 *tsubo*. Because a huge room with 1000 *tatami* is 500 *tsubo*, in the farmer's language, it will be one *tan*, 3 *se*, and 20 *bu*.

9
Announcement for Nakatsu Town School

Okudaira Masayuki, former lord of the Nakatsu Clan, was greatly influenced by Fukuzawa and established a school in Nakatsu. He asked his mentor to serve as supervisor, and Fukuzawa sent several of his disciples there, and a veritable annex of Keiō Gijuku was opened. Between 1873 and 1876, the school had some 600 students and was reputed to be the best in western Japan, stimulating development in culture, commerce, and newspaper publication in the area. However, with the adoption of the public school system by the Ministry of Education, Nakatsu Town School found its maintenance difficult. Moreover, the financial conditions of the Okudaira family no longer made it possible to continue its yearly contribution. As a result, the school was forced to close its doors in 1883. In other areas of Japan, many of the schools that were established under similar circumstances by local supporters were later forced to close or were absorbed by the public school system.

I, Okudaira Masayuki,[1] while still very young, became the master of the House of Okudaira, and consequently was appointed

"Nakatsu Shi Gakkō no Ki" (中津市学校之記), 1871. This piece is not included in *Fukuzawa Yukichi Zenshū* because it had not been recognized as Fukuzawa's writing at the time of compilation.
[1] Born the third son of Date Muneshiro, Lord of the Uwajima Clan, in 1855. When eight years old, he was adopted as heir by the Okudaira family of Nakatsu. In 1868

Governor of Nakatsu Clan.[2] However, I could not in any way measure up to this heavy responsibility. In spite of my constant efforts, little was accomplished. Thereupon, in private, I made a resolution to dedicate myself to Western studies in order to educate and cultivate myself. I thought, then, I may be able to improve myself to preserve the good name of my house and to fill the responsibilities I had been entrusted with.

And so, in January of this year, I went to Tokyo and commenced my efforts in Western studies. In July, I was relieved of the governorship, as other governors of the clans were. For me, this was a liberation from the duties which had been difficult to carry out, and it was as if I had gained peace of mind for the moment. However, upon deeper reflection, I discovered that it was only the governorship that I had been relieved of; I still had my duties as a man. Learning is for the cultivation of one's own self; it is not for the good of others. I should not measure the need for learning according to the importance of the position I hold.

Therefore, with this idea, I have petitioned the government again for a leave for study abroad. My wish is that the samurai and the commoners in my former clan will understand my intentions and will not regard my behavior as extraordinary.

To attempt a task all alone is not as enjoyable as working in the company of friends. I shall be alone in going abroad, but my

---

(Meiji 1), at the age of thirteen upon the retirement of his father, he was made the head of Okudaira family and concurrently Lord of Nakatsu Clan, and he was appointed governor of Nakatsu the next year. At sixteen he went abroad to study in the United States, accompanied by one of Fukuzawa's chief disciples, Obata Jinzaburō. They studied at Rutgers University in New Brunswick, New Jersey. Upon his return, he was made a member of the Tokyo Prefectural Assembly, and later became mayor of Shiba Ward in Tokyo. He died of pneumonia in 1884 (Meiji 17) at the age of 29.

[2] In 1869 (Meiji 2), by imperial order all clans were to return their fiefs to the emperor. This was under the policy of the new government to establish a centrally controlled, unified nation. It was readily accepted by every clan, because they were having difficulties maintaining the semi-independent status of their feudal domains. In 1870, another order made all the clan lords into governors in the employment of the central government. Finally, in 1871, the clans were reorganized into prefectures, and all the governors in office were replaced by new governors appointed by the central government.

At that time, there were more than 300 prefectures, but soon many of them were consolidated into larger units and within a few months' time, their number was reduced to 75. At the same time, the central government acquired a strong army of ten thousand soldiers—chiefly from Satsuma and Chōshū—as a safeguard against possible revolt by the former clans. This ended feudalism in Japan and brought forth a unified nation.

wish is to have the samurai and commoners of my former clan share in my attempt and to learn what I am endeavoring to learn.

Therefore, I have consulted the officials of this prefecture and have decided to donate every year one-fifth of my household income, adding to it the reserve funds[3] of the members of the former clan, for the establishment of a school of Western studies in the city of Nakatsu, and also several parochial schools in other parts of the prefecture. Thus all the samurai, high and low, and also any farmers or merchants in the prefecture should commit themselves to studying in line with my beliefs. And when I return in three to five years, they too will have advanced in their studies. I shall thus look forward to meeting my people again when both will have made progress in learning.

In connection with the schools, there is a book entitled *Encouragement of Learning* by one of the teachers, and the ideas expressed in it are already known. But I, too, would like to express my ideas here in order to give direction to the thinking of our samurai and people.

In Japan, since times of old, there has been a custom of feudal succession, and the samurai have been accustomed to living easily on the ranks and the stipends handed down from their ancestors who earned them with their meritorious deeds. This means that all the descendants live on the blessings left behind by their ancestors. If they are earnest in their duties and their behavior respectable, it will not be objectionable to allow them to retain their inherited privileges.

However, there is always a flaw in every custom. Some of the samurai and the nobles will begin to consider their ranks and income as natural privileges they possess as a matter of course; they will eat their fill, dress extravagantly, and not stop to consider why they are so privileged as to have these luxuries. In the extremes of their licentiousness, they fail to read even a single book a year or to gain a comprehensive understanding or skill in any subject in the whole of their lives. Instead they will drown themselves in wine and food, spending their families' entire stipend on luxuries and even then will not be satisfied.

[3] The financial condition of Nakatsu Clan must have been better than in most other clans. These reserve funds, created out of funds supplied by many families, had been used much like a bank for the convenience of samurai.

[59]

Such people are not only the shame of their ancestors, but in their relationships they do not respect the basic rule of earning one's living by one's own labor, and they deserve to be dismissed from Heaven's grace as veritable criminals. Moreover, this custom of hereditary fiefs itself was, from its inception, a creation against the rules of Heaven. Therefore, its rules have been changed repeatedly according to the trends of the times as illustrated in many instances in world history.

I have once heard the following account: In Europe, in the fifth century, the Roman Empire fell, to be followed by a period with no ruler and no government. This period people of later times called the Dark Ages. Many years passed, and in the eighth century, feudalism became the social system in Europe. However, its barbarism and backwardness were no different from the Dark Ages. The warrior class, which enjoyed hereditary fiefs, did not know what knowledge was. They regarded fighting as the supreme profession, and they simply oppressed the people with their armed might to gain larger incomes. Because they never appreciated the value of culture, they never considered the weight of reason. The result was that the strong would oppress the weak, the big would enslave the small, and there was not one person who could feel secure in his position.

Such a sad state of society lasted till about the year 1300 or 1400 when guns and gunpowder were invented and personal prowess ceased to be of value in warfare. At about the same time, there was another invention—that of printing—and books came to be published widely, causing a sudden dissemination of knowledge among the people. Trade and commerce prospered; money and grain acquired a new strength belonging to the common people. Hiring a gunman with a little money made it possible to knock down a brave warrior of a titled family from a distance of a hundred paces. Under such circumstances, the arts of archery and swordsmanship on horseback quickly grew obsolete, and with it the pride of the hereditary warriors waned.

In that new age, those warriors who understood the situation abandoned their militant ways and quickly turned to cultural pursuits. The prevailing peace promoted a cultured society, bringing about the present civilization.

Now turning our eyes toward trends in Japanese society, first,

[60]

in the Kaei era, trade with Western countries commenced, and commerce took a very new turn with a large share of its trade taking place with foreigners. Second, after the opening of relations with the West, the art of gunnery in Japan advanced rapidly, and people in general came to realize the uselessness of swords and spears. This condition was very similar to that in Europe when gunpowder and guns were first invented. Third, in recent years, the Japanese people have begun to have contacts with foreigners and to personally hear them speak. Some have chosen to go abroad, while others have remained in Japan to study under foreigners. This has resulted in the publication of large numbers of translated books, promoting further the cause of Western studies. This state of affairs is very much like the dissemination of knowledge and wisdom in Europe after the invention of printing.

The above three conditions make us realize that the old custom of feudal inheritance cannot continue for long. Even if it were forcibly preserved, it being against the sentiments of the public, it would certainly result in bringing harm to our country.

In recent days, there have been several proclamations from the Imperial Court, first permitting commoners to bear family names and also to ride horses,[4] and another proclamation ordering the abolition of clans. These drastic measures, I humbly surmise, were the results of an august analysis of the present situation of the country. Therefore, from now on all the samurai and commoners of our former clan must together open their eyes to the truth that the abolition of the feudal inheritance was not brought about by a human authority but that it was a natural and inevitable outcome in accordance with worldwide trends.

As a consequence, from this day on, even a commoner must realize that his position is exalted, and he is to take part in the defense of the country alongside samurai. Therefore, a commoner, too, must provide himself with the wisdom and virtue appropriate to his exalted position. Those who have been samurai, both of high and low positions, will, with the abolition of the clans, lose

[4] Bearing family names, wearing two swords, and riding on horseback were privileges of the samurai class. With the imperial order of Meiji 4 (1871), all commoners were required to adopt family names. They often adopted the name of their native village or the family name of the village headman, with the result that many families in one area came to have the same names.

[61]

the benefit of their stipends. But it is not the intention of the Imperial Court to arbitrarily deprive people of their incomes and to abandon them to the misery of cold and starvation. The true purpose is to encourage people to find a means of earning their own living and to acquire the great virtue of supporting themselves by their own labor, thus creating independent people who can stand side by side with the government in defense of their country. This being the purpose of the government's policies, the present turn is a medicine for curing old ills.

This medicine of change is bitter for the conservatives, but there is no doubt that within a few years' time the effects will be good. An old text states that the true path must not be left for even a moment; the path that one can leave without harm is not the true path. This is a statement on the value of the noble spirit.

Is it not logical to reason that to be born in this world and, without giving any service to it, be fed and clothed will mean making someone else work that much harder and stealing half the fruit? This is something that anyone should be ashamed of. The rice that the samurai of today eat is referred to with the dignified name of stipend of the house (*karoku*), but in truth it is the product of hard labor and the sweat and blood of the lowly commoners— every grain of it. To force innocent commoners into labor and to sit back lazily at home with nothing to pay in return is behavior far from honorable. The fact is that samurai strayed off the true path, which should not have been left for a moment, and stayed off for tens and hundreds of years till it became their second nature and led to today's state of affairs.

Let us take the present change as a good opportunity to alter the old decrepit ways, abandon manmade nobility and stipends, and turn to depending on one's own body and mind for acquiring knowledge and skills to operate one's family business and build up one's own fortune. This spirit may be handed down to posterity, and our descendants, too, will be able to stand independently in the world. No happiness in this world could surpass this. Compared with it, what is so precious about preserving a family name and handing it down to posterity with a meager stipend to accompany it?

According to the above ideals, this school will specialize in Western learning. Western culture will be taught and also all

[62]

varieties of translated books, thus to impart morals and wider knowledge leading to the spirit of independence and self-determination. Therefore, all people in this prefecture, whether samurai or commoner, and also older and accomplished citizens, too, if you have the desire to improve yourselves and to work for the nation, come and expend your energies in Western studies.

Okudaira Masayuki

11th month, Meiji 4th year (1871)

10
Encouragement of Learning
Essay One

This is the very first of Fukuzawa's published works in which he expresses his inner thoughts. He had already established himself as a well-known writer on Western civilization, but all his works had been descriptive pieces on the West, with no expression of his own ideas. One reason for this reticence was his fear of the new imperial government and its leaders who had overthrown the shogunate by advocating the slogan "Honor the Emperor and Expel the Foreigners." The government seemed to have changed its policy after gaining power, but Fukuzawa waited, fearing that it might turn back to its conservative ways. However, when it took the drastic step of abolishing the clans and instituting a prefectural system in 1871, Fukuzawa was heartened and felt safe in making his own ideas and ideals public.

Encouragement of Learning was published as a small pamphlet in 1872, before newspapers and magazines had come into wide circulation. It is most remarkable that the very first line of this essay, "Heaven never created a man above another..." is the most often quoted of his words.

Some 200,000 copies of the pamphlet were sold at the time. Many elementary schools, which had just been established according to the decree of the newly created Ministry of Education, used it as a textbook,

Gakumon no Susume, "Dai Ippen" (学問のすすめ, 第一編), 1872. *Fukuzawa Yukichi Zenshū*, vol. 3, pp. 29–34.

because readers for children were scarce. Delighted with the success, Fukuzawa wrote more essays under the same title, and over the next five years he wrote seventeen essays. (All these seventeen essays have been translated into English by David A. Dilworth and Umeyo Hirano as *An Encouragement of Learning*. The present translation was first printed in pamphlet form in 1960 by Keiō Gijuku University.)

"Heaven never created a man above another nor a man below another," it is said. Therefore, when people are born, Heaven's idea is that all should be equal to all others without distinction of high and low or noble and mean, and that they should all work with their bodies and minds with a dignity deserving of the lords of creation, which they are, and make use of all things in the world to satisfy their needs in clothing, food, and dwelling, freely but without interfering with others, each to live happily through life.

However, looking at this world of ours, we find wise men and ignorant men, rich men and poor men, men of importance and men of little consequence, their differences like the cloud and the slime. Why should all this be? The reason is apparent. The *Jitsugokyō*[1] says, "If a man does not study, he will have no knowledge. A man without knowledge is a fool." The distinction between the wise and the foolish is made from whether a person has studied or not.

In society, there are both difficult and easy tasks. Those who undertake difficult tasks are called people of high standing, and those who undertake easy tasks are called people of low standing. All the tasks in which one must use the mind and which involve much worry are difficult, and those requiring physical labor are easy. And so, physicians, scholars, government officials, or big merchants and big farmers who employ many workers are considered people of high standing and importance.

When a man is high in standing and importance, his house is naturally wealthy and, from the viewpoint of lowly people, he would appear to be high beyond their reach. But looking

[1] One of the most widely used textbooks for children throughout the Tokugawa period. It is made up of proverbs and old sayings. Author unknown.

[66]

at the root of it all, it will be found that the difference comes merely from whether the man has an education or not, and that there are no Heaven-made distinctions. A proverb says, "Heaven gives riches not to men but to their labors." Therefore, as I have said before, a man is not born with rank or riches. Only those who strive to be educated and are capable of reasoning will earn rank and riches while those without will become poor and lowly.

Being educated does not mean knowing strange words or reading ancient and difficult literature or enjoying poetry and writing verse and other such accomplishments which are of no practical use in the world. These accomplishments do give much pleasure to the human mind, and they have their own values, but they are not to be esteemed and worshiped as much as the usual run of scholars have tried to make them out to be. Since time immemorial, there have been very few scholars of the Chinese classics who were good household providers or merchants who were accomplished in poetry and yet clever in business. For this reason, when their children take to learning seriously merchants and farmers become concerned, thinking that their fortunes will eventually be ruined. This is natural in anxious parents and proves that such education is far removed from and quite impractical in daily life.

Therefore, this kind of learning without real use should be left for another day, and one's best efforts should be given to an education that is relevant to everyday use—for instance, the 47 letters of the alphabet, correspondence, bookkeeping, the abacus, and the use of scales. Advancing further, there will be many subjects to be taken up: geography is a sort of story and guide of Japan and all the countries of the world; natural philosophy is the knowledge of the nature and function of all things under the heavens; history is a detailed chronology and studies the conditions of every country in the world past and present; economics explains the management of a household and of a country and of the world; ethics is concerned with the natural principles of a man's conduct, his relationship with his fellow men, and his behavior in society.

For the study of these subjects, one should read the translations of Western books. In writing, one may let the Japanese alphabet suffice in most cases. If there should be a promising youth, let

[67]

him learn the Western languages, and let him grasp the fundamentals in even one field or in one subject, and according to these let him investigate the principles of things that concern his life, and thus let him fulfill the needs of every day. This is *jitsugaku*, which should be generally imbibed by all, without distinction of high or low in society. Only after this should men pursue their separate ways as samurai, farmer, artisan, and merchant, and their respective household businesses. In this way a man may attain his independence, a house its independence, and the nation, too, can attain its independence.

In the pursuit of knowledge, the important thing is to know one's proper limitations. The nature of a human being at birth is not bound or restricted; men and women as adults should be free and unrestrained in their actions. However, by stressing freedom alone without regard to one's proper limitations, one is most liable to fall into waywardness and licentiousness. What is meant by limitations is to conform to the reasons of Heaven and humanity and to attain one's own freedom without infringing upon that of others.

The boundary between freedom and waywardness lies in whether or not one infringes on others. For instance, when using one's own money, it may seem that a person is free to indulge in wine and women and to abandon oneself to licentiousness. But it is not so by any means. One person's licentiousness will become the temptation of many, causing the general degeneration of the society and the disruption of education. Even if the money he spends is his, his sin cannot be pardoned.

The problems of freedom and independence concern a nation as much as they do an individual. Since ancient times, Japan has been an island country far to the east of the Asian continent, not associating with foreign countries, living on its own produce and never being sensible of want. But after the Americans came in the Kaei era, foreign trade and intercourse began and developed to the state we see today. There has been much discussion even after the opening of the ports, some strongly advocating the closing of the ports and the expulsion of foreigners. However, these arguments take a very narrow point of view like the proverbial frog at the bottom of a well; they are not worthy of our note.

Take Japan, take any nation of the West; every nation is under the same heavens, illumined by the same sun, enjoying the beauty of the same moon, sharing the same ocean, breathing the same air, possessing the same human sentiments. Therefore, whatever we have in excess we should give to other nations, taking whatever they have in excess, teaching each other and learning together, never ashamed nor boastful, each fulfilling the needs of another, mutually praying for the happiness of all. So, according to the reasons of Heaven and the ways of man, a nation should hold mutual intercourse with all others, and when reason is against it, it should bow even before the black natives of Africa, and when reason is on its side, it should stand in defiance of the mighty warships of England and America; or when the honor of the country is at stake, all citizens should give their lives to defend the glory of the country. Such should be the ideal of a free and independent country.

But there are some people like the Chinese who think there is no nation in the world except their own, and whenever they meet foreigners, they call them barbarians, as if they were beasts walking on four legs, and despise and detest them and simply endeavor to keep them out. Such people never think of the real strength of their own countries, with the result that they are subjected to humiliation by those "barbarians." All this indicates that they are ignorant of the proper limitations of a nation, just like the person who, not knowing the true meaning of freedom, falls into the evils of waywardness and licentiousness.

Since the restoration of imperial rule, Japan's system of government has changed greatly. Externally, it associates with the world under international law; internally it guides the people to an understanding of freedom and independence, permitting common people to take family names and to ride on horseback, which one may consider the finest decisions of all times. One may say that the movement to make the four classes—samurai, farmer, artisan, and merchant—equal has now been placed on a firm footing.

Henceforth, among the people of Japan, there will be no such thing as a rank to which a person is born. Only by his ability and the position one holds will a person's rank be determined. For instance, it is proper to pay respect to a government official, but this should not be respect for the person himself. We should pay respect to the fact that he holds his position because of his ability and administers important laws for the benefit of the people. It is not the person that one is to respect; it is the law that one is to respect.

Everyone will remember that during the shōgun's regime the August Jar of Tea used to be carried along the Tōkaidō Highway. Not only the Jar of Tea but a hawk in the shōgun's household was more precious than an ordinary man; when a horse of the shōgun's household came by, all the travelers on the highway had to stand aside. Everything, even a piece of stone or tile, appeared awesome and precious when the words "belonging to the Shōgun" were attached to it. Though disliking this ugly custom, over the centuries people had become used to it, and thus the practice came to be established. After all, this did not come from the dignity of the law, nor from the value of the things themselves; it simply was a cowardly device of the government to display its power and to restrict the freedom of the people. One may call it an empty pretention without substance.

Today, such miserable laws and customs are to be discontinued throughout the country, and people ought to set their hearts at ease. If there should be the least complaint against the government, they should never hold it against the officials in secret, but they should seek the proper channels to present the case and to argue about it quietly but without hesitation. If the case should be in accord with Heaven's reason and with humanity, one should fight for it even at the risk of one's life. Such shall be the lot of those who calls themselves citizens of a civilized nation.

As I have said before, an individual person and an individual nation are free and unrestricted according to Heaven-made law. And so, if this freedom of the nation is in jeopardy, one should not fear to stand against all the nations of the world; if one's individual freedom is in jeopardy, one should not stand in awe of even government officials. Moreover, at the time when the equality of the four classes has been established, all men should feel secure in giving free rein to their activities as long as they follow the ways of Heaven. However, as every man has his position in society, he must have the ability and virtue appropriate to his position. In order to understand the logic of things, one must be literate. This is the reason for the urgent need for education.

As we look around today, the position of the three classes—

farmer, artisan, and merchant—has improved a hundredfold and soon will be on a level with the samurai. Even now, the way has been opened for drawing talented men from among the three classes into government service. All men must reflect upon themselves and the important positions they now occupy and must behave in a manner worthy of their posts.

There is no one more pitiful and obnoxious than the ignorant and the illiterate. In the extremes of ignorance, they lose all sense of shame. When they grow poor and hungry because of their ignorance, they do not blame themselves, but they envy the rich, sometimes banding themselves to force a petition or even taking to armed rioting. Shall I call them shameless, or shall I call them lawless? They owe their security to the law of the nation, and they carry on their household business under the law. They take advantage of it when they can, yet when their personal greed dictates, they break the law. Is this not an outrage of reason?

It sometimes happens that a well-established person with some means knows only how to accumulate money but is entirely ignorant in educating his children. Uneducated children will be foolish, which is not to be wondered at, and they will become lazy and licentious, finally squandering away the fortunes inherited from their ancestors like a wisp of smoke. To rule such foolish men, reason will not suffice; the only way to keep them in order is by a show of force. A Western proverb says, "Over foolish people, there is a despotic government." It is not that the government is despotic of itself, it is the foolish people who bring it upon themselves. If the government over foolish people is despotic, then reason requires that a government over wise people will be benign. Therefore, in our country, too, we have this kind of government because of the way people are.

Should our people ever sink into deeper ignorance and illiteracy, the government will become even more severe than it is today. Should people turn their minds to education, acquire an understanding of logic, and strive for civilization, the government will move toward freedom and leniency. The severity and leniency of the government are natural consequences of the worth or unworthiness of the people themselves. Who in the world would prefer despotic rule to benign rule? Who would not pray for the strength and fortune of one's own country? Who would welcome

[71]

humiliation from foreigners? This is a human sentiment common to all.

In this age, for those who have the desire to serve their country, there are no problems urgent enough to worry the mind or torture the body. For the present, the important thing for everyone is to conduct himself according to human nature, apply himself earnestly to learning in order to absorb broad knowledge, and to develop abilities worthy of his position. This will make it easy for the government to rule and pleasant for the people to accept its rule, every person finding his place and all playing a part in preserving the peace of the nation. This should be the only aim. The encouragement of learning that I advocate, too, makes this its goal.

11

The School System in Kyoto

When Fukuzawa traveled west to visit Nakatsu and the Nakatsu Town School, he stopped in Kyoto on the way for a few days to observe its school system. This was before the Ministry of Education's nationwide system of education had taken effect, and each locality was devising its own means for public education. Many areas were not doing anything at all, but Kyoto was the ancient capital and the seat of the Imperial Household for many centuries. It was truly the center of learning and the home of intelligent citizens, and a fine school system was organized there.[1]

On the first day of the fifth month, 1872, I arrived in Kyoto accompanied by a colleague, Mr. Hayashi. Though visitors usually do the rounds of historic and scenic places in Kyoto, we had no time for such sightseeing. Even a visit to the exposition[2]

"Kyōto Gakkō no Ki" (京都学校之記), 1872. *Fukuzawa Yukichi Zenshū*, vol. 20, pp. 77–81.

[1] This school system was inaugurated entirely on the initiative of Kyoto citizens and the prefectural government. In other areas of Japan, also, some former clan lords and influential people established schools, and there was an interesting development in many local attempts at education. But when the Ministry of Education commenced its activity, its influence was so powerful and overbearing that many of these independent schools and systems were either destroyed by or absorbed into its organization.

[2] Expositions had been held since the Tokugawa period though on a very small scale. This particular one in Kyoto was a large exposition of Chinese art, held for 50 days from April 17 on three Buddhist temple grounds, sponsored by an organization called Kyoto Hakuran Kaisha.

was not the purpose of my visit to this ancient capital. Above all, my purpose was to visit the schools, and, with the kind guidance of a friend, I made the rounds of various schools. At every school, I was received most cordially and was able to inspect every hall and building I wished to see. I am recording the outline of what I saw for the benefit of my colleagues and friends.

The schools in Kyoto had their beginning in the 2nd year of Meiji (1869), and at present there are 4 schools called middle schools and 64 of what they call elementary schools. The city is divided into 64 districts, an idea which probably comes from the Western system of "school districts." One elementary school has been built in each of these areas, and all the children of that area, between the ages of seven or eight and thirteen or fourteen, are allowed to attend, regardless of whether they are of rich or poor, or noble or humble, families.

All the schools have two departments, and the boys and girls sit in separate rooms for penmanship, where the students are assigned their own seats for studying. Then there is a common hall which is assigned for reading and arithmetic classes. During the penmanship lessons, the students are sent in turns to this hall in groups of ten or fifteen for instruction in reading and arithmetic. Each elementary school has a penmanship teacher, an arithmetic teacher, and a teacher for reading. There are also assistant teachers, but their number varies according to the size of the student population. Sometimes there is one, sometimes three.

The schools begin at eight o'clock in the morning and end at four in the afternoon. The lessons consist of: Japanese syllabary (*i, ro, ha*) and examples of letter writing which are copied for penmanship; then the multiplication table, addition, subtraction, multiplication, division, ratios, and other arithmetic skills; for reading, the names of the prefectures and the countries of the world; also elementary instructions in geography, physics, and economics from translated books. When translated books are not available, Chinese books are substituted.

The lessons in penmanship, arithmetic, reading, and recitation are divided into grades, and tests are held monthly in each grade. Then, twice a year in the spring and in the autumn, examinations are held. On these occasions, all the teachers and also

[74]

many others concerned but who do not take part in the daily teaching come to school. Even the governor and councilors of the prefecture and some of the town elders personally meet the students and give tests. And according to their accomplishments, the students are given such prizes as writing brushes, paper, ink stones, and books. Thus the officials and the town elders act both as witnesses to the examinations and as examiners.

The elementary schools consist of five grades, and the students are promoted to higher grades according to the results of the examinations. When they complete the fifth grade, they enter middle school. But as the inauguration of the middle schools is such a recent event, there are as yet very few students in them. However, for students who are recognized as talented, there is a regulation for admitting them to middle school before they complete the fifth grade, and their tuition is to be at government expense. At present, there are eight boys and two girls enjoying this recognition. Among them, one is said to be the child of a female hairdresser in town.

Besides the reading, writing, and arithmetic teachers assigned to the schools, there are some ten circuit lecturers who tour the 64 schools giving lectures six times a month in each. When a lecture is given, every household in that district must have one member attend. For the materials of the lectures, translations of Western books are generally used, but as necessity calls, some Chinese books may be used. These lectures do not dwell on definitions of difficult words. They seek to explain the purpose of the new civilization by giving talks on its various phases.

Concerning the expenses for elementary school education, in the beginning, the prefectural government provided half of the expenses for the establishment of the schools and the other half was donated by local men of wealth. In this way the buildings were constructed, and books were purchased. The surplus funds were loaned out and the interest earned became a permanent yearly income for the schools. Also, each household in each district is required to pay one *bu* every half year, and this is added to the interest earned on the loaned funds for the school expenses. This one *bu* every half year is assigned equally to each household in the district whether or not it has children of school age.

[75]

The income and expenditures of this school system are being managed by the town elders, and the overseer of the entire educational finances is the chief elder. Thus it is independent of the government officials. The levying of the *bu* every half year is by the order of the prefectural government, but the management of the money is entirely in the hands of the elders. This arrangement conforms with what is found in Wayland's book on economics.[3]

The number of students in these elementary schools ranges from 70 to 100 in the small schools and from 200 to 300 in the larger schools. All the schools are neat and clean; there is no writing on the walls, nor trash around the students' seats; no one makes unnecessary noise, nor runs around noisily; discipline is perfect. Also, there is an office near the school for the town assembly of that district where the officials maintain their branch office. There they may attend to the care of the students along with other business of the district. This is a very good arrangement of double benefit.

The four middle schools hire foreign teachers for the instruction of English, French, and German. The method of language teaching is about the same as in Tokyo and Osaka. The number of students in the schools ranges between 100 and 200, including both boys and girls. The school expenses are borne entirely by the prefectural government.

Among the middle schools, there is one called Women's Factory for English Studies [Eigaku Jo Kōjō]. A British teacher and his wife have been hired there. The husband teaches English to the boys, while his wife teaches the girls both English and sewing. She is the only Western woman, but there are seven or eight women in the city who know the language and are skilled in women's arts. They assist in teaching.

The girls attending the classes to learn English and women's arts number a little more than 130, their ages ranging between seven or eight to thirteen or fourteen. Some come from families of nobility, some are commoners from families in commerce and industry. Each is dressed differently according to the wealth

[3] *The Elements of Political Economy* by Francis Wayland, D.D., a college textbook from which Fukuzawa had acquired knowledge of economics and social sciences, and which was being used as a textbook in Keiō Gijuku at this time.

of her family, but all are neat and never showy; their clothes may be coarse but clean. Their language is polite, their looks modest; they may not be outspoken but they do not appear timid; they may not laugh aloud, but their expressions show their amusement. They are like flowers or jewels, lovable and respectable; they have the ideal appearance of young womanhood, not to be classed with those new women of Tokyo who cut their hair short, avoid cosmetics, and wear mannish skirts to surprise people.

This school being the most recently established of the middle schools, the skills of the students, as they are now, have not reached any stage to speak of, but with their inborn gentle and meek nature, and their studying under British teachers day after day, they must be absorbing their knowledge and be influenced by the teachers' behavior. Within a few years, these girls will probably develop a spirit of independence and self-reliance leading to their ultimate escape from old-fashioned conventions to attain a happiness unseen among other women in the country. We should look forward to such an eventuality.

The teachers in the elementary schools are appointed by prefectural government order, but as their salaries come from the office of the town elders, the teachers are not government officials; they are citizens of the district. Their salaries vary according to the size of the district and the number of students. They range from 12 or 13 *ryō* a month down to 3 or 4 *ryō*.

Among the officials in charge of the middle schools and elementary schools, there are some who, of their own volition, teach on the side, apart from their regular official work. There are about twenty officials or less. Their salaries vary according to their ranks. Large salaries may be 70 *ryō*, smaller salaries may be 15 or 20. The average is no more than 25 *ryō*, which amounts to about 500 *ryō* a month for the twenty officials. This means that the financial burden on the government is slight and the business conducted efficiently.

According to the statistics issued by the schools in April, 1872, there were a total of 15,892 students in the elementary schools and middle schools; the proportion of boys to girls was about ten to eight. All of them were between the ages of seven or eight and thirteen or fourteen. Ten years from now, these boys will have

[77]

become masters of households engaged in some business, and the girls will be married and have children of their own. Their businesses will prosper, and the education of the children will be continued in their households; what more happiness can mankind expect?

The number of students has already exceeded 15,000. By next year, it will have increased to 30,000. And there will be no prefecture in the country which will not follow Kyoto's example in promoting a school system. In the future, in this country of Japan, these boys and girls will be the ones who will know the logic of things, cultivate themselves, and preserve peace and happiness in the home. These boys and girls will be the ones who will guide society to better mores so that the laws of the government may be enforced easily. These boys and girls will be the ones who will promote industry and commerce and increase the wealth of the whole society. These boys and girls will be the ones who will promote knowledge and virtue among commoners and lead them in acquiring their rights to debate civil problems publicly. These boys and girls will be the ones to work on their own to earn their living to insure their own independence and that of their families and thus to lay the foundation for national independence. These boys and girls will be the ones who will open wide intercourse with foreign countries and maintain international trust and insure national profit in trade. To summarize, any attempt at substantiating the ideals of civilization and securing trust in Japan in the world's eyes will be in the hands of this young generation.

The education of people in schools established by the people has been my long-standing wish. Now I was able to see its actual realization on my visit to Kyoto. My joy is like that of coming home to meet old friends. Any member of our society who is not inspired upon observing these schools at work must lack patriotic sentiments.

Fukuzawa Yukichi

6th day, 5th month, Meiji 5th year (1872)
At Hotel Matsuya
Sanjō Miyuki Machi, Kyoto

12

Preface to
Methods of Bookkeeping

In the Japanese language of early Meiji, there was no precise word for bookkeeping. Fukuzawa invented the word *chōai* for his translation. Later, *chōai* was superseded by a new word, *boki*, which came from Chinese. No doubt Japanese merchants had their own ways of keeping accounts, but discovering that there was a superior and truly scientific method in the West, Fukuzawa chose to translate an elementary American textbook for bookkeeping. This was his way of demonstrating advanced methods and ideas of the West to induce Japanese people to apply them in practice and also to specialize in them. Fukuzawa himself showed no interest in bookkeeping beyond this translation.

The last few paragraphs of this preface, dealing chiefly with the translation of technical terms, have been omitted from the present translation.

1. This book is a translation of *Common School Bookkeeping*, written in 1871 by two teachers of an American school of commerce named Bryant and Stratton.[1] "Bookkeeping" means the method for keeping accounts or how to keep ledgers in order.

2. In bookkeeping, there are two methods: single entry and double entry. In the two volumes of this first part, only single

"Chōai no Hō Bonrei" (帳合之法凡例), 1873. *Fukuzawa Yukichi Zenshū*, vol. 3, pp. 333–36.
[1] Its authors were Henry Beadman Bryant and Henry Dwight Stratton.

entry will be explained. The double entry description will be published shortly as the second part; its translation is about half completed.

3. Before an explanation of how technical terms were translated, I shall describe the basic purpose of translating this book:

First: In Japan since olden times, scholars have always been poor and the wealthy have, without exception, been ignorant. The expressed opinions of the scholars were always lofty, and in their own words they would appear to be fit to rule the world. But in reality, they did not even know how to pay their personal debts. The wealth of rich men was often tremendous, so much so that they sometimes put their gold in earthen pots and buried them for safe keeping, but they had no concept of learning the economics of the world and to extend the effects of their own trade.

The reasons for this absurd situation must be that the scholars have been placing themselves too high and have decided that trading was not appropriate to the noble station they occupied; and that the merchants have been placing themselves too low to realize that they also have the right to higher knowledge. Thus both failed to learn what they should have learned and fell into these deficiencies. In short, the original sin was in giving no respect to trade and failing to recognize trade as a respectable subject of learning.

Suppose that scholars and rich men should come to learn this new art of bookkeeping. They will for the first time find the true meaning of what I call *jitsugaku*. The scholars will be surprised to discover how ignorant and foolish they have been; the rich men will for the first time learn the importance of the positions they hold in society. Thus, both will begin to study new fields; the scholars will become wealthy, the rich men will become learned, the economy of the whole society will assume a new aspect leading to an increase in national strength. All these are what this translator is praying for.

Second: It is easy to find fault with and complain about all things in society, but it is very difficult to find remedies for these faults. Examining the bookkeeping of various experts in this country, I have found all of them to be very intricate or entangled. Two months will be required to make a complete inventory of one store, even when the entire staff of the store is called forth in the work. Even then, a good deal will be left unaccounted for. This proves the inadequacy of the bookkeeping method of this country. Yet, we have not heard of anyone devising improvements in the method. This I consider a great inconvenience not only for each store but for the whole of society.

The present translation is only a beginner's attempt at Western bookkeeping; one should not expect it to revolutionize bookkeeping in all the stores and remove all the inconveniences from society. But, at least, this book will initiate a person in the science of bookkeeping. When the reader takes up the method of double entry in the second part of the book and advances further into the heart of the technique, he will be able to make both private and public accounting easy for the whole country. Therefore, this present volume, though small and incomplete in itself, has its reason for existence.

Third: As was said before, since time immemorial in Japan, education and business had no relation to each other. The more a scholar absorbs himself in his studies, the loftier he becomes, until he is ready to rise to the heavens. In contrast, ignorant farmers and merchants will grow ashamed of themselves until they want to hide themselves in a hole. Thus, these two have never approached each other. Should there be a dilettante among the farmers and merchants who tries his hand at reading some books in imitation of the scholar, he would lose himself in impractical Chinese classics and poetry and would soon forget the values of goods and the accounting of money. His studies would not in the least be helpful to his family's livelihood. Rather, his studies are liable to drag him into bankruptcy. Therefore, farmers and merchants will pay ostensible homage to scholars and call them masters of boundless knowledge, but in truth they loathe the scholars as if they were carriers of plague. They will simply keep away from them, and they will even tell their own children never to touch a book.

Even today when Western learning is establishing itself in this country and there are schools being opened in many localities, these commoners—farmers, artisans, and merchants—avoid schools because they are afraid of learning as they have had enough of the scholars in the past, and before they inquire into the merits of the new education, they will simply keep away from anything associated with it. What a loss it is that this attitude is obstructing the progress of Western learning today! After all, this is the result of the past several hundred years in which the scholars of Japanese and Chinese learning have indulged themselves in useless literature and empty theories, never looking for the real purpose of education, thus causing the general people to remain ignorant and unnecessarily cautious. All this is deeply lamentable.

The true state of affairs being as described, should the present book be used as readers in various schools, the children of commoners will on occasion go home and tell their parents what they are learning. Then the parents may discover for the first time the real purpose and true worth of the Western learning and begin to feel secure in allowing their children to continue their education. And the number of such parents will certainly increase. Then this small volume will not only be instructive in the techniques of bookkeeping but it will be standing proof of the sensible nature of *jitsugaku*, thus leading the public into the field of general education.

The sin of the scholars of ancient classics, in causing ignorance among the common people, was certainly profound, but if this little book can enlighten the millions of farmers, artisans, and merchants, the sins of past scholars will be nullified, and my efforts at the translation will be fully, or more than fully, rewarded.

Fourth: This book has made it clear that bookkeeping is a science. It leads to the idea that trade can be a science, as manufacturing, too, can be. Stretching this argument a little further, any activity that follows the laws of nature and earns compensation for labor of the mind and body may be defined as a trade. A government official who obtains a salary in return for his work in administration is involved in a trade. The profession of the samurai of former times who earned a stipend for his duties in war business, too, was a trade.

Then, why should it be that people today regard the trade of samurai and the officials as noble and those trades which involve buying and selling of goods or the trade of manufacturing goods as lowly? This comes from people's erroneous notion in not

[82]

realizing that any trade has a profound science behind it. In extreme cases of this misunderstanding, one can actually forgo the profit that is one's due.

In explaining this point, allow me to give an example: As I have said, producing and selling or buying goods is a trade and serving a lord as a samurai is a trade too. Now, let us take a household of a 100,000-*koku* lord and consider it as a trading company. Its yearly profit will be 40,000 *koku* of rice.[2] The market price of rice being 3 *ryō* per *koku*, the money value of the household income will be 120,000 *ryō*. Of this amount, one quarter, 30,000 *ryō*, will be held back for use by the lord, which will leave 90,000 *ryō* as net income of the company. The trading company will require the services of about 1200 men, from the chancellor at the top to the foot soldiers and menials at the bottom. Dividing 90,000 *ryō* by 1200, we will find that the average yearly share for the 1200 families will be 75 *ryō*. As upper-class samurai families will need a number of household servants, we will assume the average family consists of six members. This will mean that the allowance for each person on the average is 12 *ryō* and 5 *kan-mon* a year, or 1 *ryō* and 416 *mon* a month, which comes to 347 *mon* a day. The economic conditions of each clan before their abolition was similar throughout the country.

Now that the clans are no more and samurai have given up their ancestral trade as soldiers of a reserve force, they may now turn to a new trade, to producing goods and selling or transporting them. This change in trade should certainly increase their income twofold. Will this not be a great advantage to them? Assuming three members of a family of six to be old people or children or sick, suppose the other three men and women would earn 694 *mon* a day each, then their income will be equal to what they were earning as members of a clan.

Of course, the ways of free trade are not easy, but with a healthy body, 694 *mon* will not be a large amount to earn. It is the amount that a rickshawman earns by running 10 *chō* [two-thirds of a mile] in half an hour. Moreover, one must remember that the

[2] A 100,000-*koku* lord is a lord whose territory was large enough to produce 100,000 *koku* of rice a year. (One *koku* equals about five bushels.) A 40,000-*koku* profit comes from the amount of tax which the lord usually collected from the farmers every year. There was no custom of collecting tax from other sources such as commerce and manufacturing.

stipends of samurai had been reduced in recent years, and it has on the average been 10 *koku* or 20 *koku*, the best hardly ever topping 30. This income divided among the six in a family amounts to even less than what a rickshawman earns. Besides, for the present-day samurai, their work as fighting men under a lord no longer exists. They should realize that it is shameful to have an income without working for it.

Then why is it that the present samurai still long for that stipend rice and that there are so few of them trying to find an independent means of income? It is indeed strange that people's minds should be so blind and foolish, but, after all, its cause goes back hundreds and thousands of years. During all that time, the members of this class had been the masters who did not have to consider profit or loss of money and did not stop to recognize the respectable science that existed behind the trade of merchants and artisans. Such was the original sin, or cause of the behavior of samurai today.

The final purpose of this book on bookkeeping is to prove to these people the existence of a science behind commerce and industry and to guide them so that they can enter the fields of commerce and industry and satisfy their great ambitions for independent lives of their own.

The Translator

February 10, Meiji 6th year (1873)

13

Encouragement of Learning
The Social Role of Scholars

Essay Four

These days, I sometimes have occasion to hear the opinions of intellectuals who worry anxiously about the future of Japan. Of course, it is impossible to foretell the future with accuracy; that is beyond human intellect. However, these men are wondering whether there is no fear of Japan's losing its independence. Suppose Japan continues making progress as we witness every day; will it eventually reach the state of civilization? Such are their questions. There are some who sow doubts by saying that we shall have to wait 20 or 30 years before we can be certain that Japan will maintain its independence. Also, there are foreigners who hold Japan in contempt, declaring its independence precarious.

Of course, I should not waiver in my hopes at every word of these men. But the fact that there exist all these concerns proves that the independence of Japan is not without question. If there were is no doubt, no questions would be asked. Suppose one goes to England now and inquires about the future certainty of British independence; everybody will simply laugh and not give an answer. And why would they not? Because they do not hold doubt about the future of Great Britain. On the contrary, in Japan, though we do see some progress when we compare today with yesterday, we cannot help having some misgivings about the ultimate future. Anyone born in this country and calling himself a Japanese cannot help but be concerned on this point. I, too, was born in this country, and I am a Japanese citizen. As long as I am, I must do my share of duty for the country.

Gakumon no Susume, "Dai Yonhen" (学問のすすめ, 第四編), 1874. *Fukuzawa Yukichi Zenshū,* vol. 3, pp. 48–54.

Of course, governing and politics belong to the government. But there are many activities that the government is not equipped to manage. For the perfect running of an entire country, the government and the people must work side by side if any success is to be expected. Therefore, everyone must do one's share as a member of society, and with the government taking its share, all should strive for the independence of the country.

In all matters, a balance of power is necessary. Take the human body as an example. To keep fit, one must eat and drink. The body also needs air and light. Heat and cold, pain and itchiness provide external stimulation, and the body responds from within, and thus the functions of a body are regulated. If the external stimulations are eliminated and the body is left to its own vitality alone, the health of a human body cannot be preserved for even a day.

It is the same with a country. To govern it is one of its activities. To regulate this activity and preserve the independence of the country, there must be the power of the government within and the power of the people outside, the powers working on each other and keeping their balance. The government is like the power of life within and the people the stimulus from outside. When this stimulus is taken away and the government is left to take its own course, the independence of the country will not endure for even a day. Anyone who is acquainted with the physiology of the human body and knows how to apply it to the management of a country will not hold the least doubt about this theory.

Considering the present state of our country and enumerating the points in which our country falls short in comparison with Western countries, one must first consider science, second commerce, then law. Civilization stands on these three pillars, and when they are not developed, a country cannot be independent, a fact so clear it requires no explanation by an intellectual. Yet, in our country, none of these has undergone a presentable process of development.

Since the establishment of the new government, the officials have been faithful in their duties and their abilities are not by any means deficient, but there is something absolutely beyond their immediate control which has kept them from accomplishing much of what they planned: specifically, the ignorance and the illiteracy of the people. The government is aware of this and is encouraging education, discussing new laws, showing better methods in commerce. Thus they admonish the people sometimes, demonstrate new methods at times, and try many other ways, but even to this day, little improvement is evident; the government is still the same autocratic government, the people are the same spiritless idiots. Sometimes improvements are seen, but in comparison to the amount of labor and money invested, the results are very disappointing indeed.

What is the reason for this? It all goes back to the fact that the progress of a civilization of a country cannot be enforced by the government alone. One could theorize that the government is for the time being resorting to a kind of tactic in controlling ignorant people. It will wait till some progress is made and then have them seek their own way to civilization. This idea may seem sound, but it is difficult to put into practice. Our country for hundreds and thousands of years has been oppressed under despotic governments, and the people have lost the ability to express their minds, and they have become accustomed to seeking safety by deception or escaping punishment by lying, such that they have come to consider deception and artifice as necessary devices in human life, and insincerity and dishonesty common, with no one feeling shame in them or stopping to examine their propriety.

Thus with the sense of personal honor having fallen in disgrace, how can people have the broadness to turn their minds to the welfare of the country? The government, in its endeavor to correct this attitude, puts on airs and scolds the people and threatens them into becoming sincere and loyal. But this only results in further distrust among the people, the situation being like an endeavor to use fire to put out another fire. Finally, a gulf between the two has developed, both with distinct dispositions. Disposition is what might be called "spirit," something that cannot be altered easily. Recently the organization of the government appears to have changed to a great extent, but the policy of oppression and despotism still remains. And the people, too, remain as conniving and distrustful as ever, despite the rights they have acquired. This disposition is intangible and amorphous, impossible to explain with the behavior of one person or the process of one event, but its influence is extremely powerful, which will be seen when its effects upon the whole of society are examined.

To give one example: Anyone will agree that there are many respectable people among the officials in the government, whose words and deeds indicate that they are of broad minds and magnanimous personalities, with nothing to be criticized, sometimes even deserving respect. In the same way, the common people are not entirely made up of spiritless ignoramuses; there are some with open and sincere minds. Yet, when these fine people combine their forces in the government, the resultant administration often is something far from what I would admire, and those fine and sincere commoners, too, when they come in contact with the government, quickly cast away their principles and begin using crafty pretexts to deceive the officials, and they show no sign of shame for it.

Why do these officials fail thus in the administration and honest commoners resort to miserable acts of deception? Both are like a person with one body and two heads. In private, they are wise; in office, idiotic. When separate, they see; when gathered, blind. The government may be called an office where the wise come together and act like fools. One is obliged to wonder at this strange phenomenon. The reason for all this must be in the atmosphere, or the general disposition, which restrains each one from acting freely as an individual. The same must be the cause for the failure of all the attempts of the government since the Restoration in promoting learning, technology, law, and commerce.

Yet, it has been claimed that the government may very well resort to a temporary ruse to govern the people and wait for improvement in their intellect and morality. This is tantamount to threatening people into civilization or cheating them into becoming honest. When the government resorts to force, the people will turn to deception to escape; when the government resorts to a ruse, people will cope with it through pretense. These cannot be classed as good policies. However cleverly executed, these policies will not contribute to civilization. Therefore, I believe that for the promotion of civilization, one must not look to the power of the government alone.

Reasoning from the above discourse, we are led to the conclusion that the first requisite for civilization in our country is the eradication of the roots of the disposition that permeates the minds of our people. For this, a government order will not do; nor will private admonitions. What we need for this purpose is a person to stand before others as an example toward which all others may endeavor to strive. Where are we to look for such a person? He will not be found among the farming class, not among the merchant class, nor among the scholars of Chinese and Japanese learning. The only area one may hopefully find someone will be among the scholars of Western learning. And yet, there is a reason for not pinning my hopes on this group.

The number of scholars of Western learning has greatly increased. Some of them are teaching, others are studying books translated from Western materials, and they appear to be devoting all their energies to this purpose. But these scholars either do not understand the real meaning of what they read or they lack the good faith to put the knowledge into practice. In their attitude and behavior, there is too much that gives me misgivings. These people, supposedly scholars, seem to recognize the importance of the government alone and do not seem to realize even the existence of the citizenry. They are competent officials in the government but do not know what it is to live under the government as a citizen. This means that they are still captives of Chinese learning; or they may be described as possessing the body of a Chinese but wearing Western clothing.

Allow me to illustrate with realistic examples: Today most Western scholars in our society have obtained government posts, and few of them work privately. The reason is not only greed for better incomes but because of their inborn inclination, nurtured by their education, to have eyes for official positions, believing that no worthwhile work can be accomplished except through the government. Thus their only and life-long ambition is to join the government and to obtain as high a position as they can. Even renowned scholars are guilty of this, but one should not despise them too much as they are simply following the general trend of society and they are not conscious of their own behavior. Even people recognized by society are like this; the rest of society naturally would follow their example.

Young men, after reading a few books, begin looking for an opening in the government; an ambitious merchant, when he accumulates a few hundred yen of capital, will seek advantageous government connections to promote his trade; a school wants government sanction; preaching would do better with government sanction; cattle raising, too, must have government sanction; the raising of silkworms, too, is the same. All in all, seven or eight out of ten private enterprises have some government connections. The whole of society is leaning more and more toward the government, longing for it, depending on it, fearing it, and flattering it—there is not the least show of the spirit of independence among the people. Their behavior is too obnoxious to observe.

The newspapers published these days and petitions and memorials are good examples. The regulations on publication are not strict by any means, but the newspapers simply will not touch upon a sensitive issue for fear of losing government favor. When there is a praiseworthy deed on the part of the officials, the papers will praise it to the skies with exaggerated language very much like a harlot coquetting with her customer. Also, one may see in those petitions and memorials that they are written in a despicable style with excessive reverence for the government as if it were a god to be worshiped; at the same time the writer belittles himself as if he were a criminal using a language unsuitable for relations between equals in society. And yet, there is not the least sign of embarrassment on the part of the writers. A glance at these papers would lead one to judge the writers as nothing but insane.

Even then, the publishers of those newspapers and the writers of the petitions and memorials are, in most cases, those recognized by society as scholars of Western learning. And when one looks into their private lives, they are by no means harlots or insane. The reason why these men have fallen to the extremes of insincerity and falsehood must be that there have been no advocates of popular rights in our country. These men have simply been made captives of the servile spirit which permeates the whole nation, and they are unable to express their true selves.

To put the situation in a simple statement, the only tangible existence in Japan is the government, and the people have not yet attained their "existence." Therefore, it must be declared that to revolutionize the people's attitudes and strive toward civilization, one cannot expect much from those who now pose as scholars of Western learning.

Should the statements in the above paragraphs be true, one will have to concede that the government by itself is powerless to develop Japan's civilization and to preserve its independence. Also, little can be expected from the scholars of Western learning. All this leads to the conclusion that I will bear the responsibility for initiating the movement, not only to guide the ignorant but to march before the scholars who claim to be studying Western learning and demonstrate to them what their true aim should be.

I must admit that there are limits to my knowledge, but I have been studying the West for a number of years, and I have been recognized as above average among the scholars in the field. Many of the renovations in our country in recent years are what I had advocated first or indirectly helped to bring about. Even granting that my influence has not been much, because I am satisfied with all the developments, it is natural that the general public regards me as a reformist. So, I already enjoy a reputation as a reformist and my position is above the average, and there probably are people who regard me as their model. I therefore consider it my task to demonstrate with my own behavior and actions the proper path of progress for the members of our present society.

It is true that to promote an idea it is better to teach it than to command it; it is still better to demonstrate it than to teach it. The government, of its own nature, possesses no other function than one of authority. Teaching and demonstrating are functions belonging only to private people. Therefore, I intend to remain a private citizen and continue teaching the new learning, or engage in commerce, or discuss law, or write books and publish newspapers. Thus I intend to be active within the sphere proper to a citizen, never fearing the contempt of those in authority, strictly observing the law in all activities. If I am suspected by the untrusting government, I shall defend my position with rightful arguments, sharply criticizing the government if necessary.

Such endeavors to remove the present evils and regain the people's rights are our immediate and basic necessities. It is very true that any business of a private nature has many problems, and each individual is gifted with different talents. It will be impossible for a small group of scholars to attend to all problems, but my purpose is not to demonstrate expertise in accomplishing things.

[91]

I only wish to demonstrate to our society the attitude of a person who seeks to be an independent individual.

One example in actual life is better than a hundred lectures and admonitions. My intention is to demonstrate that example and to prove to society that the government is not the only responsible organ in the activities of society and that scholars can accomplish work independently, and merchants can conduct their own businesses individually. The government is Japan's government and the people, too, are Japan's people. The government is not to be regarded in awe from a distance. It is not to be suspected but should be approached; it should be made friends with.

When these principles are understood, people will learn how to behave and the present atmosphere which separates the people and the officials will gradually disappear, causing the emergence of what may be called the true citizens of Japan, citizens who will not be playthings but stimulating agents of the government, and the people will be their own true masters. This will balance the powers of the government and the powers of the people, and thus the true independence of the country will be assured.

To summarize the above discussion, my endeavors have been to compare the advantages and disadvantages of a scholar working as an official within the government and as a private citizen in his efforts to ensure the independence of this country. And the present essay sides with independent activity.

As with all things in the world, when studied thoroughly, whatever is lacking in advantage will be found to be harmful; whatever brings no gain will bring a loss; there cannot be anything half-way between. I am not by any means advocating my opinion for any personal reasons. I have only been exhibiting the convictions I have always had. If someone disagrees with me and provides firm proof of the disadvantage of independence, then I shall willingly accede to his opinion and cease to cause harm to the world with my arguments.

14
Encouragement of Learning
Essay Five

As Fukuzawa himself notes in his opening paragraph, this essay is a transcript of a talk he gave to his students and friends at a New Year's party. From this essay we can observe that Fukuzawa and his colleagues were serious in their concern to preserve Japan's independence, and they were impatient with their countrymen, still dazed by the new civilization yet never realizing the importance of the spirit behind it. In his discussion, Fukuzawa brings forward his concept of civilization represented by the spirit of independence.

Encouragement of Learning was first started as a popular reader for a general audience and as teaching material in elementary schools. Therefore, the first to third essays were written in a somewhat colloquial style in order to make them easy reading. But in the fourth essay, I changed my style and used some scholarly words. This fifth essay, being a summary of a talk given at the meeting of our colleagues on New Year's Day, the 7th year of Meiji (1874), is worded like the fourth essay, and I fear it may be difficult in parts. The fourth and fifth essays were organized and written for scholars, hence the difficult style.

The scholars in our society are mostly cowards, and they haven't much mettle to be counted on, but their ability to decipher difficult texts is always admirable. And so, in these two essays, I

Gakumon no Susume, "Dai Gohen" (学問のすすめ, 第五編), 1874. *Fukuzawa Yukichi Zenshū,* vol. 3, pp. 57–62.

did not adopt a style to facilitate reading. The contents are high-sounding, which is against the original idea of *Encouragement of Learning*: to provide reading material for the populace. Deep apologies are due to beginning students, but this wrong will be amended from the sixth essay on. I will return to the former style and care will be taken to make all the points understandable to beginners. Readers are requested not to judge the whole by the present two essays.[1]

Observations on New Year's Day

Today we are celebrating New Year's day of the 7th year of Meiji in our school, Keiō Gijuku. This era, Meiji, is an era in which our country stands independent. This school is an independent school run by the combined efforts of our colleagues. Is it not a joyous occasion that we are able to assemble in our independent school to greet the New Year of our country's independence? Whatever we are happy to possess will cause sorrow when it is lost. Therefore, on this occasion of happiness, we must not forget the possibility of disappointment in the future.

Since times of old, our governments have changed hands countless times due to wars, but up to this day this country has never lost its independence in its long history. This may be attributed to the fact that the people have been satisfied with national isolationism, and warfare and the rise and fall of powers have not involved relations with foreign countries.

When foreign relations are not involved, peace will mean peace within the country; warfare will only be a disturbance within the country. Independence, too, which was preserved through peace and war, was an independence enjoyed within the confines of the country and was not won or proved in conflict with foreign powers. We are like a child brought up in a family with no contact with outside people. The weakness of such a child may well be surmised.

Now that foreign intercourse has suddenly commenced, we

---

[1] This difference in style is not apparent in the translation. Also, the Japanese language has evolved so much since Fukuzawa's time that present-day Japanese find all his writings difficult to read. Today, his "easy style" is almost as difficult as his scholarly style.

find that nothing can remain unaffected by it. In this age when everything must be measured against foreign equivalents, the level of civilization which the Japanese have reached with their own power appears to be very inadequate in comparison with its Western counterparts. We are even beset with a sense of despair while endeavoring to imitate the West, and we are all the more reminded of the weakness of our independence.

The civilization of a country must not be gauged by its appearance alone. The schools, the industry, the army, the navy, and all such institutions that people boast about are, after all, mere appurtenances of civilization. It is not difficult to create these appurtenances. Money can buy them. But there is one thing intangible—not to be seen by the eyes, not to be heard by the ears, not to be sold or purchased, not to be lent out or borrowed. Yet, it presides over the people everywhere with such a powerful force that without it even the schools and other institutions of civilization cannot function. Indeed, it is the most important and indispensable thing—in one word, the spirit of civilization. What should this spirit be? It is none other than the people's will and belief in independence.

In recent years, our government has been most active in establishing schools, encouraging industry, and reforming the army and the navy, and thus the appearance of civilization has taken some form. But among the people, there is hardly a person giving thought to securing our national independence in the face of foreign powers or to competing with them. Not only will they not compete when some of them, by chance, come to learn about the West; they are first frightened before they comprehend the details. When one is beset with fear, even when one obtains useful knowledge, one cannot apply it in actual policy against the foreigners. All this illustrates that when people lack the spirit of independence, all the flowery advancements of civilization are reduced to uselessness.

To look into the cause of why our people are as spiritless as they are, one will note that all the power and leadership of the nation has been concentrated in one government since many hundreds and thousands of years ago. Not only military power, culture, and learning, but industry, commerce, and even minor details of human affairs have been the concern of the government. People had no choice but to act according to the government's will.

It has been almost as if the country was a private possession of the government with the people dependents of the country. If people were simply dependents with no residence rights of their own, living on a sort of charity of the country, then they would regard their country simply as temporary living quarters. Naturally, they would not feel any devotion for the country, nor have the opportunity for creativity, the result being the present attitude of the people.

Moreover, something even worse is happening. Everything in society that does not advance recedes, and everything that does not deteriorate is sure to flourish; nothing remains stationary. Examining the state of things in Japan today, I find that the appearance of civilization seems to be advancing, but the virility of the people which should be the spirit of civilization is regressing day by day. Allow me to discuss this point.

During the Ashikaga and Tokugawa periods, the government used force to control the people, and the people obeyed because they did not possess the power to resist. This kind of obedience is not true obedience; the people were simply obeisant out of fear. The present government is not only powerful; it is very quick in intellect too and never misses a cue. It has not been ten years since the great Restoration, but already we see in this country astounding improvements in the school system, national armaments, the inauguration of railway and telegraph systems. Concrete buildings have been built and steel bridges now cross rivers. The speed of the decisions and the wonders of their successes have startled the eyes and ears of all who observe. However, all these schools and armaments are government schools and armaments. The railways and the telegraph systems are government railways and telegraph systems. The concrete buildings and steel bridges, too, are government buildings and bridges.

And how should the people regard all this? They are all saying that the government has power—not only power, but sagacity. The government is something beyond their reach; it stands above the clouds to rule the land; the people stand below, and all they can do is to obey and depend upon it. Concern for the country is the affair of those above; the people below have little to do with it! In short, the government in old times used power, but the present government uses both power and wisdom. The former governments were ineffective in controlling the people, but the present government is highly efficient in it. The former governments broke the people into submission; the present government steals their hearts. The former government violated the physical freedom of the people; the present government controls their inner minds. The people used to fear their government as if it were a demon, but today they worship the government as if it were a god.

If things continue as they are, unless ways are reformed presently, the people will lose their vigor and spirit each time the government starts a new project. Though each project will contribute to the appearance of civilization, the spirit of civilization will be receding at each turn.

There is now a standing army under the government. People should be proud of this army as the mainstay of national defense. But the fact at present is that the people regard the army as a force to intimidate the people; fear is the only sentiment that lurks in their minds. Many schools and many miles of railway have been built. People should take pride in them as symbols of civilization, but in truth they regard these as special favors of the government, the result simply being that their sense of dependence on the government increases.

People are overwhelmed with a sense of awe and recoil in the face of their own government. In this state of mind, how could they compete with foreign people in the development of civilization? To conclude, I believe that unless people have the spirit of independence, the appearance of civilization will be of no use, however elaborately it develops. Rather, it will contribute to the gradual loss of the people's spirit.

By the above discussion, I trust it has been made clear that a nation's civilization cannot be started from above by the government, nor can it be engendered from below by the lower classes. It has to start in the middle of society to indicate the path for the majority and stand side by side with the government in this attempt. Then, and only then, may one expect progress.

In the histories of various countries of the West, there is not one example of new developments in commerce or industry created by the government. The origins of such developments are always found in the innovation of thinkers from the middle class of society. The steam engine was an invention of a man named Watt; the locomotive was the devising of one Stephenson. The person who for the first time discussed the laws of economics and brought about a change in commerce was Adam Smith. All these prominent men belonged to what is called the middle class. They were not the rulers of the country, nor were they people who lived by physical labor. They were from the middle class, and with their wisdom gave guidance to a whole generation.

When their new ideas or inventions were completed in their minds, they formed private companies of friends and put it in practice to promote the scheme further and contribute to the general populace and to posterity. The government's role is to allow this business to progress unhindered and understand the people's intentions. Therefore, it is the people who actually carry out the activities of civilization and the government that protects civilization.

In this way, the people of a country would care for their civilization as their own; they would compete for it, fight over it; envy others or show off to others. When there is one event in the country to tickle their pride, the whole people would rise up to cheer, their only care being not to allow other countries to surpass them. Then every activity related to civilization would invigorate the people, and every act and aspect of civilization would help ensure the independence of the country. All these, I regret to say, are counter to what we see in our country today.

Those in the middle class and who occupy a position to advocate civilization for the preservation of the country's independence are the scholars. But too many of these scholars either lack ability in comprehension or concern for the country, or they are simply following the trends of the times, believing that everything will come out well when left in the hands of the government. These scholars often grow restless and take the first opportunity to obtain positions in the government. They become preoccupied with trivial business, which is simply ludicrous. But they themselves are satisfied and the people do not question this. The most extreme among them will boast that the government is vastly endowed in talent and there is no talent left outside of it.

This trend, after all, is a phenomenon of the times and no in-

[98]

dividual should be blamed, but for the country's civilization, it is the most deplorable state of affairs. Indeed, it is sad to see the daily deterioration of the scholars whose duty should be to nurture civilization, and there is no one to express concern.

In this state of dire distress, our colleagues of Keiō Gijuku have barely been able to escape the calamities, and in the past several years, have preserved our independence. We are in this independent school, nurturing the spirit of independence, our one purpose being to preserve the independence of the whole nation. However, when the trend of the times overwhelms the society, its force is like a torrent of water or a wind storm. It is not easy to stand up against its fury. Unless one has a very courageous mind, one will unconsciously be carried along the stream or converted to the trend, thus losing the basis of one's beliefs.

Spiritual strength cannot be acquired from the reading of books only. Reading books is one of the means for learning, and learning is one of the means for accomplishing things. Unless one experiences work, a true spiritual power will not be cultivated. Those among our colleagues who have solved the secret must seek to apply their knowledge and wisdom for the realization of civilization even if they have to suffer poverty and privations. There are countless fields in which to work. Commerce must be attended to; law must be studied; industry must be started; agriculture must be encouraged. Publication of books, translations, and newspapers, and all phases of civilization must be absorbed and made part of our activities. We must stand at the forefront of our people in all walks of life in cooperation with the government, the official power and the private power maintaining a healthy balance to promote national prestige and transform it from its present feeble state of independence into a solid and immovable one so that we will not budge an inch in competition with foreign powers.

Several dozen years in the future when we recall how things were on this New Year's Day, suppose instead of relief and elation over the safety of our country that we feel now, we were to recollect with pity the lack of independence! Would that not be a joyful prospect to look forward to? All people of intellect should select and work toward their own objectives with firm resolution.

15

Outline of Civilization

Outline of Civilization is recognized as Fukuzawa's most scholarly work. It contains discussions of all the elements of civilization in general and their implications for Japan's own civilization. Fukuzawa regarded civilization as a continuous growth and introduced a concept of history that was new to traditional Japanese thought.

One may regard *Outline of Civilization* as the culmination of Fukuzawa's studies and thinking up to that time, or perhaps his thoughts ripened to maturity in this book. All his subsequent works are expositions of each individual subject included in the book.

Translated here are Fukuzawa's Preface to the book and a selection from the ninth chapter, which deals with education.

Preface

A discourse on civilization is a discourse on the development of the human mind. It does not deal with the development of the mind of an individual but the minds of people as a group in the whole of society. Therefore, it would be well to call a discourse on civilization a discourse on the development of the group mind.

Bummeiron no Gairyaku (文明論之概略), 1875. *Fukuzawa Yukichi Zenshū*, vol. 4, pp. 3–6.

In their daily lives, people are liable to be misled by the immediate interest in minor problems and lose sight of the true path. People become so habituated to old customs that they are often unable to distinguish between natural and artificially induced behaviors. At times one discovers something to be a custom though it had been thought of as natural. Sometimes a circumstance quite in reverse may be seen. Under such complicated and confused conditions, the purpose of this discourse is to discover a precise and consistent principle. Such being the case, this deliberation on civilization is a truly difficult process.

Western civilization has a long history of development dating back to the fall of the Roman Empire a thousand years ago. Japan, too, has had a history of 2500 years since the founding of the nation. Our civilization has developed on its own to its present state. Naturally great differences exist between the two civilizations.

In the Kaei era, the Americans arrived, and soon thereafter treaties of communication and trade were signed with several Western countries. Then for the first time, our countrymen realized the existence of Western peoples. Comparing our civilization with theirs, they have been both surprised and disturbed by the great differences. No doubt, there had been many earlier instances of surprise among the people by the warfare within the country and the rise and fall of rulers. But the first instance of wonderment which reached deep into the people's inner sentiments was the introduction of Buddhism and Confucianism from China, and the second instance was the recent encounter with the West. These were the most profound instances. However, the teachings of Buddhism and Confucianism were of Asiatic origin brought into an Asiatic country. It was not difficult to accept them, because the differences were only in the degree of refinement. It may well be said that to us those teachings were new but not foreign.

Our encounter with the West, however, was not of the same order. The birthplace of the new civilization was distant, its origin was foreign, the subsequent development it took and the degree of development were different. An unknown culture was to be met and to be closely associated with. No wonder the whole experience was strange: every one of the things and ideas brought in was surprising to see and startling to hear. To use a simile, it was like the meeting of the hottest fire with the coldest water. It never ceased to confuse the people, it even went to the bottom of their minds and caused a turnover and a great revolution.

This great revolution resulted in the imperial restoration of the other year, followed by the abolition of clans and the organization of prefectures. Thus the nation survives, but the disturbance was not to stop with these changes. The warfare itself has been forgotten as a thing of the past, but the turbulence in the minds of the people is still there with no sign of abating. After all, this turbulence is a manifestation of the people's efforts to advance higher or their dissatisfaction with their own civilization and endeavors to assimilate the Western civilization. And they will not cease or be satisfied till they bring their own civilization to the level of the West and stand abreast with it or surpass it. And because the civilization of the West, too, is advancing constantly, our people will be vying with it in a race with no end. Indeed, the coming of the Americans in the Kaei era proved to be the kindling of a fire in our people's minds which, once kindled, is never to be put out.

Such being the confusion in the people's minds, the turmoil in society is almost beyond imagination. At such a juncture, to clarify the concept of civilization and to provide it with a proper definition is a serious and difficult undertaking for a scholar. The scholars in the West are introducing new ideas daily. Some of them are novel and curious or even startling. But they are, after all, products of studies which have a tradition of a thousand years. Even if they are novel, they are outgrowths of the same civilization, and to the scholars of the West not a fresh creation.

In comparison, the state of things in Japan is by no means of the same order. Our civilization today is like fire trying to change into water, or turning something void into existence. This transformation can be called neither sudden progress nor reformation. Perhaps terms such as "initiation" or "origination" would be more appropriate. This underlines the difficulty of writing a discourse on the subject.

The scholars of today are obliged to face these difficulties, but at the same time, they are blessed with a fortunate circumstance which is theirs by an accident of history. This accident of history

[103]

came about thus: Since the opening of our ports, many of our scholars devoted themselves seriously to Western studies, and though the results are still negligible and rudimentary, they have at least grasped the outline and some elements of Western civilization, if but vaguely. At the same time, these scholars, until twenty years ago, lived in a purely atmosphere Japanese civilization. Not only were they able to learn about Western civilization, they actually worked in it and worked for it. Therefore, in their study of a foreign civilization, they researched every fact and facet thoroughly. On this point, their understanding might be more accurate than that of their Western counterparts who were born and bred in that civilization and did not have to study the state of things in foreign countries.

This is what I call the fortunate circumstance of the scholars in Japan today. And after the passing of this generation, this fortunate circumstance will not be had again. This generation is truly a blessed one.

To illustrate, every one of our scholars in Western studies today was once a student in Chinese learning, and every one was either Shintoist or Buddhist, and either a samurai or a commoner in a feudal society. Now that he is a scholar in Western studies, it is for him like living two lives with one body or having two bodies in one person. Suppose he compares the two lives or two bodies, or matches the experiences received in the former body with Western civilization, which he is receiving in the present body, and see how the memory of the past compares with the reality of today. What impression will result? Whatever observations he may make will have a ring of truth and value.

The reason for my writing this book is simply to take advantage of the situation which I am enjoying and which later generations cannot. Therefore, in composing the materials for this book with my still insufficient knowledge of Western learning and my meager scholarship, I did not translate the original works of the scholars of the West but applied their general ideas to the actual situation in Japan. All this is to record the thoughts of men of this era for the generations that will follow.

However, I am very conscious of my superficial reasoning and of my many errors, and I apologize for my limitations. Therefore, those scholars who succeed me will study more, read books from the West in depth, observe conditions in Japan further, expand the scope of their mental domain, excel in their studies, and complete a work truly worthy to be a dissertation on civilization so as to renew the appearance and reputation of Japanese scholarship. This is my sincere hope. I still am not too aged. I shall endeavor in my own studies to be of some aid in that attempt which I know will one day be realized.

In the present work, whenever a book is quoted for translation, the original source is given, but when the general idea is translated or where several books were used in forming my own opinion, the original sources are not recorded. It is like eating food and digesting it: the food certainly was something foreign, but when digested, it became a part of me. Therefore, whenever there is a good idea in this book, that idea is not originally my own, but it was the good food which gave birth to it.

In writing this book, I have many times consulted my colleagues and benefited from their readings. In particular I am indebted to Obata Tokujirō, who read my manuscript and made corrections which improved the academic value of this book.

Fukuzawa Yukichi

March 25, Meiji 8th year (1875)

Education as a Tool of Despotism

... Thus in Japan, religion has had no authority of its own. How much truer this is of Confucian learning! Confucianism came to our country many centuries ago. In the imperial age before feudalism began, there were "learned men" in the employ of the government and the emperors themselves were tutored in the Chinese classics by them. During the reign of Emperor Saga [809–23], the chief councilor of state, Dainagon Fuyutsugu, established a school called Kangaku-in for the education of members of his house and clan. In Emperor Uda's time [887–97], the councilor of state, Chūnagon Yukihira, also established a school called Shōgaku-in. As such instances prove, the study of Chinese

Selection from ch. 9, *Bummeiron no Gairyaku, Fukuzawa Yukichi Zenshū*, vol. 4, pp. 159–61.

classics gradually spread. Japanese poetry composition was even more prevalent and began earlier than Chinese studies. However, all these educational activities were confined to the children of titled families, and the writing of books was monopolized by the officials. This being before the invention of printing, there was no possibility of education to reaching the common people.

In the Kamakura period [1185–1333], with the beginning of the warriors' rule, such scholars as Ōe no Hiromoto and Miyoshi Yasunobu were appointed for their knowledge in Confucianism to work in the government, but there was not one scholar known among the people. In the third year of Jōkyū [1221], Hōjō Yasutoki, who was the government chief, led his troops to Kyoto. On the way, he was met by a messenger from Gotoba Jōō[1] with an imperial rescript. The general sought among his troops of over 5000 for someone who could read this rescript and found one Fujita Saburō of Musashi province who was able to read it for him. This is a good illustration of how illiterate common people were at the time.

From this time till the end of the Ashikaga period [1333–1573], the situation remained basically unchanged, and education continued to be the monopoly of Buddhist priests. Anyone who wanted to learn to read or study had to depend on the temples. In later years, children who were taught to write came to be called *terako* [temple children]. This must have developed out of the above situation. According to a certain scholar, the first printed books in Japan were produced by the five great temples in Kamakura. That is probably true.

At the beginning of the Tokugawa period [1603–1867], the first shōgun, Ieyasu, appointed Fujiwara Seika and later Hayashi Dōshun as chief scholars under him. In the long period of peace that followed, Confucian scholars flourished and thus the tradition continued into the modern age.

As described above, the rise and fall of learning was affected by the state of war or peace in society, and education could not progress of its own independent power. Learning was entirely in the hands of the priests who stood more or less aloof from society. This I consider a disgrace to the cause of learning. And from this

[1] Retired emperor who held actual power.

one instance, one may see that Confucianism was not the equal of Buddhism.

However, it is not only in Japan that the cause of learning suffers during disturbances or warfare. All the countries of the world are the same. In Europe, too, from the medieval age, called the Dark Ages, to feudal times, education was entirely in the hands of the priests, and it was only in the 1600s that the general public began to take interest in it.

Also, the styles of learning were different in the East and the West. The main stream in the West depends on experimentation, while in Japan the doctrines of Confucius and Mencius were valued. The two cannot be compared according to the same standard, for one finds value in verified truths while the other pays respects to given theories. One must not find too much fault with Confucianism, for, after all, what brought the Japanese people from their absolute ignorance to the civilization of today is the achievement of Buddhism and Confucianism. Particularly, in recent times with the rise of Confucianism, superstitious Shintō and Buddhist practices among the populace have been eliminated. From this one instance the influence of Confucianism can be recognized. Its positive influence must not go unnoticed.

I shall leave off discussing the comparative merits of learning in the East and the West and turn to the outstanding differences between the circumstances under which both existed. What are the differences? When learning rose after a period of disturbance in society, in the West it rose among the general people while in Japan it rose within the government. This was the difference. In the West, learning has been an enterprise of the scholars and in its study there is no distinction between official and private—it is in the domain of the scholars. In our country, learning has been within the domain of the rulers. It has been, so to say, only a part of the government.

For instance, in the 250 years of the Tokugawa period, every institution in the country which can be called a school was either a government or clan establishment. There were famous scholars, certainly, and outstanding publications, too. But these scholars were always vassals of a ruler; the publications were official publications. There were, of course, scholars among the masterless samurai [rōnin] and some private publications. But the masterless samurai

[107]

were those who wanted but failed to become vassals; the private publications were results of failure to obtain official sponsorship. A scholars' association was simply unheard of. No newspapers or publications for the expression of opinions ever existed. No training schools for arts and crafts existed, nor assemblies for the discussion of public opinion. In short, there was not one private attempt at intellectual development.

On rare occasions, a great scholar would establish a school of his own, but the only students who gathered were of the samurai class whose livelihood was assured by the stipends from their lords. They were to study in between their service to their lords, and the subjects of their learning, too, were geared to the needs of the ruling class. They learned the philosophy of ruling, which was the essence of Confucianism, and even when they mastered the study of a thousand books, unless they found a position in the government, their studies would be of no use. At times, there was the scholar called a "hermit sage," but in truth he was not living a hermit life out of preference; he may have been either secretly lamenting his fate and envying or reproaching others, or he may have retired from this society. To summarize the circumstances, the scholars in old Japan were confined within a cage called the government, regarded this cage as their universe, and fretted and struggled in this little universe. Very fortunately, there were not too many scholars taking Chinese studies seriously. Suppose those teachers were able to train as many scholars as they had wished; they would all have been crowded in that small cage with no room to satisfy everyone, resulting in growing envy and grudges which would have accumulated without end. A pitiful prospect to imagine, is it not?

Being ignorant of the world of human beings outside, these scholars failed to carve out positions of their own. They depended only on the administrators of the time, never realizing that they were being humiliated by those in power. In the Tokugawa era, those scholars who considered themselves successful were those appointed official Confucians of either the shogunate or the clans. They may have had official titles, but being of a category called "long sleeves,"[2] they were not respected at all. They were taken

[2] In the early days of warrior rule, scholarly and cultural activities were the monopoly

advantage of and never appointed to administrative positions, which they would have liked, but they were given stipends of perhaps half a *koku* and made to teach young men. In an age when only a few were literate, these scholars were convenient tools for satisfying this need, but it was exactly like the *eta*[3] being hired for working on leathercraft, a shameful circumstance for a scholar's livelihood. What can we expect of such people? What could we blame them for? There is no wonder that no independent association could grow or that no firmly rooted opinions developed.

On top of all this, there is more to be considered. At times some spirited scholars did speak out against the despotism of the government. But when the very root of it all is studied, we realize that the seed was first sown by the scholars themselves and that they were themselves being bound by the "vines" which grew out of it. Who, in the first place, taught the doctrine of despotism to the government? Granted that a government, by its very nature, contains the seed of despotism, what was it that nurtured this seed and embellished it? It was none other than Confucian doctrine. Those Confucian scholars who were said to be the ablest and the most successful were those most knowledgeable of despotism and most highly promoted in the government. From this point of view, one may declare that Confucianism is the master and the government its pupil.

The people of today should be pitied. Who among them do not have forebears? All those in this age who hold high positions and practice despotism or those who suffer under this despotism, no one must blame contemporary Confucians for the state of things. They must realize that all this came from a poison inherited from their distant ancestors. And who helped to increase the power of this poison? The scholars of Confucianism, above all, have contributed to this cause.

---

of the imperial courtiers. The samurai held power but they were all rough and illiterate, and they had a way of belittling the courtiers as good-for-nothing slowpokes in feminine dresses with long sleeves.

[3] The lowest caste in the feudal Japanese society, an outcast who specialized in the slaughter of cattle and the curing of leather.

16

On Moral Education:
A Letter in Reply to
Nakamura Ritsuen

Nakamura Ritsuen was a noted scholar of the old
school in the Kyoto-Osaka area and had been a close
friend of the Fukuzawa family since Yukichi's father's
time. To Yukichi, Ritsuen was like an uncle and a
senior scholar, but by 1878, when this letter was written, Ritsuen regarded Yukichi as the most noted scholar
and educator of the new age. The correspondence
between the two was published in a periodical of the
Ministry of Education, and it provoked lively discussions
among the scholars in Japan, dividing them into two
major currents through the Meiji era, classical moralists
against liberals, until the issuance of the Imperial
Rescript on Education in 1890, which stopped the
public discussions.

In recent years, there has been a remarkable growth in the establishment of elementary schools throughout the country, but
instruction provided in these schools gives one much cause for
concern. You have expressed your wish that I should undertake
the publication of a manual on school education and demonstrate
the ways filial piety and brotherly harmony should be given
preference over technical instruction, and that if this idea were
advocated among the officials responsible for education, it would
serve to improve public education.

"Nakamura Ritsuen Sensei ni Kotau" (中村栗園先生に答), 1878. *Fukuzawa Yukichi Zenshū*, vol. 4, pp. 491–96.

Your cordial letter I read with deep respect, and I do not know how to express my appreciation of your kind sentiment toward me. I, too, have been concerned with the same problem, but I have been consoling myself with the thought that when the time comes, society will adjust itself to the needs of the times. Allow me here to express my humble thoughts.

During the Tokugawa period, those who became scholars were confined to the samurai class, and very few among the lower classes were literate. It was not only that there were few who took interest in learning, but the policy of the government and the prevailing customs made it almost prohibitive for commoners to seek an education. The samurai alone occupied an advantageous position in society and enjoyed a monopoly over education, refinement, and the arts. We may safely say that the civilization and education of the whole nation were private possessions of the samurai class. This is the reason why, even today, those men with noble demeanor are found almost exclusively among former clan samurai.

However, the samurai class was not large. Estimating the whole population of Japan to be about 35 million, the samurai class occupied only about one-seventeenth of that number or less. Therefore, the diffusion of education covered only about one-seventeenth of the whole nation. And only the number of scholars and teachers or books and instruments of instruction sufficient to answer the needs of the one-seventeenth was required. Such was the general condition of education in Tokugawa times.

Since the Restoration, the general population has gradually come to recognize the importance of education, and the farmers, artisans, and merchants, along with the samurai, began to realize that all their children must be educated. A Ministry of Education was established in the government, and it began promoting universal education; people with ideals began writing books or in newspapers to promote this growing interest in education, finally bringing about the splendor we enjoy today. However, the prosperity we see today is a prosperity of appearance only, and the true fruition has not yet been attained. And there is a reason for this.

The publication of books for the encouragement of learning and the government officials' advocacy of education have been effective, but what they have accomplished thus far has only been to make people realize the importance of education or eliminate the restraints of the Tokugawa period. They have not had time as yet to consider the contents of education. Even if they have thought of it, there were reasons for their inability to deal with them. For instance, as was said before, in former times only the samurai were privileged to an education, and among them those who chose to pursue scholarship numbered between 100,000 and 200,000. This means that there were only 200,000 or fewer students in the whole country, and the number of teachers, too, was correspondingly small. Estimating that one teacher was reponsible for 50 pupils, 4000 teachers would have been more than sufficient to satisfy the needs of the whole country.

But then, according to the report of the Ministry of Education for 1874, the number of students in both public and private schools in all the prefectures of the country was 1,730,179, and the number of teachers was 37,736. How and where were these 37,736 teachers obtained? There is no doubt that such a large number of qualified teachers could not have been hired all at once. Metaphorically speaking, this is like guests arriving at a party, only to find that the host is not there to receive them. If the party does not even have a host, the quality of the food need not be questioned at all. The only thing to be done would be to have the guests sit at the table and feed them and keep them from going hungry.

In the elementary schools today, the curriculum is not perfect; the only thing they do is to teach children how to read, write, and count, and that under a regimented rule as in the army and never in an atmosphere congenial to true education. All this is due to the lack of qualified teachers. It is not that the schools do not look for such teachers; they do, but there are not enough of them.

When there are no qualified men among the teachers, no matter how much the school curriculum is improved or whatever textbooks are published, no great results can be expected. Especially, the moral education of filial piety and brotherly harmony cannot be taught by formal instruction. It has to be transmitted to the pupils informally or unawares through the personality of the teachers. If there were an ideal personality who was truly capable of being a teacher, even under the present school system,

[113]

with the same books and the same curriculum, this teacher would certainly be able to influence his pupils in the ways of filial piety and brotherly harmony. There are even examples in which there was not even a book to read and yet good education was provided. Therefore, one may safely assert that the present deficiency in elementary school education is due not to the faults in the system of instruction but to the lack of qualified teachers. Such has been the general trend of education since the Restoration.

Without question, I do not make light of the teaching of filial piety and brotherly harmony. Since my childhood to this day, I have believed it to be an essential element in the morals of human nature. And I am sure that I am not alone in my beliefs: a large number of people will share the same beliefs. Even those who fail to practice the precepts themselves must be reassured when others do. Therefore, it is clear that disloyalty to parents and brethren is what people detest. If the whole world hates it, what can stand against it? The general sentiment will certainly be united on this point sooner or later.

Now, allow me to illustrate my point with some facts. In recent years, the need for teachers in schools has been so acute that the school authorities could not afford to be selective. A person had only to be literate to be employed as a teacher, even when his personality did not qualify him to become a policeman. But this practice is not to continue for long. The science of economics dictates the theory of supply and demand. When the supply of teachers increases in our society, the urgency of the demand will decrease accordingly, and with it the standards for their selection will become higher. When a man is thirsty, he will drink anything, but when his thirst is satisfied, he will become discriminating about the quality of the drink.

Elementary school teachers today are taking advantage of the thirst of the society and are proudly occupying their positions, apparently with no cares. In extreme cases, some young teachers with all nonchalance purposely act and speak in defiance of the established customs in order to bewilder the public. But such bewilderment is a temporary thing. The mind of the public, though not adept at times, is in truth sensible and powerful. It will not tolerate such frivolity.

In the future, as the supply increases, the day will certainly

[114]

come when higher standards in selecting, testing, and judging between the jewels and bricks will be applied. Even today, the administration of education has improved, and in areas where there is a large number of teachers, the moral behavior of the candidates is weighed when there is a choice between two whose age and scholarship are equal. In some cases, even when one candidate's scholarship is somewhat wanting, if his moral character is sufficient to make up for it, the public seems to prefer such a person in spite of his lack of scholarship. With this example, the tendency of public preference may be surmised. And this is my humble expectation of the general trend in education in the future.

You have told me to petition to the responsible government officials concerning the education in our country. However, according to my observation, it is not that the officials are not conscious of the problems; they are unable to cope with the times. Outstanding intellectuals are not lacking among the officials. Indeed, there are some with whom it would be worthwhile discussing the issues of the times, especially education, which they seem to be studying seriously. Yet, the trends of society are not steered by just one or two officials.

The situation is comparable to a great ship that carries the whole of society, and the officials are no more than the boatmen. All they can do is steer the ship so that it will not run into too rough a wind or waves. Such matters as the speed of the ship are not within the powers of these one or two boatmen. I have heard that there soon will be a reformation in the educational regulations. In this reformation, there is sure to be a return to the moral teachings of filial piety and brotherly harmony. It will be a commendable attempt, but from my own point of view, I cannot believe that it will have much effect, even if the regulations order it. The best I can hope for will be improvement in the wording of the regulations and to wait for the time when the moral level of the teachers rises and they begin to give life to the regulations.

You also wrote that if I had decided that the moral doctrine of filial piety and brotherly harmony was too narrow to be taken seriously, that would be going against the will of my late father, and you hinted that this would be unfilial toward my father. I am always driven to shivers at the simple mention of undutifulness to parents. It was my misfortune that within 18 months of my birth, I lost my father who was 45 years of age. In my whole family (one elder brother and three elder sisters), I am the only one who does not remember our father's face. Not only am I an unfortunate orphan, I am the most unhappy of the five siblings.

Because I was unable to serve my father while he was in this world, I am ever careful not to tarnish his name and reputation after his death, and there has not been a minute, day or night, I have not honored this. Four years ago, I lost my mother, too, but I may consider my having served her for 40 years as one fortunate circumstance in my generally unfortunate life. I learned all about my late father's words and deeds in great detail from my mother while she was living. My father was upright in his moral behavior, yet very remarkable in literary talent, which I deeply esteem, and I trust that you, too, will acknowledge the love I have for my father. If you regard my father as a person who endeavored to follow and study Confucianism and was assiduous in literary activities, then I am the son of that very person, and I earnestly admire and believe in his words and deeds.

I went into Western studies while I was still young, and I have not been able yet to delve deeply into the inner philosophy of Confucianism. Moreover, being of shallow intellect and of simple reasoning, I do not yet know what exactly is the true way. But should my forebears' words and deeds be truly in accord with Confucianism, then I, too, am a believer in Confucianism with no vestiges of doubt.

I think there is a reason for your believing that I am against Confucianism. When I first began studying Western learning some twenty years ago, it was very much against the times, and very few relatives and friends approved my choice. Only with the approval of my late mother and late brother was I secretly able to begin my studies, and after much hardship, just as I was beginning to grasp an understanding of Western learning, the slogan "Drive Out the Foreigners" was raised.

Scholars in Western learning were held in contempt, and in extreme cases, some found their lives in danger. Since time immemorial, most men in the world of learning have sought fame, but the Western scholars of those days were anxious to conceal their names and their abodes as much as possible. The advocates of "Drive Out the Foreigners" were mostly from the schools of

[116]

Confucianism and their doctrines were based on filial 'piety, brotherly harmony, and loyalty to the master. We, the Western scholars, had no wish to approach them and to listen to their arguments; we only sought to avoid them.

After all, the doctrine of "Drive Out the Foreigners" and our doctrine of the extension of national rights were both founded on patriotism. My advocacy of national rights has never altered in the past twenty years, and I expect it will not change till the day I die. But then, it was inevitable that the anti-foreign arguments of those days were as contrary to our Western scholars' ideas as water to fire. It was impossible at that time to discuss anything with adversaries. And we simply chose to stay away from them.

Therefore, I wish to state that I was not against the Confucian doctrine; I was simply avoiding the Confucian advocates. Or rather, I was afraid of them, and I simply kept away from them. These probably are the circumstances for my reputation as anti-Confucian. All that belongs to the past now, and I no longer need to point out the differences. Western and Confucian teachings have now grown into one, and no contradiction is seen. This is a fortunate outcome for society.

My sole interest today is to continue my work in education and to improve my moral behavior. I do not dare instruct or lead, but my life-long endeavor will be to preserve for my mind and body a position of my own and to respect the family tradition that I inherited from my ancestors and thus to prevent shame upon my father's and mother's memories. Yet, what am I to do when there is so much to regret in my own deeds in spite of my trying so much to protect my parents' honor.

I pray for your generous tolerance.

Very respectfully,
Yukichi

January 25, Meiji 11th year (1878)

17
A Bequest of Old Coins to Children

Probably prompted by his correspondence with Nakamura Ritsuen on the moral issue, Fukuzawa wrote the
following article and handed copies to each of his children along with coins which their grandfather had
collected. Eighteen years later, in 1896, it was made
public in *Jijishimpō*.

To Ichitarō and my other children,
Your grandfather, Fukuzawa Hyakusuke, was a samurai of
the former Nakatsu Clan. He was stationed in Dōjima of Osaka
on official duty from when he was 24 years old, and all of us, two
sons and three daughters, were born there. And your grandfather
died at the age of 45 on the Dōjima Clan estate.
Your grandfather was fond of learning. He studied under
Nomoto Setsugan of Nakatsu and Hoashi Banri of Bungo, and he
was recognized as an outstanding student. It was not for his
scholarship alone that he was noted; he was known to be good,
considerate, unaffected, and tolerant of all things, also morally
pure in his private life, which won him the respect of all who
knew him. He died more than 40 years ago, and I am not privileged to remember anything about him—not even his features.
Yet I have learned of his words and deeds in great detail from
your grandmother.
While grandfather was in Osaka, he took pleasure in collecting

"Fukuzawa Shi Kosen Haibun no Ki" (福沢氏古銭配分之記), 1878. *Jijishimpō*, March
11, 1896. *Fukuzawa Yukichi Zenshū*, vol. 15, pp. 394–97.

old coins. In those days in Osaka, the custom was to tie copper coins, which had holes in the center and were called green coins, together with a string. A string of 96 coins was used as a unit of currency. People would accept it simply by glancing at its length but seldom bothered to actually count the number of coins on the string. Even when a few coins were missing, no one cared, and there was practically no one conniving enough to steal a few coins from the strings for gain.

One day, grandfather found some interesting specimens. He slipped several coins off the string, retied it, and went out on some business, forgetting to tell his family what he had done. After returning home at sundown, he inquired where the money was and found that those strings had already been handed to a fishmonger in payment for that day's purchase.

Grandfather was annoyed and asked which fishmonger had been paid the money. Unfortunately, it was not the usual fellow. It was a different man who happened to stop by, and no one, not even the servants, could tell who he was. Grandfather's concern grew all the more. He called together all the members of the household who saw the man and inquired about his appearance, age, clothing, the size of the packs he carried, and even about the pole from which he hung the packs.

All these he noted down, and then he called in a laborer [nakashi] who transported rice for the clan estate and ordered him, for a certain sum, to go to Ajikawa or Zakoba to look for the fishmonger, because grandfather reasoned that most of the fishmongers who came to sell in Dōjima were likely to be from either of those two places. The estate laborer took two or three days before he finally brought back the right person. Grandfather told him the details of what had happened and paid him the 5 or 10 mon which were missing from the strings of coins. He also paid him for coming at his call and apologized for his neglect.

This story was never told to anyone in the clan estate or outside. We children were too small at that time to understand what had happened. The only person who knew was your grandmother. I imagine that grandfather disliked having his deed known and gossiped about by the public, which was his nature. The incident belongs to the past now, and he departed from this world 40 long years ago. I cannot bear to let this story disappear into

[120]

oblivion, for it is not only the pride of the Fukuzawa family, it is indeed a touching story for the whole of society.

When you children reach adulthood, I want you to share this story with others to exalt the virtue of your forebears. As you do so, reflect upon your own behavior. What kind of grandchildren are worthy of such a grandfather? You are descended from an honorable family. As descendants, whether to exalt your ancestor's name or otherwise depends upon your conscience.

Remember that your grandfather did not simply find pride in being honest. In his early adulthood, he was appointed official in charge of the clan's finances, stationed in Osaka, and associated with the big and rich merchants of the day. To manage the clan's finances, he sometimes sold the clan's rice or raised bonds for the clan, arguing over interest rates and discussing the terms of loans. At times, in order to approach the moneylenders, he had to drink with and entertain them. Thus he spent some twenty-odd years associating with the most vulgar of the Osaka merchants. Yet, he retained the latitude of mind to nourish his interest in literature and learning.

He studied in the school of Itō Jinsai and Tōgai, father and son, who specialized in scholarly analyses of the Chinese classics. Besides, he was skilled in writing classical Chinese as well as poetry. Men like Noda Tekiho were among his intimate friends. Therefore, grandfather was an ordinary clan official in status, but he was also a scholar, a literary person, and a poet. His interest was widespread, his mind capable in a large variety of subjects, never inclined to a single direction.

The episode of the fishmonger is simply an incident in which his nature was revealed in a casual event, and it does not by any means imply that his daily behavior was consistently upright. I do not think that honesty is the only virtue nor consider my life and conduct perfect. However, in my personal feelings toward my children, I wish to hand down this episode, even if it is a small matter, as an admirable example of our forebear's conduct.

Very fortunately, I have here today 87 *mon* which grandfather gathered together in his life. Among them must be the same coins from the string which was handed to the fishmonger. I have always kept them close to me, even while I was away from home for studies. But because you are now all growing up and in a few years you will be joining adult society, I intend to divide the coins among you, two sons and four daughters, for you to keep as reminders for your moral conduct, and I shall continue to treasure a few myself, as I always have.

The house of Fukuzawa was of poor samurai origin with a small stipend, and it possessed no property to speak of. When I inherited the household, all there was in the house were several hundred volumes of Chinese books, a few scrolls of paintings and calligraphy, and some swords. All these were sold off to defray expenses while I was studying. Today practically nothing remains of inherited objects to be handed down to you. Even if there are a few, they are all ordinary objects which can be purchased today, and I hold no regrets for this meagerness.

As for the old coins, however, they are something that cannot be purchased, however many thousands of gold pieces you may expend, a treasure retaining the glory of our forebears. And here you are to share with me their afterglow. Your inheritance is indeed great! Be reverent in retaining this treasure. Be reverent in remembering the spirit of this treasure. When you beget children, let them inherit it. When grandchildren come, have them follow in this inheritance. Thus generation after generation, the line of Fukuzawa shall endeavor in being earnest, independent, and self-sustaining. Direct your households well, though that will be a matter of course, but by chance if you fall into poverty, never shall you forget the great cause of independence and civilization or sink into the misery of spiritual starvation.

Yukichi

February 5, Meiji 11th year (1878)

Note in Jijishimpō: The statement of two sons and four daughters in the above article was correct in Meiji 11th year. But one daughter and two sons were have been born since, and at present there are four sons and five daughters.

March 11, 1896

18
The Importance of
Physical Sciences

Physical science is a branch of learning that clarifies the characteristics of physical matter, studies their workings by means of the laws of nature, and puts them to the use of human purposes. Therefore, this subject, of its nature, is different from all other subjects. For instance, economics and commerce are both regarded as subjects, but as they are today, they do not work according to the laws of nature. For example, there exist a school of free trade and a school of protective trade, both finding the basis of their arguments on different reasons. While British scholars advocate free trade as standing to reason, American scholars side with protective policy. Listening to their arguments, both seem to be true to reason. Therefore, one will have to regard the basis of economics as different in England and in America.

Physical phenomena are not like that. Since the beginning of the world up to this day, anywhere in the whole world, the laws governing physical matter have been the same with not a single change ever. In the ancient period of the gods, water boiled when it reached 212 degrees Fahrenheit, and in this Meiji era, too, water boils at the same temperature. Steam in the Western world has the same power of expansion as steam in the Orient. Men in America die taking an excessive dose of morphine, and Japanese also die taking the same dosage. This is what we call physical law. The learning that studies these laws in order to apply them to human advantage is called physical science.

Nothing in human life can be an exception to this law. If there

"Butsurigaku no Yōyō" (物理学之要用), *Jijishimpō* editorial, March 22, 1882. *Fukuzawa Yukichi Zenshū*, vol. 8, pp. 49–52.

should be anything that appears to be otherwise, it will simply mean a lack of research concerning the subject. The one enemy of physical science that hinders its development is the infatuation with such superstitions as cosmic dual force and the five-element theory of old Chinese philosophy. Fortunately, among the upper class of our society, there is very little of this infatuation.

In my former publication, *Jiji Shōgen* [Commentary on Current Problems, 1881], fourth chapter, I made the following remarks:

After all, the above is the result of the Chinese people's excessive confidence in the size of their country and their total belief in the cosmic dual force and five-element theory and their neglect in seeking the true and basic law of matter. For them, astronomy was one of the means of divination, and they worried about their fortunes when a change in the positions of the planets was observed. They took the legends of the dragons, the fiery horse [*kirin*], or phoenix, symbols of peace and good fortune, and ghostly demons and godly spirits very seriously. Even today, members of the Chinese upper class are slaves to these beliefs, and it seems that very few people hold doubts about them. All these are powerful deterrents to scientific truth, and as long as they remain, the Chinese cannot make any progress in civilization. It is not that these enemies did not exist in Japan, but historical circumstances created a completely different scene.

Here, in our country, most of the superstitious tales of fearful gods and ghosts were what the Buddhists first believed and circulated among the people, but from 300 years ago, Confucianism spread and, in its competition with Buddhism, criticized the nonsense about gods and ghosts. Later, in their enthusiasm for this attack, the Confucians began to discredit their own cosmic dual forces and five-element practices. For instance, Confucian scholars would study the philosophy of *I-ching*, but they would be ashamed to practice divination by turtle shells and bamboo sticks. In their criticism of Buddhism, the Confucians saved themselves from superstition. This one may call an accident of good fortune.

The Confucianism of China values the teachings of Confucius and Mencius; and the Confucianism of Japan studies the works of the same great sages. They share the same sources of doctrine, and yet the results of their propagation in society are quite contrary. What can be the reason for this? It cannot simply be accidental. As I consider the situation, Confucianism in China became intoxicated with itself because it had no competitor. In Japan, Confucianism was able to guard itself against corruption because it had a formidable competitor to cope with. Also, in Japan, Confucian scholars came mostly from the samurai families, and they naturally retained healthy and active interests in literary and artistic pursuits. With that spirit, they guided their pupils toward a vigorous life style, and all the people in the country above the samurai class were naturally influenced in this way. Therefore, one may see that the whole society of Japan was ready for new developments and reform.

As described above, very few of our upper class are susceptible to superstitious nonsense, but the cause of it all is simply a temporary rivalry with the Buddhists, and it did not arise from their knowledge of the truths of natural phenomena. Therefore, they have a very superficial knowledge of physical science, just as they are indifferent about superstitions.

Confucians denounce the Buddhist tales of heaven and hell as irrational, but then, in the past several hundred years, not a single Confucian scholar has seriously studied the process of how rain falls. They would simply say that rain falls from the heavens and that clouds condense and turn into rain, but have never come round to seeking theoretical and quantitative research on evaporation and rainfall.

They use water every morning and night and talk about its hardness and softness, but they never seek the facts on what substances combine to make up water or what substance or lack of it makes the difference between hard and soft water. I have never heard of a scholar who took interest in calcium bicarbonate, which when dissolved in water makes it hard and which in time solidifies into the dregs on the bottom of kettles. These scholars are trained to consider these phenomena as trivial. But they are wrong. In the recent civilization of Europe, there is nothing that is not based on physical science.

[125]

Those great inventions of steamships, steam locomotives, and guns and other weapons or telegraphy and gas lights—they all appear grand and formidable, but they all emerged from minute studies, analyses, and inferences of seemingly trivial principles that scholars applied to human affairs. One must not be surprised only by the greatness of results; one must never neglect seemingly trivial ideas. Neither the great nor the small was stumbled on by accident.

For a person to be ignorant of science and to be taking advantage of the conveniences of civilization without being conscious of their nature is like a horse that eats its feed without knowing anything about the nature of the feed, consuming only what it finds tasty and avoiding the untasty. Yet, a horse has the instinct to tell good feed apart from poisonous feed. However, today's unlearned people are riding on steam locomotives without understanding how steam works, and using telegraphy without knowing anything about electricity. An ignoramus would know nothing about himself and even have unhygienic habits, to the detriment of his own health. Worse, one would declare that the cure of a disease comes from one's state of mind, and, considering a doctor's treatment a mere conjecture, would take nonsensical Chinese herbal medicine to satisfy oneself. The worst one would take a cure-all medicine, believed it to be effective for every disease under the sun. Even among the upper class, the meagerness of medical knowledge is amazing. This is all the result of their neglect of physical science, and these people, who are no better than horses, will have no way of maintaining healthy bodies.

For all these reasons, in our Keiō Gijuku, physical science is taught as the first subject to beginners, and it has been made a prerequisite for all other courses. There will be another occasion to expand on the details of the curriculum.

19
Social Sciences Shall Also Be Studied

There was a certain person who argued as follows. He had read the curriculum of Keiō Gijuku and heard what is being said about its method of instruction that teaches the freshmen physical sciences exclusively. And he heartily approved of the approach. However, he had also heard that when the students advance to upper grades, they are taught the outlines of philosophy and law, and they are even supplied with books on politics and economics for study. However, of those students, even the oldest must be around 20, and those over 25 will be rare, admittedly a very young age. Even if highly gifted, they will necessarily be lacking in life's experiences; that is, they may safely be rated as youths devoid of judgment. Is it not dangerous to let these young people study politics and economics? Of course, politics and economics must not be regarded as dangerous in themselves. However, it depends on whether the person who studies them uses the knowledge to contribute to the peace of society or disturb it.

In that person's opinion, it is too early to let young men under twenty take up such studies. The danger is like letting young children play with a sharp sword. Moreover, in these days, political discussions are rampant in society and the arguments are very radical. In education, there is the possibility of leading young men astray and into danger rather than guiding them.[1] Speculating over the above advice, I can clearly see that that man

"Keisei no Gaku mata Kōkyū Subeshi" (経世之学亦考究すべし), *Jijishimpō* editorial, March 23, 1882. *Fukuzawa Yukichi Zenshū*, vol. 8, pp. 52–56.
[1] This fear that social sciences could lead young men into revolutionary action remained, especially government officials, until the end of World War II. The basic

is quite aware of the usefulness of political and economic studies. But because the choice of using the knowledge for constructive or destructive use depends on the student himself, and because young students are usually devoid of sound judgment, he believes that they are not fit to study those subjects.

This argument is certainly correct. It is clear that handling things without proper judgment of what is right and wrong will certainly bring harm. Riding without choosing the proper horse will entail the danger of being thrown. Eating without choosing the proper food will entail the danger of poisoning.

Judgment is important; that is clear. But simply to declare the importance is only half of the argument. One should go into the cause of how a person acquires or fails to acquire good judgment, and the ways and means of cultivating such judgment, and thus go through all these problems before closing one's argument. In all cases, it is important to learn the nature of a thing to decide whether it is safe or harmful. To learn the nature of things, it is first necessary to observe them. People in tropical regions have never seen ice. Therefore, they are ignorant of its nature. Because they do not know it, they cannot tell whether ice is harmful or not.

People are by nature fond of something different. Mountain people rejoice on seeing the sea, and people living on the seashore enjoy viewing the mountains because these are scenes their eyes and ears are not accustomed to. And this love of the exotic will increase in proportion to the degree of exoticness of the object, and at times it will cause a person to lose his reason.

The southern region of France is known for its production of grapes and plentiful wine, but among the natives of that region there are very few heavy drinkers. However, when people of the north, where wine is scarce, move to this southern region, they are liable to be caught by the tantalizing taste of the good wine to such an extent that they lose their self-control until they are stripped of their property and even their lives.

In Japan, when a poor man's son is hired at a confectionary store, he cannot resist the sweet taste in the beginning. The only cure for it is to let him eat all he wants and wait till he grows tired

---

reason for it was the possible denial of the emperor system. The Restoration had destroyed feudalism and abolished the rigid class system, and there was always the fear of the movement evolving into socialism.

of it. It is said that in Tokyo, those who amuse themselves in the gay quarters and lose themselves to the extreme are very rare among the natives. The quarters are more often frequented by those from the countryside, and in the bygone days those country boys were mostly from very proper samurai families and today from rich, exclusive landowners' families, very protected sons who have had little contact with the worldly atmosphere. The instances are too many to raise, but this is a well-known fact among those acquainted with such affairs.

All these instances illustrate the aspect of human nature that is attracted by something unusual and results in a loss of good sense. Therefore, whoever engages in bringing up young men and women should realize the importance of acquainting them with worldly affairs as they approach adulthood. Modest and serious-minded parents may disapprove of drinking and theater going, but they should not be fastidious. Let their children take liberty in wine and theater according to their taste, but advise them on the importance of proper restraint. According to a certain Westerner, children should be allowed to drink and go to the theater, but the parents should accompany them on the first occasion, and they should gradually be allowed liberty and independence. This idea appears to be very sound and proper.

If the ideas expressed above are deemed correct, what should be the procedure for developing the power of reason and clear sense of judgment in youth? Suppose they are to be restricted all their lives from reading books on politics and economics? The young will not stay young all their lives. In three to five years, they are to turn into full-grown adults, and they will be inconvenienced by not being familiar with politics and economics, for they are very necessary disciplines.

Let us retreat one step and suppose that in a human life, morality comes first, followed by the physical sciences. These two will produce a fine and respectable citizen. As for the social sciences, one may not receive instruction in them as such; they can be learned from actual experiences without difficulty. For instance, in our present government, the officials in the Ministry of Finance did not necessarily study economics; the officials in the Ministry of Education have not necessarily done research on education. But they seem to be carrying out their duties quite

[129]

successfully. In the final analysis, social sciences are "living" sciences; they are to be mastered in the experiences of real life and not to be learned at school.

Thus one may try to console oneself, but there is one situation which will not allow this easy relief. It comes from human nature which is attracted to the novel and strange. Even when young men are brought up with sound moral education, braced with training in the physical sciences under a strictly secluded school atmosphere, as if they were precious treasures in a jewelry box, there will be no way to prevent a sudden breaking out when the occasion arises, for after all no jewelry box exists in this world to really contain men. Moreover, this breaking out will be more severe in proportion to the solidness of the box and the length of time of containment.

To illustrate, suppose a special school is set up where the students are strictly prohibited from learning social sciences, and books on the subject and even history books kept from its library. After a few years, the students graduate, and at that moment, these students brought up strictly on morality and physical sciences will be fine and responsible citizens. Then, suppose these students, going home, come across a book on political or social problems, or suppose one evening on a casual visit outside, happen to hear a political speech; and suppose that book or the speech happened to be provocative People's Rights propaganda, cleverly designed to excite its listeners.

Then what will be the reaction of that fine and responsible citizen? The new experience will certainly startle him in the way a blind person would be on suddenly meeting the mystery of light and color or a dumb person on suddenly hearing a voice. When the mind is upset, clear judgment is lost. This occurrence may well be described as the complete loss overnight of the several years of hard work in bringing up a good and dutiful student.

It will not stop at a complete loss. The turn from extreme goodness to extreme sophistry will be like the northern Frenchmen intoxicated with the wine and the workers in a sweet shop lost to the sweets. They will not know where to stop. All this may be described as the effort to produce good students resulting in aiding their fall into sophistry. There can be no greater failure or miscarriage of purpose.

[130]

After all, society is a living society; those who teach in a school are living beings, and so are those who are being taught. The behavior of these living beings is difficult to control, even between parents and their children, and more so in teaching children who are not related.

Instruction in a school can seldom go the way the teacher plans. When the teacher realizes that his plans are going wrong, he should prepare to cope with it. As was said before, the basic reason young men harangue on social problems or bustle about for political propaganda that happens to be in vogue and thus busy themselves for no good cause, or in a worse case fall into the vice of disturbing the peace of the nation, is simply the young men's inadequate power of reasoning. What is the cause of this inadequacy in reasoning? It is their ignorance in the real social sciences. By all means, those provocative speakers are to be detested, but they are not speaking in their style because they know their subject. Rather, they are speaking eloquently because they do not know.

Therefore, in our Keiō Gijuku, the reason why books on philosophy and law or social sciences are permitted is to give the students an opportunity to understand the true reasonings of those disciplines, and thus to clarify judgments between right and wrong. Experience tells us that those who have read and learned deeply turn reticent in speech. However, this reticence does not mean loss of speech. When the time comes, their speech will prove most appropriate and candid, sometimes surprising to the ears of the unlearned, but that is because of the ignorance on the part of the listeners.

A good example is near at hand: What is the reason for the prevalence of the People's Rights movement in our country, something never seen elsewhere? It is because those advocates came across the idea recently and were surprised by its originality and startled exactly as the blind and dumb upon suddenly becoming able to see and hear. Of course, some of the activists are knowledgeable as a result of their long and serious study and observations of society, and give their best efforts to the movement. I do know such people. But all in all, I believe the reason for the popularity of the present movement is the large number of ignorant people among its supporters.

[131]

Though what I am suggesting here is something difficult to carry out in practice, suppose statistics are taken of the political speeches made throughout the country, for their degree of leniency or severity in their criticism as well as their levels of refinement and vulgarity. I am sure that the more vulgar and critical the speeches are, the less educated the speaker is. The reason for the differences in presentation can only arise from the speaker's competence or incompetence to judge.

Therefore, in Keiō Gijuku, until graduation, we concentrate on training the students to acquire good judgment. When the training is completed and the students graduate, we let them go their own ways, and we do not interfere in their behavior in any way, praying only for prudence in their behavior. We hope our true alumni will be outspoken when they express themselves, but when they stay silent, truly silent. We do not take interest in this random world where the advocates are ignorant, the listeners, too, are ignorant, and the unlearned and unreasonable masses are heading toward no clear goal.

20

On the Imperial Household

This essay appeared in *Jijishimpō* as a long editorial in twelve installments in April and May of 1882 (Meiji 15) and was later republished in book form. The Preface, a portion of the first installment, and the last four installments are translated here.

At the end of World War II, when the entire country came under the supervision of the Supreme Commander for the Allied Forces, General Douglas MacArthur, it was imperative that Japan reorganize its emperor system to comform with the spirit of democracy. At that time, the most puzzled and troubled person was the emperor himself. He consulted Prime Minister Yoshida Shigeru, who was unprepared to offer a clear answer. After requesting a few days' time to ponder the question, Yoshida Shigeru met people in the government and outside to discuss this. His personal physician, Dr. Takemi Tarō, was a professor at Keiō University, Faculty of Medicine. He remembered Fukuzawa's *On the Imperial Household*. He brought it from his library and, taking it to the prime minister, told him to spend two hours reading and studying the book. Yoshida did so and, feeling enlightened, took the book to the emperor. And a new world is said to have opened before the emperor's eyes. Thus the present order of the Imperial Household came to be. (This

"Teishitsuron" (帝室論), *Jijishimpō* editorials, April 26, May 6, May 9–11, 1882. *Fukuzawa Yukichi Zenshū*, vol. 5, pp. 257–62, 281–92.

is the gist of Dr. Takemi's reminiscences presented at
a meeting of the Fukuzawa Yukichi Society in 1983.)

Preface

Among the affairs of state in this country, there is none weightier
than the Imperial Household, but few critics venture to discourse
on this subject. The reason probably is that they lack a true understanding of the nature of the Imperial Household. Recently,
some newspaper articles, purportedly on sovereignty, were published. But one faction of the writers based their discourse on
the thousand-year Confucian and classical Japanese philosophies,
as though preaching a religious doctrine. They were hardly
worth attracting the interest of an enlightened mind. The other
faction appeared to have the intention of attacking the first argument, and yet was unable to express itself boldly, or probably
their line of logic was bungled. In any case, their arguments
were very puzzling. In short, all goes back to the timidity or lack
of logic on the part of the writers.

My learning, after all, is limited, and my views are shallow.
Yet, I feel I must speak my mind without modification. Beginning
today, I will write a discourse entitled "On the Imperial Household" in about ten installments. Whether or not my arguments
are fair and worthwhile will be left to the judgment of my readers.
My approach will be straightforward, and nothing will be left
under the cover of ambiguity. The writer solicits the understanding of his readers on this point.

Installment One
The Imperial Household is an entity outside of the political
world. It has been my constant thought that all men living in
Japan who discuss politics or who hold positions in government
must not exploit the dignity and the sanctity of the Imperial
Household. Referring to the examples in the history of Japan,
there has not been a single instance of a person who took advantage
of this dignity and sanctity against the people, nor has there been
an instance of the people uniting in an attempt against the Imperial Household.

Setting aside the ancient times for the moment, we recognize that there have been men called rebels and traitors since the Kamakura period. But these men were never rebels against the emperor in the strict sense of the word. Even the so-called cardinal rebels, such as the Hōjōs and the Ashikagas, in reality had their own sense of loyalty toward the sovereign. The truth is that these epithets were given them by men of different principles who would label anyone a rebel and a traitor unless he shared the same form of loyalty as theirs.

I do not tolerate those rebels and traitors; I personally hate them and condemn them no end. But I must recognize also that these are the arguments only among petty citizens. Observed from the exalted position of the Imperial Household, all the people must be regarded as equal, including the rebels and traitors. From the omnipresent benevolence, there is no difference in its blessings for all the subjects. Some subjects may at times go astray in their behavior, but they will simply be scolded for the moment, the admonition of a loving father whose children are quarrelling noisily among themselves. It is not from hatred but only for restraint, and in time, the incident will be forgotten and the children will remain the same citizens of Japan and the subjects of the emperor.

For instance, at the time of the Restoration, there were some men who fought against the Imperial forces. At that time, they appeared to be rebels against the emperor, but in truth it was not so. As soon as the disturbance was over, the men were pardoned, and now they live under the loving care of the emperor. Those members of Shōgitai, who fought the one battle within the city of Edo, appeared at that time to be a band of outrageous rebels, but in the eyes of the emperor at present, they are only members of a particular faction when people had differences and resorted to armed conflicts during the difficult times fifteen years ago. There were brave fighters on both sides—indeed, Japan had many courageous men. Looking back today, those who died are to be mourned. The emperor must now be happy to recall the large number of brave men and at the same time be sad to count the dead among them.

Here Fukuzawa commences his discourse on why the Imperial family should stand apart from and above political schemes and strifes and why it should be the source of honors and rewards granted to the people by the state, but never of punishment or dishonor. This discussion leads to his contention that the Imperial Household should also be the patron of education and learning, and he advances the following proposition.

Installment Nine

The encouragement of learning and the arts, too, should be left to the Imperial Household, and the country will benefit much from it. The administration of education and the encouragement of learning and arts are presently in the hands of the Ministry of Education. However, only a few schools are under the direct management of the ministry, and the number of students enrolled in them are but a few hundred. This is by no means sufficient to foster the number of intellectuals needed in the country. Also, because the ministry is a part of the government, its activities are subject to the changes in government. Whenever there is an upheaval in the government, the ministry is affected. In an extreme case, when a new minister of education is appointed, many of the officials are replaced, and even the school teachers are open to attack. Shifting the teachers, revising school rules, one change after another every three to five years—this is the least commendable policy in education.

Moreover, after the establishment of the National Diet, why should the government subsidize only the few officially established schools? That should not be the case. Even if the Ministry of Education is not to be abolished after the establishment of the National Diet, it will be limited to supervising educational activities throughout the country, and I believe direct government administration of schools will cease. The government schools will cease to exist, and even if some remain, they alone will not suffice to provide education for all the students of the land. They will realize that they will have to encourage private schools and allow them to increase in scale and number. But, for the present, the existing private schools in various parts of our country are

[136]

few and insignificant. Only a handful have enrollments of several hundred students and have successfully preserved their reputation for a dozen years or more. Lower-level education may be left to the elementary schools under the sponsorship of local councils, but technical and advanced training or anything beyond the elementary-school level cannot be left to the few private schools.

Therefore, what I wish to propose here is for the Imperial Household to put its energies into opening schools, and rather than calling them imperial schools, give them the status of private schools by calling on scholars throughout the country to take charge of them, thus establishing the education and learning of this country as independent of politics. When the general culture advances and people come to realize the importance of learning, men of wealth will donate money to the cause of learning, but the people have not arrived at that stage yet, and I see no other way but to rely on the Imperial Household to serve as an example.

Thus new schools with high standards will be established and the existing private schools will be aided, or at times some of the present government schools may be selected as the first to be transformed into imperial schools with the status of private schools and their teachers taking over the management. I will not go into the details of institutional changes here, but in the general plan described above, I am certain that this arrangement to encourage learning by allowing it to remain outside of politics will not only be of benefit to the country but our Imperial Household will acquire a reputation in the world for its role in promoting education and its high regard for scholars.

In England, all the great schools and universities are private establishments, but when one looks into them, their histories will reveal much patronage from the Royal family. In more recent history, Prince Albert, the queen's consort, is said to have had little to do with politics but was active throughout his life in encouraging learning and the arts, and it is said that there is not a scholar of note nor a person excelling in an art or craft who did not enjoy his personal hospitality. Indeed, the social peace and prosperity of England in the past several decades are said to have depended much on the prince's sponsorship, though his contribution was indirect. Here we see an example of how a Royal family or Imperial household may take advantage of its position in promoting education in a country and how far-reaching and enduring such promotion can be.

Now, allow me to advance another idea from a new point of view. It is said that a scholar's life is quiet and a politician's life is active, but this should not mean that an active life is more interesting, for each life has its own attractions. Of course, a politician wielding his power in government and a military officer vanquishing the enemy have exhilarating experiences. But a scholar, too, may have his ecstasy and triumph unknown to anyone but himself: when he studies the profound laws of nature and in a chemical experiment or the testing of the precision of a mechanism and, by a stroke of unexpected chance, solves a century-old mystery; or when he delves through an unfathomed philosophical question and meditates alone in the quietude of his study and, with a single publication, influences the thinking of society, the satisfaction he feels would be incomparable. Even a jewel worth a dozen castles or even the whole world would not be too large for comparison. When the mind reaches this stage, no minister, no general, no prince, nor even a king can awe a scholar. This, I call a scholar's happiness. Therefore, personal happiness is different according to the nature and profession of that person. And so, a profession should be chosen according to one's inborn nature. Then, the scarcity of people going into the scholarly profession will disappear, for many will join it and remain satisfied.

People watching the state of things these days are surprised by the number of scholars engaged in political discussions, and sometimes they are worried that Japanese scholars have an intense interest in politics. The fact is not that they have a disposition inclined toward politics; it is caused by the lack of a certain understanding in society. This society is devoid of respect for scholars, and thus scholars find it difficult to make their living by their profession alone. They are intelligent, but that intelligence does not provide them with a satisfactory living. Under such circumstances, how can they remain silent even if they wish? And they of necessity become politically active. It is not that they do so of their own inclination, but rather there is something that induces them to do it.

If the Imperial Household leads the way by demonstrating a respect for scholarship and the situation improves so that scholars are able to remain in their own professions, the whole nation will follow and provide a way for scholars to establish a society outside of the political world. And then, for the first time, we shall see the independence of learning in our country.

Scholars differ from politicians. They care little about the appearance of their homes and dress or how they live; their work does not require them to spend money on their appearance. They are different in their looks and ways from average people. That is, they are young on the outside but very refined within. They may look poor, and yet they command deep respect in society. Such scholars will stand out as models for society, which would be an extra benefit.

As things look today, the number of students is increasing by the day, but it appears that very few among them will devote their whole lives to scholarship. The reason is not that they do not care for the quiet life of a scholar; it is because there is no security in that life. The more they submerge themselves in academia, the less they benefit from it and the farther fame moves away from them. They are simply forced to withdraw from the scholar's life. And this is the reason why I wish to solicit our Imperial Household to be the central sponsor of learning for the whole nation.

Installment Ten

In the last installment, I wrote of my wish to have the Imperial Household as the central sponsor of learning in our country. This idea also includes my wish to keep Japan's learning independent of government and politics. Though the new learning will adopt modern Western civilization as its principle, I want it to gain independence just as did Chinese learning, which had its origin in ancient China but which Japanese scholars made into an independent study of their own. I first intended my idea to be applied to a rather high level of learning, but great varieties of arts on a much lower level, too, require imperial sponsorship.

The civilization of a nation is composed of diverse elements, or rather, every element in human society is a component of civilization. For instance, compare the inhabitants of Japan proper and the aborigines of Hokkaidō. It is obvious that Japan proper is civilized and the northern island uncivilized, because life in Japan proper is diversified and life in the northern island is simple. The inhabitants of Japan proper, in preparing their three daily meals, will set the table with bowls and chopsticks for each person, while the northern people often will not go that far in preparing a meal. Therefore, in human society, the use of a single pair of chopsticks indicates the level of civilization. Chopsticks are products of civilization; their use is a civilized action. Their manufacture and sale are, again, civilized actions. This illustration will apply in greater degree to items of a higher level than chopsticks. The more such items multiply, the more advanced the civilization. It will be safe to say in short that civilization means increase and sophistication of human activities.

In a sweeping statement, the way to advance civilization is to encourage complexity in all affairs of human life. Twenty years ago, two soups and five dishes were considered a sumptuous feast. But now people have added Western-style dishes as well. This means that our people have expanded their knowledge and taste to Western foods and thus advanced their civilization. Twenty years ago, a man was able to pose as a scholar with only his ability to read Chinese, but now one cannot join the class of scholars without knowledge of Western books as well. Our people have advanced civilization by increasing their knowledge of Western things.

I shall leave further discussion on this point to some other day, because it involves the great problem of bringing in a new civilization and adding it to the old. What I wish to discuss at present is the preservation of aspects of our ancient civilization. And for this purpose, I shall again have to look for aid from the Imperial Household. There is nothing that overturns a nation's spirit more than a revolution. When there is a change in government, people's ways of thinking will change with it and sometimes even their tastes and their sense of values will be renewed. Even that recent revolution in our country did not stop at just a change in government. It opened up new intercourse with foreign countries. Thus a good many new and strange things were introduced to upset the old and established way of things. People acquired the habit of putting the word "outmoded" after the word "old" to describe anything dating back from the ages before the revolution. This phrase, old and outmoded, has spread even to the lower reaches of society, and people who throw away everything old as being obsolescent are considered enlightened. Thus the minds of the people were bewildered by both the foreign influences and the extremists who believed in adopting anything new and Western and discarding the old and traditional; it was like a fire destroying a field of withered grass in the autumn.

The damage seemed to have no end making us feel that Japan's old civilization was being swept away. The solar calendar was adopted, and in the process the five festivals of the year were done away with; the 300 clans were abolished and their castles demolished; a ban prohibited Buddhist temples and Shintō shrines from sharing their premises, thus destroying the beauty of the old temples. All these will be difficult to restore at this late date. And considering the present state of things, there may be little advantage in attempting their restoration. I shall leave them to their fate without protest. But I do have a special concern for the indigenous arts of our country, for they can be preserved without difficulty if people have the mind to do so. And yet, they are in danger of disappearing if left unattended.

The following are my special concerns: In Japanese art, calligraphy, painting, sculpture, fencing with swords or spears, horseback-riding, archery, jūdō, sumō [wrestling], swimming, various ritual ceremonies, music, Nō drama, go and shōgi [chess], flower arrangement, tea ceremony, incense burning, etc. Then also, there is carpentry, plastering, dwarf-plant growing, gardening, cooking, lacquer and gold-inlay lacquer arts, weaving and dyeing, ceramics and copperwares, sword making, etc. There are too many to enumerate here. These are the arts precious to our civilization, and they are gradually declining after the upheaval of the revolution, and I strongly urge that they be saved before their complete extinction.

The reason that art is different from such disciplines as mathematics, mechanics, and chemistry is that art cannot be measured in terms of number and time, nor can it be handed down by instruction through textbooks. It has been the custom from old times for even mechanical techniques, which could be reduced to

[141]

written rules, to be kept as secrets of the artist or his house, preserved only in the mind. When the artist died, the art perished with him unless it was taught to and inherited by his followers. Today, very few of these gifted artists remain, and in time they will die, taking their precious knowledge with them.

What will be the way to save the arts in such an emergency? We cannot depend on the Ministry of Education for this, for by its nature the ministry is not fit for the purpose. Particularly after the establishment of the National Diet, the ministry will be made to act according to the bureaucratic and impersonal laws and regulations for administering what they profess to be the interests of the people. The officials working under such conditions cannot be expected to be concerned with the dying arts which are not essential to everyday life. The only hope I might rely on at this time is the gracious aid from the Imperial Household. The Imperial Household can stand aloof from the political world and make itself the central sponsor of lofty learning and at the same time preserver of various arts, saving them from decline and extinction.

Installment Eleven
A person, while agreeing with this proposal of depending on the Imperial Household for the preservation of the various arts described above, may have some differences and may question the validity of preserving those arts that are entirely useless in modern times. Is it not wasteful to give so much attention to and spend money on useless arts? Those who argue in this way are people who live only for today with no foresight for tomorrow. The civilization of human beings is an eternal thing; its domain is widespread. It advances in leaps, each leap spanning a thousand years, which in terms of a whole civilization will appear to be a mere day. Why should one cast away the material of an eternal civilization for the simple reason that it is valueless at the present moment?

Those prehistoric crescent-shaped jewels and gold rings being unearthed today may have been regarded as useless luxuries by the economists of the day, but several thousand years later, the excavated rings prove to our scholars today that prehistoric Japan already had the technique of gold-plating, helping them to determine the level of civilization of that time. Therefore, there is no telling if a useless thing today may become useful tomorrow. Now, consider how calligraphy, paintings, and old curios are valued today. A dozen years ago, they only collected dust. At that time, a fine set of crimson-corded armor was priced at 2 *shu* [less than one U.S. dollar] and even at that price, there was no one who cared to buy it. The screen paintings by noted artists with gold-foil decorations were burned for their gold. But today, the opposite is true. Old armor and swords are valued as curios; as for the paintings and calligraphy, a small piece on paper or silk may sell for several thousand yen.

In a mere dozen years we have witnessed such a change. After a hundred years or a thousand years, what will be the difference? The changes in human sense of appreciation are unpredictable. Therefore, it is important that all forms of art be preserved and all techniques be handed down, thus saving the wealth of our civilization from extinction.

There are also many forms of art among those mentioned above that are of purely Japanese origin, entirely new and foreign to Western people. There is the art of tea drinking called tea ceremony; the arranging of flowers has been developed into a refined art; the burning of incense, too, has its own art. There are endless varieties of this sort, and Western people have a difficult time understanding some of them. The art of ink brush writing, calligraphy, was first brought in from China, but original styles have been developed and passed down to succeeding generations. This, too, may be called Japan's own and a very important field in the graphic arts. All of these are treasures of Japan's civilization, of which we should be very proud.

As for other fields of art such as *makie* [gold-inlay lacquer], lacquerware, ceramics, copperware, plant culture, cooking, etc., I am not qualified to explain them all, and as they are beside the purpose of this article, I shall leave them untouched. The one point that I earnestly wish to make is that these arts shall not be lost in a small disturbance such as this political revolution.

In the era of feudalism, the life styles of the 300 clan lords [daimyō] were very elegant, and it is well known that these noblemen sponsored the arts, and their contribution in the development of these was considerable. Many of the clan lords had among their retainers makers of arms and armor to begin with, then some

[143]

experts in tea ceremony, carpenters, plasterers, *makie* artists, gardeners, cooks, cabinet makers, etc., all of them hereditary retainers. Many of them were true artists and cared more for their reputation than for wealth. Such an environment occasionally fostered an exceptional genius who would produce some lasting masterpieces. In calculating how much these masterpieces cost the lords, suppose all the stipends for several generations of these artists were counted; the cost would have been enormous. But the lords of those days had their own way of accounting. They never considered the income before spending, and they did not mind investing any amount in the arts.

In the future, there may be wealthy men whose riches surpass those of the former clan lords, but if such modern men follow the rule of estimating the income before investing, we cannot expect them to contribute very much to the arts. And we cannot hope, in these modern times, to establish life stipends for artists, but it will be possible to establish a way to encourage the aspiring hearts of the artists. What will this be? I have said that the Imperial Household is the fountainhead of honor. Therefore, honor for the artists may well issue from it.

To cite some examples, in the Tokugawa period, whenever there was a famed scholar or a physician among the samurai in service or even among those without masters [*rōnin*], special summons were sent them for an audience with the shōgun. Sometimes gifts of garments with the shōgun's crest were presented to them. Any man who had even once had the honor of an audience was given status equal to or above those who had the official privilege of audience with the lord, and they would be respected above the vassals of the clan lords, equal to the shōgun's immediate vassals. Such was the honor, the highest that any scholar or physician could attain, and it was open even to the masterless samurai. Naturally, after the audience, his fame and reputation among the populace would rise high.

Not only these intellectuals but those skilled in *go* and *shōgi*, if they were renowned, would be granted audiences. Also, "master families" were appointed for *go* and *shōgi* with sumptuous stipends. Tournaments would be held in the shōgun's castle every year ("Games Before the August Presence"), and the shōgun attended the games in person. Not every shōgun could have been fond of

[144]

these games. Some of them would have found this custom tedious, but the attention of the whole society was concentrated on these games. As for the players, the one game in the castle was to determine their fates. In an extreme case, a player, fatigued with mental concentration, is said to have vomited blood and died. Also, Nō players were granted stipends and swordsmiths and sculptors were provided financial aid.

Thus, throughout the fifteen generations of the Tokugawa shogunate, this policy was ideal for the promotion of the arts. Now the shogunate is no more, and neither are the clan lords. Under these conditions, suppose the Imperial Household, which is the springhead of honor and the heart of the nation, should recognize the wishes of the people and create a law to confer medals of honor or grant Imperial gifts in the form of yearly stipends to outstanding people of learning or art or grant audiences to those prominent people or collect objects of arts and crafts from periods old and new. Then the hearts of the people will all be drawn to the center and the aspiration for distinction would rise toward this springhead of honor. The arts would revive from their impending fate of decline, the adoration of the Imperial Household would gain in fervor, and its dignity and sanctity would grow ever more prominent in the hearts of the people.

Installment Twelve
The Imperial Household should be the symbol of the nation; command the spirit of the soldiers of the navy and the army and give purpose to their devotion; commend loyal children and faithful wives in order to raise the moral standard of the nation; take leadership in the encouragement of learning and recognition of able scholars so as to promote the independence of education, save the arts from the brink of extinction and increase our wealth in civilization. The list of merits is too large and varied to be enumerated.

Presumably, saucy political advocates do not realize these great merits and are silent on them. When they allude to them, their discussions are as colorless and spiritless as water. Such is the sin of ignorance. As for our senior citizens, who are said to be courteous and firm, they are in reality very hasty. When they are enthused, they are liable to turn extreme, and, forgetting

[145]

their blessings, they are simply flustered in awe. This, too, is from ignorance. The blunders of ignorance may be pardoned, for they are not intentional and may be corrected.

So, let us imagine that the whole society has been enlightened, and the Imperial Household is about to embark on the activities described. We will first need the capital to work from. According to the national budget of Meiji 14th year [1881], the earmarked budget for the Emperor's family and his relatives is 1,156,000 yen, of which the Ministry of the Imperial Household is allocated 354,000 yen. Let us consider whether this amount is sufficient.

The king of Italy's household account totals 3,250,000 yen, of which the king's brother's share is 60,000 yen. The expenses for the king's tours of the country and the construction and repairs of the palace are borne separately by the national treasury. The national account for the king of England appears to be small in proportion to the wealth of the country, and it is actually 2,000,000 yen, but he has a separate income from the estate of Lancaster. The German government provides 3,080,000 yen for its emperor. On top of this, he owns extensive property which brings in sufficient income for the expenses on the palaces and for imperial relatives. In Holland, the budget is only 312,000 yen, but the king's family has possessed a great amount of property since the time of King William I.

After examining these examples in different countries, Japan's budget for the Imperial Household cannot be considered very large. Besides the smallness of the budget, one must take into account the absence of imperial property. After the establishment of the National Diet, it is certain that the accounts of the Imperial Household and of the government will be separated. I believe that the share for the Imperial Household should be increased now. Fortunately, there is a good deal of government-owned land in the country. Some tracts of such land should be ceded to the Imperial Household as permanent property.

In Bagehot's book on English government organization, it is said that public opinion on royalty varies greatly, some insisting that the king's household should be lavish and extravagant, others insisting it should be plain and frugal. Arguments for a royal monarchy will always be countered by advocates of the abolition of the king's regime; all these are mere arguments on paper. What is important in the preservation of peace and security is to gauge the people's sentiments and to take the middle road. From the point of economy alone, if one million pounds are spent on the king's household and this contributes to winning the people's hearts, this will be a very wise investment. The one million pounds would have performed a worthy service. Suppose a little economy is practiced and the budget is reduced to 750,000 pounds, and it fails to attract the people. This 750,000 pounds will be a total loss, and the policy will prove itself very uneconomical.

The above is Mr. Bagehot's opinion, very simple but precise. After all, the expenses for the Imperial Household are a very special consideration. Some of it will be for public affairs, but there will be some spent freely, not to be recorded on the ledger, and this will be the most important portion. For instance, in the history of France, Josephine, the first empress of Emperor Napoleon I, was a person famed for her integrity. She helped the emperor from behind the scenes, always making amends for his small oversights and maintaining ties with the officers and people in the palace and outside. But when the emperor had a change of heart and deposed the empress, he quickly lost the people's esteem. More recently, there is the example of the queen of Italy, Margherita, who is known for her wisdom and generosity. She won the people's hearts, assists the king, and indirectly influences politics by helping to pacify political conflicts.

Therefore, the way the virtues of the Imperial Household touches the people is an almost mystical way, and they may bear an influence completely unnoticed by outsiders. A sovereign emperor touring the country incognito could help a person in poverty and increase the productivity of the whole province. He might inquire after one wounded soldier, and the whole army would be consoled. All activities such as a party under the spring blossoms or a banquet on a moonlit night should not be judged as a king's mere pastime. In all such activities, the first requirement is money. And when the funds are expended, some of the items may not be of the kind to be entered on the ledger. I am not concerned with these. I am simply praying for an increase in the imperial account.

A man may theorize that it is well to win the people's hearts

[147]

with the great name of the Imperial Household. But in giving recognition to the meritorious and in encouraging the arts and sciences, there is the strong possibility of partiality toward traditional and classical persons and subjects because it is customary to see people of traditional schools associate with the Imperial Household. For instance, in recognizing those of distinguished service, the old loyalists of the imperial cause are likely to be chosen, and for scholars, those of classical learning only will be recognized. What about the sciences of modern civilization that are making rapid progress daily?

Such arguments are being made, but I am not perturbed in the least because, after all, since the opening of the country in the Kaei era, what changed the course of our country is the modern civilization of the West. In the course of advancement, there naturally will be some mishaps and some obstructions, but they will simply be problems of a temporary nature. Classical learning may appear to be an obstruction to modern learning, but its influence is limited to a small area and for a short duration. What can a hundred, or a thousand, old scholars do to the great movement of society? Moreover, this classical learning, too, has an important value of its own (when the portion concerning natural science is excluded). I wish to aid efforts to preserve it.

What I am looking for in the Imperial Household is an impartial benevolence with which it will bless us in its broad and fair embrace. My prayer will not be futile. The Imperial Household will not side with the new nor with the old. Calm and impartial, it will grasp the heart of the nation and act in unison with it. It will stand apart from politics and factionalism. Why should it create factions in people's minds? We people should stand back and accept the truth in deep respect.

21
Questions on Moral Education

This essay first appeared as a *Jijishimpō* editorial (October 21–24, 1882) under the title of "School Education" (Gakkō Kyōiku) and was later republished in pamphlet form as "Questions on Moral Education," which is the title used in *Fukuzawa Yukichi Zenshū*. Fukuzawa discusses the changes in moral standards accompanying the changes in society, and he promotes the principle of independence and individuality in place of Confucianism as the basis of moral behavior for contemporary people.

Installment One

Cyanide is a fatal poison. Its effect is instant: the moment it touches the tongue, it kills. The effects of morphine and arsenic are somewhat slower, and a laxative such as rhubarb takes two or three hours to show its effects. These are illustrations of the time it takes chemicals to take effect. As for fertilizers, they will show their effects on vegetables within three days by turning the leaves green, but those for trees are given in winter and their effects cannot be seen until the spring or summer of the following year.

The human mind can be likened to trees, and education to fertilizer. In providing education to the human mind, can we expect to see any results in three days? The answer is no. Providing it in winter, can we expect results in the spring or summer? The answer is, again, no. Entering young men in a school, beginning with lessons in reading and penmanship, and advancing in time

"Tokuiku Ikan" (徳育如何), 1882. *Fukuzawa Yukichi Zenshū*, vol. 5, pp. 349–63.

to higher levels, it will be some five years at best, usually seven years, before they begin to understand and reason. In comparison with the fertilizing of plants, this is the slowest of all reactions.

Plants are helped in their growth by fertilizers, but it is only assistance that the fertilizer gives; the source of the plants' growth is the air, sunlight, warmth, and nourishment in the soil. When the air loses its balance in humidity or the sun's rays are obstructed or nourishment in the soil becomes insufficient, the application of fertilizer will not be effective—sometimes not at all. The case of education, too, is very similar. It is true that education will help people's intellectual and moral growth, but its role is in assisting only. The basic factors that determine the state and level of the human intellect and morals are determined by heredity, handed down from one's ancestors, the family tradition, and the general environment and opinions current in society.

Even if one provides a son of the Ezo people[1] with education, it will be impossible to make a first-rate scholar out of this boy in one generation. In our old history, we find that there were many great warriors among the descendants of Hachiman Tarō Yoshiie [1039?–1106] of the Minamoto family. This is proof that courage and ability are hereditary. On the other hand, when the son of a warrior is adopted into a merchant's house, he will naturally grow to become a man of merchant-like disposition; when a merchant's son is brought up in a literary man's home, he will naturally advance into a literary career. The home atmosphere is very powerful in influencing the mind, for it is well known that the natural character of the parents, even if they are foster parents with no blood relations, is passed on to the child.

In the age of wars, all of society was warlike, and even the priests, who had supposedly renounced worldly affairs, carried arms and warfare was part of their lives. This we learn from the histories of the temples of Hiei-zan and Mii-dera. Thus the power of public opinion and the spirit of the times influenced Buddhist priests into taking up arms and committing the crimes of fighting and killing.

These are illustrations of causes that promote and retard or sometimes alter the intellectual and moral behavior of human

[1] More generally called Ainu, a people racially distinct from the Japanese, living on the islands in the north of Japan, including Hokkaidō.

[150]

beings. And they are much more powerful than education in schools. Schools should not be taken lightly by any means, but those educators of today and yesterday, who advise parents to place their children in schools and claim that any kind of personality may be developed by proper training, are certainly victims of an illusion. This is tantamount to believing that plants will grow on the strength of fertilizers alone, with no regard to the basic requirements for air, sunlight, or soil.

According to a popular saying, "an urchin hanging around the temple memorizes a sutra without being taught." The meaning of this saying probably is that children who play around a temple unconsciously absorb religious ways and mannerisms; that is, children are won over by Buddhism. Indeed, when exposed to Buddhism, they become Buddhists, when exposed to Confucianism, they become Confucian. This influence of the environment is natural and cannot be prevented by human power. Even the most independent and individualistic of characters cannot stay absolutely aloof from his surroundings; it is as difficult as remaining immune to a contagious disease when it is rampant.

An individual preserving his high morality apart from the society is to be admired, but there is a limit to his independence. For instance, in language: while living in a certain locality, even a person who claims to be absolutely independent, different in every act and behavior from other people, will speak the local dialect, recognizable even when heard behind a wall. From whom did this man learn the dialect? From no one in particular. Yet, he acquired it somehow. We will have to conclude that he learned it from his immediate environment. Or we may say he absorbed it willy-nilly from the environment.

Not only in language but in all other things, the same phenomenon can be observed. From clothing and food to house and garden construction, decorative designs, and toys and other pastimes, one cannot escape the influence of the times and of fashion. A person will wear stylish clothes, eat popular food, live in a fashionable house, and enjoy the amusement currently in vogue. Observed from this point of view, we are veritable slaves of society, never free from its oppression, and not even the most determined person has ever managed to be free from it in the whole history of the world.

[151]

Such is the case with material things. When it comes to the abstract, to intellect and morality, there is no reason for us to expect freedom from the oppression of society. We may gain knowledge without being taught, and morality is imbued without training. Both are implanted in the minds of the people exactly in the form and to the extent of the current trend. Society may be described as a great arena for intellectual and moral training. Within this arena, individual institutions of education are capable of influencing the students' minds to a slight degree, whatever curriculum or whatever facilities they may have. This should be obvious to anyone even before they are taught the logic of things.

Installment Two

There are educational critics who accuse our youth of having grown frivolous—they no longer follow their parents' advice nor heed the admonitions of their elders. In extreme cases, these rash young men, regardless of their tender ages, will discuss politics, sometimes even infringing upon the sanctity of the emperor. All this is the result of school education that neglects moral instruction. For moral education, these critics always promote the teachings of Chou Kung and Confucius as the basis of instruction and codes for conduct and behavior in present-day society. I am entirely sympathetic with their sense of anxiety, but I completely disagree with their ideas on how to correct the situation.

What these critics are concerned about is that young men these days lack respect for their elders and that they are so insolent as to discuss politics. This argument is quite correct, and I, too, agree. Yet I am more concerned about the question of whether or not school education alone is responsible for this insolence and flippancy we see in youth. If it is, how did it come about? We must study and determine its cause. If schools are at fault, it will mean a lack of moral sense on the part of the teachers and the lack of proper textbooks. Then who is responsible for appointing such immoral teachers and adopting such textbooks? Perhaps the cause of all may be found in the regulations issued by the Ministry of Education. Why did the ministry issue such regulations? All these must be examined and clarified.

In my opinion, the real cause is not in the ministry's regulations nor in the teachers' lack of moral sense nor in the textbooks, although these are all related causes. Unless further research is done to determine the basic cause which brought forth these related issues, no true understanding of the situation will be reached nor a decision on how to cope with the problem. What, then, is the basic cause? It is none other than the opening of the country and the revolution in the government.

Since the opening of the country to the West, the Japanese people have been hard at work absorbing the new learning of those Western countries, but most of the information has been communicated by hearsay. They learned what was meant by "freedom" and "independence," but no one as yet has tried the new ideas in practice nor observed their actual workings. Then, fifteen years ago, the great revolution, the Imperial Restoration, took place.

In actuality, this revolution was brought about by the samurai of various clans, and these samurai were men who had been trained for generations over centuries in the strict doctrines of Chou Kung and Confucius. They were indeed loyal men, and there was very little in their minds or hearts other than the ideal of working for their masters, offering their lives in service. Yet, once they were awakened to the new cause of resuming relations with the world, they found themselves being swept by the tide of the times; they overthrew the old shogunate and established a new Imperial government. In the beginning, all the work and the fighting was carried out in the name of the lords of different clans, but as the work came to a successful conclusion, the lords received no honor, and the benefits of the revolution, along with fame and material profit, fell into the hands of their erstwhile subordinates, the samurai.

A few years later, there came the sweeping abolition of clans, and the lords were deprived of all their ancient privileges and left to the world like drifters. Some of the lowly samurai, who had not been privileged to a formal audience with the lords of their clans, were now riding the tide of the times, had joined the new government and secured positions of dignity, and now not only were they seated in the Imperial Court side by side with their former lords but at times had risen to higher positions. In an extreme case, a lord was forced to accept orders from his former vassal or to privately visit him at his house to solicit favors.

[153]

The equality of all citizens was proclaimed, and merchants and farmers are no longer considered simple townsfolk or country bumpkins. They no longer fear the samurai of the clan to which they once belonged, and sometimes they sue their former lords in court and force them into poverty when they win. The sons of farmers, who would have been cut down on sight when found riding on horseback in former days, are now seen riding about on rented horses. If they, by accident, trample a former samurai to death, the only thing the law can do will be to order indemnity in money from these arrogant farmers' sons.

Heredity was a cornerstone of feudal society, and second and third sons had no way of establishing themselves. Their only hope was to be adopted into families that were not blessed with heirs. Then they would be made the masters of those houses. But the demand and supply were not in balance, for very few families were without sons, while there were many second and third sons. Many were forced to live as poor dependents in their fathers' or eldest brothers' house, or when outliving them, relied on the second generation, finally ending up in their nieces' homes, still dependents. These men were called *sune-kajiri* (hangers-on), and no one in society respected them. Whatever intelligence, whatever powers they possessed, they were obliged to live the lives of neglected souls.

This being the custom among the samurai class, it spread to the farmer, artisan, and merchant classes and until recently it was the custom for all classes to hold the housed in esteem and have the eldest son inherit all the property and the authority belonging to the house. This custom was rigid and inviolable. But a new age in which ability is respected has set in. As long as one can make his own living, all doors are open to him. If the eldest son is slow and poor, his younger and cleverer brother may become rich and look down on him. It is not only among brothers; even an adopted son, who married the daughter of a house to continue the line, may succeed in business, meet a beautiful woman in the gay quarters, and begin to find his wife an obstacle to his pleasures. He will approach his parents-in-law and ask them to disinherit him for his misbehavior. This, in other words, is a situation in which the son banishes his parents and wife.

Between father and son,
there shall be love and harmony;
Between lord and vassal,
there shall be loyalty and discipline;
Between husband and wife,
there shall be discretion and discernment;
Between elder and younger,
there shall be order and discipline.

These are the venerable words of the ancient sages Chou Kung and Confucius. Yet today, as I have described in several examples, there is little evidence of these teachings being followed in our society.

Installment Three
The examples I have given above are actual situations seen in the past fifteen years, permitted by law and tolerated by the customs of today—truly surprising in the eyes of older moralists. Suppose people of the Genroku era [1688–1703] could be revived to observe our society; they would certainly be astonished and think that humanity has taken the wrong path and the world has receded into darkness. Yet the truth is not that the Japanese people have neglected moral instruction in the past fifteen years.

The truth is that popular opinion has been transformed under the influence of the new open-door policy. Popular opinion involves all that concerns the affairs of the people, and school education is but a tiny fraction of the great scheme. Therefore, in my opinion, the arguments of the educational critics are nonsensical.

It is very well that they are disturbed by the arrogant and frivolous attitude of present-day people. It is natural that they should be surprised, but in their anxiety, they are trying to push the youths back to the behavior of olden times. In other words, they are endeavoring to revive the old moral philosophy of loyalty and filial piety of the Genroku era. They seem to be advocating the classical teachings of ancient China as opposed to what is often written in recent newspapers and publications. Do they truly believe that classical philosophy is powerful enough to win over modern theories? Moreover, whenever they disagree with something in today's society, they are quick to blame it on the schools. Do they consider schools so powerful that they can influ-

[155]

ence the moral trend of society? I totally disagree with them. To begin with, the Meiji era is different from the Genroku era. The root of the difference is not in the education, but in the general trends and the public opinions of the two eras. And the differences in the two societies and times produced different educational policies. What made Meiji society and its public opinions what they are is the opening of the country 30 years ago and the revolution in government that followed. These events brought forth the present trend in public opinion, causing the whole nation to idealize liberalism and progress. In the process, some obnoxious trends were born and, one must admit, some unworthy moral practices. But they are not prohibited by law, and society does not censure them. In some cases, even among those who discuss moral issues like accomplished gentlemen, there are pretenders who have ridden the tide of progress for material gains, and, on the pretext of liberalism, sometimes commited unmentionable breaches of moral conduct.

When measured against the old laws of morality, these men would be condemned for breaches of all the codes in their relations with parents, lords, spouse, and friends. Yet, they seem to succeed in deceiving society and proudly continue their careers, for they identify with the powerful tide of progress and liberalism. In society today, to try for betterment by mere improvement in one phase of school education is like trying to control the growth of plants by changing fertilizers. Granting for a moment that education can be effective when combined with other human activities, even then one must remember that it takes years to see the effects of education, much longer than it would any fertilizer. This fact is another demonstration of the stupidity of the argument.

Therefore, it is clear that if our present-day youth are arrogant and frivolous, they were taught in the great school of society and public opinion, which leads to the conclusion that unless the great school itself is reorganized, the youth will not reform. But will it be possible to fight against the present trend and push society back to its old ways? Can the present law be reverted to the old law? Should the commoners be prohibited from riding horseback? Should the second and third sons be held from going their own ways? I strongly believe that having come this far on the road of progress and liberalism, to return to a society of feudalism and family stipends will be like making a bird fly away from a great tree into the gloom of a valley—absolutely impossible, whatever forces are applied. This, I am sure, the advocates themselves fully realize.

Therefore, if there is no way to reform the great school, it is obvious that there is no use devising changes in the individual little schools. I am not satisfied with the society of today; I do not admire the behavior of today's youth. Yet, I do not seek improvements in individual matters; I intend to follow the trend of society in leading the youth and allowing them to go as far as they can, and just as one would manage a river according to its natural flow, I hope to let the youth find their own natural way.

Suppose a senior gentleman active in the present society should admonish the youth of today, saying, "You young men are presumptuous. Why don't you obey your seniors and honor those who should be respected? You men are too young to meddle with new-fangled theories and give your opinion on the politics of the day."

Then the young men would most likely answer thus: "Why then, sir, did you in former days approve the abolition of clans and allow your former lord to lose his exalted position? Moreover, you are now moving in society on equal terms with your former lord, or sometimes even above him, and do not show the least bit of embarrassment. Why is this? Here is another question: When you were immersed in politics around the time of the Restoration, how old were you? Didn't anyone take exception to your hasty actions and give you advice as you are now giving us? And did you accept the advice? I surmise that you are not the kind to calmly accept advice of that sort. You must have privately despised him and sneered at him as a temporizing blockhead. I may be young, but you were about the same age twenty years ago. My actions may be rash, but compared with your activities twenty years ago, there should be no reason for me to accept rebukes from you. You might argue that your challenges were different: you lived through the troubled years of the shogunate and then worked to build the new government. Yes, the times are different and the circumstances are not the same, but my enthusiasm is equal to yours of yesteryear, and it is an enthusiasm I acquired from you."

[157]

Thus attacked with torrential eloquence, the senior gentleman would find it difficult to make a retort and perhaps have a hard time extricating himself from embarrassment. The situation will be similar to that of an old man advising a young man on his loose behavior, who finds himself counterattacked by exposure of his promiscuity in youth and blushes with the sweat of shame on his grey-haired head. A direct admonition seldom produces a favorable result even in a personal encounter. More unlikely will it be effective with the youth of society. Not only will it be a lost effort, it is more likely to bring anger and revolt from the youth.

Installment Four

In a previous section, in alluding to education, I did state that what I wished was to let our youth be influenced by popular trends and have them find their own way to the best destination, just as one would manage a stream of water according to the nature of its flow. However, I am conscious of the vagueness of my discussion, and I will cite several examples to illustrate my point. In my judgment, the teachings of Chou Kung and Confucius are truly effective in moving the hearts of people, but they are by no means infinite in effectiveness. The teachings have their limits, where their effects cease to extend. They are valid as long as they are confined to situations in which the general sentiment and popular opinion are sympathetic to their ideals.

For instance, take the difference in customs between China and Japan. Most conspicuous are the morals of feudalism. Both the Chou period in China and the Tokugawa period in Japan were feudalistic, but when the behavior of people in the two societies is compared, we see that in China an official disappointed in one regime would easily leave for another position; his movement was very free. Confucius is said to have served twelve masters, one after another; Mencius was disappointed with King Hsüan of Ch'i and easily turned his allegiance to King Huei of Liang. A man like Chü Po-yü boasted, "If the country is honorable, I will willingly serve it; if the country lacks morality, I will roll it up and put it away in my pocket," exhibiting his very meager respect for his country. Yet he was never blamed for disloyalty; rather, he was respected as a sage.

On the contrary, in Japan, the behavior of an official was very strictly restrained. "A loyal vassal never serves a second master; a faithful wife never marries a second time" is a precept which spread even to the lower strata of society, and except in very special circumstances, a breach of this precept was not countenanced. The above is an example of the different nature of public opinion prevailing in the two countries. The difference between the two is amazing. And yet, the foundation of morality in both countries is the same. The Chinese worship the teachings of the sages, as do the Japanese. These two peoples, who are brought up on the same moral philosophy, react in completely opposite ways in real-life situations. A most surprising phenomenon, but it is proof that a moral teaching, after all, influences people only to the extent tolerated by popular opinion, and not beyond. When it does go beyond, it will conform to popular opinion, freely interpreting the precepts and giving itself an agreeable appearance to survive.

The barbarians' destruction of the peace of the Hsia dynasty was what the sages feared. But the barbarians, after all, occupied the country and usurped the throne, which now has become the present Ch'ing dynasty of China, and the people of China continue to read and follow the teachings of the sages. In Japan, too, the Tokugawa government had been loyal to the Imperial Household according to the precepts of loyalty. But later, the popular opinion rose to topple this government, and the new regime is, in turn, very loyal to the Imperial Household.

Thus in China, the free movement of officials is seen as honoring the precepts of the sages, and in Japan such acts are censured for going against the precepts of the same sages. When a horde of barbarians invade a country, the government may defend itself with the teachings of the sages, but once the barbarians take over, they will justify themselves with the same teachings. The teachings can serve one's own side; they can also be useful to the enemy. They are effective wherever they are applied, for they will change their form according to popular opinion. This is what makes the sages' teachings what they are, and they are veritably beyond the comprehension of ordinary, small scholars.

(Some scholars in Japan avoid books by Mencius because they contain statements justifying revolution against evil rulers. But this is the worthless and laughable argument of small scholars.

[159]

In the past several hundred years, the Japanese people have been reading Mencius, and no one is known to have acquired disloyal concepts from him. Suppose every word, every phrase in a book were to affect its readers, any book by Confucius would be taboo in Japan as the author served twelve lords and even considered accepting invitations from Kung-shan Fu-jao and Pi Hsi. Arguments of those narrow, obstinate scholars are not worthy of consideration.)

Since the opening of the country and the subsequent revolution in government, the trend of the whole nation has turned toward development and progress; nothing can alter the force of this trend. With this overwhelming change in popular opinion, moral doctrines must readjust drastically in order to conform with the current social trend though the need for moral education will not by any means disappear in the new age.

For instance, in former days, there were 300 clans in the country, and the solidarity of the lord and the vassals was by clan unit. Today the whole country has become one unit, and the idea of loyalty had to take on a new form, the old type of loyalty being no longer appropriate. Peoples' concerns used to be confined to the conflict of interests between clans, and no one knew of a country existing outside of the 300 clans. Now the entire country has become one great clan, and the old loyalty of defending clan rights must be transformed into defending national rights.

Discipline in society was based on the spirit of mutual dependence—lord and vassals, parents and children, husband and wife, elders and youths all depended on each other, loved and respected one another. All moral teachings were built on such mutuality. But today under the philosophy of individual independence, one must first become independent, develop self-respect, regarding oneself as pure and precious, and on this basis build relations with others and thus preserve discipline in society.

Because of one's pure self-image, one must avoid the smallest flaws or defilement. One must not be dishonorable or sink to pettiness. The woman in the gay quarters may be attractive, one's old wife serving in the kitchen may no longer be lovable. Yet for an honorable person, it is not appropriate to dismiss the old woman. The elder brother may be a fool and the younger brother may be rich and clever, but for the younger to make light

[160]

of the elder is unthinkable in view of his self-image. Fame and riches may be within reach by compromising one's principles slightly and currying favor with the men in power, but if compromise means marring the self, this cannot be tolerated. One cannot exchange even the riches of the world or the position of a general or a premier for the smallest injury to one's pure image. Once one reaches this stage of thought, the entire world appears small, the kings and the princes appear lowly. Nothing worthy exists outside of oneself, only the purity of self.

Thus when one's independence is attained, the independence of one's fellow citizens should be sought, and finally forces should be joined in securing the independence of the country—this should be the natural order of progress. One may follow this principle of independence in serving a lord, in caring for parents, in preserving relations between husband and wife, in maintaining discipline between elder and younger, and in consolidating fellowship between friends; thus from minor events in everyday life to the great policies of the world, this will serve as a guiding principle for all.

Therefore, I shall not reprove the endeavors of the present moralists for trying to apply the classical books in moral instruction, but I pray that the classical principles will be left to naturally adapt themselves to the contemporary trends of society and popular opinion, and only influence certain quarters where they may be effective. In other words, my wish is to let Chou Kung's and Confucius's teachings be absorbed into the principles of independence, because this is the time when moral teaching will undoubtedly be changing according to popular opinion. If the present trend is toward arrogance and shallowness, that is because of the lack of the spirit of independence. If the critic lacks power and his arguments and his speeches do not inspire the audience, that is because of his failure to grasp the principle of independence. Popular opinion at present is turning toward the principle of independence and progress, and this tendency cannot be altered. When it is understood as inalterable, it will be the wise policy of the sensible person to follow it. This is exactly what I mean when I say that school education should follow the times, just as water may be controlled by complying with the law of its flow.

[161]

22
The Independence of Learning

The following essay first came out in 1883 as a series of
Jijishimpō editorials between January 21 and February
5, under the title of "Learning Shall Be Separated from
Politics" (*Gakumon to Seiji to Bunri Subeshi*). In the
same year, it was reprinted in pamphlet form as "The
Independence of Learning" (*Gakumon no Dokuritsu*)
with a preface by an editor of *Jijishimpō*. The *Fukuzawa
Yukichi Zenshū* version is based on the pamphlet. Fukuzawa proposes to separate all the public schools in
the country from the Ministry of Education, placing
them under the supervision of the Imperial Household,
which will grant control of each school to a private
citizen of recognized ability and provide financial aid
from the Imperial Household treasury.

Installment One
Learning and politics share the same ideals, for both seek to
promote the fortunes of a nation. But learning is not politics, and
scholars are different from politicians. What are their basic differences? The interest of scholars is far removed from the realities
of society today, and the work of politicians is concerned with
everyday matters of the people. To use a metaphor, a nation is
like the human body, and both scholars and politicians strive to
keep it in good condition—politicians attending to medical cures

"Gakumon no Dokuritsu" (学問之独立), 1883. *Fukuzawa Yukichi Zenshū*, vol. 5, pp.
365–90.

when the body is ill, and scholars teaching personal hygiene. Since the beginning of history, human beings, imperfect as they are physically and intellectually, have always had afflictions somewhere in their body. Naturally, a politician is kept busy restoring health. But suppose scholars give instruction on how to preserve health—and to keep society in good order. Perhaps the disease may be prevented, or even when it is contracted, it may be cured without becoming serious. This might be called preventive medicine, the true strength of learning.

As was discussed in an earlier editorial of *Jijishimpō* [January 11, "Ushiba Takuzō goes to Korea"], even while anti-foreign sentiment ran high when the country was opened in the final years of the shogunate, scholars of Western learning persisted in advocating things Western, which proved to be the "hygiene" lectures for the Japanese people, preparing them for the open-door policy. Without these hygiene lectures, there is no telling how many Japanese people might have died of the diseases of antiforeignism and closed-door policy.

The influence of learning can thus be immense, but this does not imply that the scholars themselves would be efficient administrators if charged with practical daily matters. This can be seen in the histories of many lands, and it is the same reason why a hygiene specialist is inefficient in bedside treatment. Therefore, separation of education and politics and strict prohibition of their intermingling will be an advantage to society as well as to the happiness of the respective specialists. In the West, there have been instances of harm done by men in the government meddling with academic and cultural affairs, and of some noted scholars taking positions in the government and making laughingstocks of themselves. In the feudal clans in Japan, too, there have been examples of famed scholars being appointed to high positions in the clan governments but who proved to be useless; rather, they placed the clans in awkward situations, resulting in the scholars' loss of reputation. All these are instances of failures caused by the confounding of hygiene and clinical specialists.

If my belief in the separation of learning and politics is truly for the advantage of the nation, I pray that in our country learning will be made independent of politics. To be more specific, I wish to see those schools now under the direct control of the Ministry

[164]

of Education and the Ministry of Industry separated from those ministries. At the time of the Restoration, everything was being initiated anew, and no one distinguished items to be placed under government control from those to remain in private hands. Every new enterprise was under the control of the government, even minor details in industry and commerce come under its scrutiny. Therefore, it was natural that schools under the modern system were established by the ministries. However, in sixteen years, we have gradually reached a point in government organization and society where present conditions must be reconsidered from all angles and also in reference to the West. It is a very rare instance in any advanced country that the government itself establishes schools, gathers students, and permits government officials to teach under the direct control of the ministry. This practice, I judge, has become inappropriate for Japan today.

Of course, learning is learning, and one is liable to presume that it is the same whether taught in a government school or in any other kind of school. But in actual society, it does not work this way. The politics of a country are concerned, as was said earlier, with day-to-day affairs, attending to emergencies as they occur. For instance, for famine, relief must be arranged, and against foreign threats, armaments must be readied; when the value of paper money falls, gold and silver must be obtained; tariffs must be raised or lowered according to the growth and decline of foreign trade. In short, politics is a busy transaction in haggling, to use a vulgar term. And so, when the nation's schools are placed under state control, the school administration, too, will naturally be swayed by this busy haggling. Haggling is the most important part of politics and government as it tends to emergencies day and night. And politicians and officials must be alert at all times. However, education is not the concern of just one day, nor should it be altered so easily.

Of course, the school regulations laid down by the Ministry of Education, as they are now, are not related to politics, and the curriculum, too, is in agreement with my ideas. It places emphasis on moral education and on intellectual training, and most of the material originating from Western civilization covers all subjects, down to the details of physical education. All these appear to be perfect. But even then, the men who administer these

[165]

regulations are officials; even the teachers who come in contact with the students are government employees. And because the details of instruction and school atmosphere cannot be stipulated in school rules, the actual school spirit will be created by the current political situation. Politics, by its very nature, is constantly changing, and it is something that should not stagnate. Therefore, the result will be that the school spirit will change from time to time, which is against the true character of learning. In short, politics is of an active nature, and it must continue to move, but learning is profound and quiet. They are incompatible, and it will be impossible to avoid harm in having these two keep an unnatural alliance.

For instance, it is not commendable for young students to discuss politics in excess or to read political newspapers and harangue the public, and I myself dislike to see them indulging in such activities. To prohibit such activities is to help the students, who are supposed to be docile, regain their natural outlook. But as a prohibition from government officials, it may not be taken simply as advice for the good of the students; it will more likely create suspicion of political intervention. Furthermore, because the government changes its policies from time to time, it can very well happen that an order banning political involvement will be issued at one time and then another allowing it at a later date. A total lack of political opposition to a party in power could cause some students to overstep the line and become reactionary. For these very reasons I strongly object to the collaboration of learning and politics.

Installment Two

The danger of collaboration between learning and politics is not a discovery of my own. Since olden times in Japan, although no one actually put it down in words, it is interesting to see that the idea was actually practiced. In the Tokugawa period, there was a custom of appointing a chief scholar to the central government as well as in each of the 300 clans to oversee the education of the sons of the retainers. The scholars were highly respected, with even the clan lords honoring them as "masters." But this respect was confined to scholarly matters alone, and they were strictly kept from having a say in politics. Rather, the scholars were called "long sleeves" and placed in a category along with priests and physicians. In extreme cases, they were not admitted inside government offices or allowed to associate with the samurai, except in a professional capacity.

The head of the Hayashi family was for generations the chief scholar under the Tokugawa and ranked next to *rōjū* and *wakatoshiyori* [ministers], that is, near the top of the immediate retainers. Yet they were not allowed to hold the least amount of power in the administration. In an emergency, this scholar might be consulted, but his role was strictly limited to giving advice. Some regretted this practice of the Tokugawa military government not placing sufficient emphasis on cultural knowledge. However, I think that it would have been harmful to have a scholar in the government, and I am certain that this rule and custom of the Tokugawa regime was wise and appropriate.

Suppose in those days the chief of learning and education, the head of the Hayashi family, had been given a position in the government. His numerous disciples, all well versed in politics, would certainly have formed a faction in the government, but its power would not have been sufficient to dominate the whole nation and would have come in conflict with other powers. The result would have been that all the schools run by Hayashi disciples would advocate one policy while other schools under independent scholars, which were quite numerous, would have opposing ideas, thus turning the schools of learning into an arena of political arguments, spreading conflict even into the government itself. In an extreme case, it could cause armed conflict throughout the nation. The fact that no such misfortune ever occurred during the long regime was the result of keeping scholars out of politics.

Some theorists may argue that learning and politics are two completely different disciplines; therefore, there should be a law prohibiting schools of learning from giving instruction in politics and reading books on the subject. With the enforcement of the law, the distinction between the two will become clear and there will be no confusion or trouble. However, this argument is plausible only in theory, and it does not apply to the reality of education. Whatever law may be created to restrict the schools of learning, as long as the principals of the schools are

[167]

government employees, it will be more than impossible to keep politics off the minds of the students. Even when the principal criticizes the evils of politics and warns his students against imitating loose-tongued politicians or fanatics of certain factions and succeeds in quelling any political thoughts in the students, some students will understand the principal's words as political opposition against a certain party. Therefore, the result of the prohibition will only be an outward dissociation from politics which may lead to the formation of group of students of similar political beliefs who will not discuss politics openly.

To give another example, the differences in political factions are like the differences in religious sects. When a priest of the Hokke sect tells the people not to recite the *nenbutsu* [the invocation of Shin and related sects], he may not be advocating the invocation of his own sect, and yet his intention to convert the crowd to his sect will be clear.

One must realize that for an education devoid of political atmosphere, we need schools run by principals and teachers who are totally unrelated to the government and whose minds are devoid of prejudice in politics. For prohibiting *nenbutsu* and for cleansing people's minds of sectarian prejudice, the policy will have to either prohibit prayers of all sects or to refrain from commenting on the outward acts of religion and to teach people not to promote one's own sect alone. As long as the head of the school is free of politics both in mind and in position, no harm will arise from studying or discussing any subject in school. Rather, the true nature of learning requires such studies and discussion from a free point of view and at a distance from actual political situations. This will nurture far-sighted views to the benefit of those in power.

The instances of the Hayashi family and other scholars in the Tokugawa period, or in an earlier period—the case of Tenkai Sōjō,[1] who had no connections with the administration—will show that at times scholars can be helpful to the government. And all these were not accidental cases.

[1] Tenkai Sōjō [1536?–1643]. An able and learned priest of the Tendai sect, personal advisor to Tokugawa Ieyasu. Influenced Ieyasu's religious and philosophical thoughts and those of the second shōgun, Hidetada, and the third shōgun, Iemitsu, whom he also served as advisor.

In contrast to these, there are examples in China from the Sung era and, in more recent years, in the Mito Clan of Japan, where scholars formed political parties and caused much turmoil. All of these are instances in which men in education meddled in politics, sometimes using their schools as bases to form political parties or to agitate students with their own political thoughts to bring harm on all of society.

It is natural that the head of a school should guide his pupils freely according to his ideals, and sometimes his school can come into opposition with other schools, in extreme cases becoming hostile to them. As long as the conflict stays within the bounds of learning, no harm can be done to society; rather the competition will stimulate further studies, just as competition among different schools of military arts, calligraphy, or painting help the advancement of the arts. However, as soon as the scholarly groups acquire a political interest, the tranquil and profound nature of the scholars is transformed into activity and severity, which will lead to no end of harm. The leaders of society will do best to keep this in mind.

Installment Three

The prediction currently prevailing is that within a few years' time a National Diet will be opened in this country, and there is already some discussion of forming political parties in preparation for this event. It will launch an era of party politics, something unprecedented in our country, and there is no telling what may happen after the opening of the Diet. We should expect people to divide into factions and have strong disagreements and much strife over political principles. The government will probably change hands from time to time, as they do in Western countries; or perhaps this will not be the case. Whatever form the government may take, its policy will certainly change from time to time. That will be inevitable. Under such fluid conditions, suppose the schools throughout the nation are run by the Ministry of Education and their teachers officials of the ministry; they will be obliged to change their policy each time the government alters its course. Nothing would be more unfortunate for the cause of the nation's culture and education.

For instance, when the authorities discover that the foreign trade balance is disadvantageous and that the cause for this imbalance is the backwardness of industry and commerce in Japan, they will adopt a policy encouraging industrial and commercial education. Then when all the young students in the country are redirected in accordance with the new policy, a new report will be received from foreign countries describing an unhealthy political atmosphere—the state of affairs in Europe is such and such; even in our neighboring country, China, Minister so and so has taken over power and his policies are such and such; there is no telling when war clouds might cover the whole of the Far East! To be prepared for the worst emergency should be fundamental in a nation's policy; school education, too, must follow the trend of the times. Prevent the students from turning into bookish weaklings. Promote the military arts!

The students who had just started to study industry and commerce would now have to throw away their books on economics and take to books on military tactics, abandon the pen, and turn to the sword. The minds of youths are as pliable as the willow in the wind; they will be easily swayed by instructions from above. And in this case, what has been the cause of these instructions? Nothing more than a few years of imbalance in foreign trade and the promotion of one minister in a neighboring country. These matters in foreign trade and the politics of a neighboring country are important to government officials who must make immediate policy decisions on them. However, is it not tragic to let such transient matters influence education, which deserves serious and long-range planning? When politics and education are interlocked, a change in one would cause a commotion in the other, and when the change is large in scale, the commotion will turn into an upheaval.

To provide an example, the old shogunate-sponsored school of Western studies, called Kaisei Gakkō in Edo, was the central authority on Western studies in the country, a large organization with many students. However, with the fall of the shogunate, the school simply disintegrated; all the students and teachers dispersed and disappeared. The Imperial forces entering the city of Edo showed no signs of singling out Kaisei Gakkō as an object of attack, but the scholars were frightened and deserted the school in one confused retreat, allowing this center of Western studies to fold.

[170]

How did this happen? Because Kaisei Gakkō was a part of the shōgun's government and very closely tied to the politics of the day. In other words, the school was an appendage of the faction that ran the government, and the teachers and the students themselves were members of that faction. Or it could be that these teachers had forgotten the true spirit of scholarship, overcome by the confusing changes in society, lost themselves in the arguments over expediencies of the moment, some siding with the Imperial cause, some with the shōgun, and thus placed themselves in the arena of politics.

Suppose Kaisei Gakkō had been independent of the powers of the government, free to roam the world untainted by political strifes, truly unprejudiced and unattached. For the members of the faculty, in reality brave and independent men, the Imperial forces entering the city would have posed no cause for fear. A school worthy of its name would have continued its studies in the face of raining cannon balls, and inside its walls the voices of students reciting lessons would have been heard. But because of its affiliation with the government and the cowardice of the scholars on the faculty, the school disintegrated in the most shameful manner and allowed the cause of learning to fall back for several years until the Imperial government revived the school after the Restoration. This incident was a great misfortune for the cause of learning.[2]

Without doubt, the present government is different from the old shogunate, and there is no fear of another revolutionary disturbance in the future. Yet the disadvantage of close ties between politics and education is obvious, regardless of the type of government.

Now, let us examine what exactly this religion called Shintoism has done for the society of Japan in the first few years of the Restoration. Before merits of this religion became evident, it had begun demanding the expulsion of Buddhism. Backed by the government, this new movement prohibited the coexistence of

---

[2] There was good reason for Fukuzawa to make such a strong statement in this paragraph. On May 15, 1868, during a pitched battle in Edo when the Imperial forces attacked and destroyed a pocket of the shogunate diehards in the area now occupied by Ueno Park, Fukuzawa continued teaching in his school, actually within sight of the battlefield. His own account of this incident is in his autobiography, ch. 10, p. 210.

Shintoism and Buddhism in the same premises. This placed great hardships on Buddhist priests, offended the pious sentiments of the faithful, and ruined the scenic sites in shrines and temples throughout the country by destroying parts of the buildings where the two religions had coexisted This was all the doing of Shintoism in the critical days of the Restoration.

I know very little about Shintoism, but I presume it is a discipline with principles of its own. I shall have no objection to its competing with other religions or schools of thought with its principles, or even to being hostile to other groups, because as long as there is no involvement of government authority, the rivalries will be no more than competitions between the schools of learning themselves. However, at the time of the Restoration, Shintoism became affiliated with the government and acquired power with which it disrupted the whole country, wholly out of proportion to its position. This again is an example of the evils caused by the alliance of learning and politics.

The above are examples taken from periods of disturbance, but in times of peace, too, there is no escape from political activity in the schools when arguments among politicians grow heated. When administrative officials themselves conduct classes, there is always the temptation for politicians to draw schools into political strife. Although schools should be immune to politics, the opposition party in local politics will not limit their activities to political matters alone; they will include schools among their targets as the schools are part of the administration.

Today, we already see that when a schoolteacher is being interviewed for a position, his political beliefs and connections are questioned. Sometimes, candidates with connections with a certain political party are rejected; or the committee will acknowledge the candidate's fine political speech at a meeting under the sponsorship of a certain party and therefore employ the person at a somewhat higher salary. Thus, instead of the candidate's academic accomplishments, his oratory skills at political meetings become the criterion for his selection. Learning, of its nature, has no relation to politics, much as such other arts as the fine arts and military arts do not, and as long as a person has the ability to teach an assigned subject, he should be considered qualified to work as a teacher, regardless of his political beliefs. Yet today, when he is being employed, it is his political beliefs and his skills in making political speeches that are the foremost criteria. Such a practice makes schools the veritable tools of politics. Most people let this pass nonchalantly, but I fear it is a visible sign of a calamity to come. I am afraid that the nation will fall into the extremes of misfortune, such as was seen with the Sung dynasty of China and the Mito Clan of more recent Japan.

Installment Four

To prevent this misfortune is a matter of urgency that we are confronted with today, and it must not be neglected by any means. How can it be prevented? My constant advice has been to separate all the schools from the Ministry of Education or the Ministry of Industry, and place them under the supervision of the Imperial Household. The Imperial Household will grant the control of the schools to private citizens of recognized experience and willingness and let them reorganize the schools into private schools under cooperative management. At the same time, the schools should receive financial aid from the Imperial Household, either in one-time grants of large sums sufficient for permanent support of the schools or in yearly grants out of the Imperial finances. Either arrangement will be satisfactory. Even the one-time-grant method will not pose any difficulty for the following reason.

The annual expenditure of the ministries on the schools they administer is about 500,000 yen. Thus, if five million yen is granted as a common fund for the schools, government bonds worth that amount can be purchased and deposited with the government. The bonds will earn about 500,000 yen in annual interest. On the ledger, this sum of five million yen will appear to have been used in one large payment, but in reality no cash will be transferred; the only operation will be transferring the ownership of the government bonds in the Ministry of Finance. Of course, this will grant a tremendous sum to private hands, but as long as it is to be under cooperative management, no one individual will be able to appropriate it for private purposes. And this capital of five million yen will enable those schools to finance themselves permanently under private control.

After schools have been organized as described above, let us consider establishing a council of scholars of high reputation from

[173]

throughout the nation for regular academic conferences. This council will be the center of learning and education of the nation and it should be granted the authority to supervise all literary and scholastic activities and study methods in education, judge books, do research on ancient history, study new theories, serve as the final authority on language usage, edit dictionaries, and such myriad cultural activities without government interference. This council shall be a kind of supreme overseer of Japan's culture.

An episode in the Treasury Department (Kanjōsho) of the old Tokugawa government tells us that there was a custom in this department for retainers of the shōgun, upon receiving their stipend of rice, to present receipts stating "so many bushels of rice" using the character "rice" written with one stroke shorter than in the normal way of writing. One day, a receipt submitted by the family of Hayashi, the chief of learning [*daigaku no kami*], was found to have written the character in the usual way with the stroke in question long. The official of the Treasury Department refused to accept it because, as he said, it was against the established rule of the department. The official of the Hayashi family objected, and a dispute arose between the two which grew more serious as the trouble was referred to higher officials. The situation finally called for a direct confrontation of the minister of the treasury and the chief of learning. At this confrontation, the chief of learning expounded that the final authority on how a Chinese character should be written resided with himself, as granted by the grace of the shōgun, and he declared that his way of writing was correct! This settled the question, and the most powerful official in the government, the minister of treasury, was, for once, defeated in argument.

Whether this is a true story or a creation of a storyteller is not known, but it is a good illustration of where the final authority on letters resided in those days. Times have changed, and there is no possibility of such an incident occurring today, but if fortune favors us with the establishment of a scholars' council, I pray that its authority will be like that of the Hayashi family of bygone days.

I pray also that while the scholars' council will be the supreme authority in matters of learning, it will not have any say in political matters. Under any circumstance, those in the administration of

[174]

schools should never hold power in politics or in government; this shall be a taboo. Those men in learning and in education, from the point of view of politicians and officials, shall remain those out-of-this-world "long-sleeved" men. In short, learning should never be allowed to interfere in politics, and politics should never be allowed to obstruct the free activities of learning. The two shall stand side by side, each finding its proper place for the progress of the society. The paths of politics and learning will be unobstructed, and nothing could be more to the advantage of both.

I am not advocating the abolition of the Ministry of Education. The ministry is an administrative office, and it is needed to oversee the hundred and one items of education. For instance, issuing orders to various areas to survey the children of school-going age, or considering the increase or decrease in children and the proportion between the general population and school-age children; surveying schools on their status and their history, and their capital and its management; or at times sending officials out for on-the-spot supervision—such activities cannot be done without the authority of the Ministry of Education. In particular, compulsory education cannot be realized without the authority of the government. I, of course, believe in compulsory education, for it is very important for all boys and girls born in Japan to attend school when they reach a certain age, and they should be forced to go, if necessary.

But decisions on what kind of education, on books to be used for instruction, on books to be kept away from the children, and on actual instruction in the classrooms must not be made by the ministry. In short, all the important decisions on learning should be left to the scholars' council, while the reports, supervision, and other administrative chores should be managed by the ministry. In other words, matters on learning and matters of administrative business should be handled separately, each depending on the other. Thus, and thus only, can education function well.

For instance, in the navy and army, those who serve on warships and those who command soldiers in the field on horseback are thorough naval or military men, and only those properly trained in the arts of war and with actual experience are able to carry out the duties. Yet, the navy and the army cannot carry out their duties by depending on military men alone. In a military court, lawyers are needed; in caring for the injured and sick, a medical staff is required; when the army is on the march, acquisition and transportation of food and munitions are a major concern; in times of peace, too, there is the keeping of books and finances. All these and a myriad other things are businesses outside of actual fighting, yet their importance is no less than those of fighting proper. The two complement each other, and the military is enabled to function to full measure, a fact well-known to all.

The same logic applies to the education of a nation. To select the path of education and to lead young men accordingly, instruction in reading and writing, or advanced arts and sciences is possible only by those who have received education themselves from their early years and have experience in actual classroom teaching. This is why professional men of learning should be responsible for education and learning. But, from another point of view, the education of a nation cannot be left in the hands of scholars only. For organizing them and providing them with satisfactory facilities, we need the authority of government administration and the assistance of business managers.

A scholar forcing learning upon people by assuming governmental authority or an administrator without the true knowledge of learning trying to teach can be compared to military men trying to manage the business end of the navy and army or the office workers without knowledge or experience of military tactics attempting to command an army on the battlefield. The results will never be in proportion to the labor; rather, they will only result in disasters. People are well acquainted with the difficulty or inadvisability of army surgeons or army lawyers training soldiers or in making battlefield decisions. By the same token, they should be convinced of the inaptness of political administrators meddling in the instruction methods or specifying advisable and inadvisable books for the students. I trust that some of my readers will see the wisdom of my arguments.

Installment Five

There will be questions asked on how the funds will be appropriated if the Imperial Household is to sponsor all the schools that are to be made private organizations. This can be solved very easily. In my personal opinion, the present budget for the Imperial Household is overly small. I have expressed my opinion many times that either the Imperial Household budget should be increased a great deal or property should be presented to it. If by some good fortune this idea of mine is realized, the sponsoring of schools will be a small matter, for the entire expense of the re-organized schools throughout the nation will be only a few hundred thousand yen a year. Even the policy of granting a lump sum will require no more than a few million yen, which is to be lent out without interest for an indefinite period. Neither way would be a heavy financial burden for the Imperial Household.

Another argument will be that the present government is financially too pressed to attempt an increase in the Imperial Household budget. In that case, there is a way of attaining the same goal without increasing the national budget at all. The way is simply this: When the schools are separated from the Ministry of Education and the Ministry of Industry and transferred to the Imperial Household, the two ministries will have surpluses in their budgets, and these surpluses naturally will be returned to the Ministry of Finance. The Ministry of Finance may then use these to increase the Imperial Household budget, and the Imperial Household will be able to use it to sponsor schools. This process will work without affecting the total national budget.

Not only will it bring no change to the national budget. This transfer of schools from an official status to a private one will influence the school masters toward a frugal policy and will result in a substantial decrease in school expenditures. If the expenditures are not decreased, the school masters will launch new or larger activities on the same budget. I am not intimating that the government schools of today are loose in spending money, but in reality expenditures do differ in government schools and private schools, a fact understood by society. Therefore, by good fortune, if the present proposal should be realized, it will be discovered that the national budget for schools has been more than generous in the past years.

Some may agree that while the present proposal of turning government schools into cooperative private schools, of employing the same principals and teachers in the new schools, and of having a scholars' council make decisions on policies on learning and

[177]

education is very fine, those principals and teachers who enjoyed their privileged positions as government officials in the past would suddenly be deprived. Their demotion to the status of private school teachers would cause much disappointment. My first reaction to this argument was to dismiss it as something born out of petty-official psychology, oblivious of the sentiments among men of learning. Yet, upon second thought, I remembered that there are quite a number of gross men among us; there certainly will be cases, though rare, of men who enjoy boasting about their promotions to their present status of such-and-such grade in such-and-such service.

However, this problem can be solved easily and with perfect satisfaction. First of all, their remuneration will remain the same whether they are in government service or employed in private schools. On the question of official rank, too, the Imperial Household can very well grant ranks and medals of honor to all the men of learning in the country according to their merits. This honor should satisfy any scholar or teacher.

Ranks and medals, of their own nature, should not be monopolized by officials in the government. When an official resigns, he leaves the government, but he does not lose his court rank or medals. The members of noble families may not serve in government posts, but they are always granted ranks. This, I believe, is in recognition of the honor inherited by the family. Therefore, the ranks and medals are not tokens of reward for the men in office; they are in recognition of ordinary citizens of Japan for their distinguished achievements as proven by their appointment to government posts. Among the officials, those called first-rank officials hold very responsible positions which are difficult for ordinary people to fill. These men hold them successfully without mishaps, proof of their rare quality of heaven-granted talents enforced by first-rate education. These must be the reasons for granting them a first-class medal and an exalted rank.

Officials are compensated for their labors by salaries. Using numbers to explain this, a salary of 100 is paid for the labor of 100, which is comparable to a business transaction. From this point of view, to hold an official position is one way of earning a living, but the granting of ranks and medals is to classify and arrange people according to their merits and personalities, apart from the quantity of work performed. And because there naturally are a large number of outstanding men serving as officials, one may expect a large percentage of officials to receive ranks and medals. But this large percentage should not come from partiality toward the government. Thus, because government service is a kind of scale against which men's merits are measured, once the scale has been set and ranks and medals awarded, the status stays with them for life, without regard to their subsequent conduct. This will be illustrated by the fact that the men are not deprived of their ranks and medals when they resign from their positions in government.

Installment Six
The ranks and medals are honors granted directly by the Imperial Household, and the government officials should not be concerned about their granting at all. The Imperial Household is the Imperial Household of the whole nation; it is not the over-lord of government officials alone, nor should it favor the government as a special organ. Absolutely impartial, the Imperial Household will shine over the whole empire, never favoring one party nor slighting another. In its eyes, all sectors of the nation, the political circle, scholars' circles, or religion, arts, farming, commerce, and everything will be of equal importance. When-ever there is a person excelling in any one of these fields, the Imperial Household will recognize his merits. Here lies the basic principle of the ranks and medals, I presume. The affairs of human society are complex and varied, and the government is not society's sole organization. The activities of individuals, too, must be distinguished according to their myriad varieties. This is called division of labor.

As long as there is division of labor, there will naturally appear in each division a person excelling in it—some excelling in farm-ing or commerce, some in industrial arts, or some in learning or in politics. Their superior performance being in different fields, they cannot be compared with one another. Therefore, it will naturally follow that recognition be given to each separately as champion in his field. For instance, an *ōzeki* in Japanese wrestling is the strongest man in that world, and the man holding the ninth grade has the greatest skill in Japanese chess [*shōgi*]

[179]

world. Their holding those positions of honor is exactly like the first-rank officials being the most honored men in the national government. Therefore, those who have devoted their lives since youth to scholarship and to its instruction and attained fame in that field are the honored champions in the world of learning, and there should be no question of their deserving honor on the same level as the first-rank official in government.

Then, why is it that the champion of wrestling and the holder of the ninth grade in chess are not honored to the same degree as the prime minister [*dajō daijin*]? The reason is that wrestling and chess are in themselves not as weighty as politics, and it is impossible to compare the head of each on the same basis. However, when the development of civilization is taken as the measure of comparison, I presume that it will be very difficult to decide whether government or learning is of greater importance.

When a scholar is allowed to express his opinion on the importance of learning, he will certainly make government and politics appear like child's play, while a politician, when asked his opinion on scholarship, will belittle it as empty meddling in outdated theorems, far from practical value to everyday life. These are, after all, one-sided arguments of biased partisans. From an unbiased point of view, both government and learning are necessary activities of human life which cannot go neglected for even a single day. Government is important in attending to practical day-to-day affairs; learning is important in forming long-range plans for the future. Government ensures peace so that scholars are able to engage in their work without a care; scholars educate people and supply the government with intelligent men. This is a perfectly just and fair verdict on the equality of the two, with which both sides should be satisfied.

Thus the importance of learning being clear, it follows that those in this world of learning should be honored with ranks and medals, a recognition that should be welcomed by the people. In short, those in the higher echelons of learning should rank equally with those in the higher echelons in the government, and there should be no difference in importance between the two. But the two should not interfere in each other's activities. An old proverb says that in the Imperial Court, ranks are honored, and in local communities, age is honored. This saying probably means that even with the importance of Imperial Court ranks, the values of local society cannot be disregarded. This concept applies with greater effect in the world of learning. Even when a scholar finds a position in the government, the true value of that scholar does not increase in the least.

In a certain university in France, it is recorded that Napoleon I succeeded in obtaining membership to the academic society, but Napoleon III was not able to obtain the honor. This is evidence of the powerful authority that scholars hold in that country. In our country, suppose there were no order of nobility and the government ranks were applicable only while the men were in office. In that case, the ranks would function exactly like those in commercial companies, and their effectiveness would be markedly less. However, as long as the order of ranks of honor exists, I hope that this system will extend to all the people in the country with no distinction between those in government service and those not.

Officials serve the government of our society; scholars are in the academic branch of our society. Their professions are different, but in their value as people, there should be no distinction. The only distinguishing point would be that one happened to go into scholarship and was never given the opportunity to obtain honorary ranks, while the other, having joined government service, came into both lucrative remuneration and honorary titles. This state of things cannot be called fair and just. From a very philosophical, high-minded point of view, ranks and medals are the most mundane symbols of this society, not worthy of commanding attention. However, such a rejection is too often the boasting of a proud, common scholar which does not necessarily reveal the truth. A scholar with a truly lofty point of view, who really does not care for the petty honor and glory, is very, very rare—much less than ten out of a hundred, or even one or two in a thousand or ten thousand! If there were no system of recognition in the country, one might have to resign oneself. But precisely because there is one, one to which only select countrymen are privileged, the unprivileged ones only naturally feel deprived. Under these circumstances, one cannot expect present-day scholars to be immune to the temptation of glory.

As described in detail above, it will not only be natural to grant

[181]

ranks and medals to the scholars in recognition of their merits, but it is also a bewilderment to the people to have only government officials monopolize the honors. Therefore, if by good fortune, those government-administered schools are to be reorganized into private schools, the teachers in those schools should be granted ranks and medals according to their merits. These teachers have been in the field of learning from their childhood, cultivating their own wisdom and sharing it with their pupils, and are highly skilled. They deserve to be called senior leaders in the field. If they are humble men without rank at present, they certainly deserve proper honors. This act will not only make those teachers happy, it will prove that the omnipresence of the emperor's benevolence extends to every sector of the nation without favoritism.

Installment Seven
When the Imperial Household becomes the sponsor of all the private schools of Japan, I wish to promote a system of honor in addition to the one described above: selecting the most outstanding scholars in the country and bestowing on them special honor and yearly stipends, allowing them the freedom to devote all their attention to the studies of their own choice. The development of learning in the West has been particularly rapid in recent years. Not only have discoveries in science been remarkable; their application to human welfare has become particularly conspicuous. All the machinery for use in factories and in agriculture and even those for manual work—those used in such daily chores as gardening, cooking, and lighting—have come under scientific scrutiny. Indeed, in every sector of human life, scientific principles are being applied.

In short, the West in recent years has passed the age of scientific studies and has entered the age of scientific application. Or, in a more figurative description, they are like army men graduated from the military academy and marching into the battlefield. In contrast, our scientific studies, though much advanced in the past dozen years or so, have not graduated by any means. They are still at the stage of drilling exercises to learn from other countries, far from actual battlefield experience. They are still unable to discover new facts in science for themselves. It will be

[182]

many years yet before they will become capable of applying their discoveries to practical life.

For instance, medicine has had a much longer history than any other physical science in our country, and it is therefore more advanced than other sciences, but at present it is still struggling to catch up with the ever-advancing medical research in the West. In the past several hundred years, not one new discovery in medical science has been heard of. Even the cause and the transmission of beriberi, a disease common among the Japanese, has not been thoroughly researched. This is not because of inaptitude on the part of our medical scientists; they do not have the time or funds to carry out the research they wish to do.

As soon as our doctors acquire the rudiments of medicine, they are either placed in a government office or they are obliged to open their private practices. Then they become so occupied in their daily work, and though their work, either in government or in the private sector, may not be to their hearts' desire, they have no choice because they must earn their living. There are many in the medical field who spend their lives rushing about every day without finding even half a day in a whole year to study new advances in their field. This is a deplorable state of affairs.

(Tapping the chest and listening to its sounds are the most important techniques in the diagnosis of diseases, but because a physician's hearing ability is limited, errors or oversights are invariably made. I once suggested using blind men in this technique: Select some blind men with musical talent and first have them listen to a healthy heart and healthy lungs. Then have them listen to various kinds of diseased hearts and lungs. These blind men with their sensitive ears would probably be able to distinguish the sounds of varieties within different diseases—for instance, distinguishing two or three different kinds out of one that the physicians formerly were able to identify. This will mean that where the physicians formerly had divided diseases into five kinds, the new technique would divide them into fifteen, thus offering a wider field for research in diagnosis. If this supposition of mine is valid, the new subject of acoustics will be offered in medical schools for the training of young physicians while their hearing faculties are still sharp. Probably, some of the talented ones will make this tapping and listening their specialty. I believe some

[183]

secrets in medical science will be uncovered by these alert physicians.)

It is not only in medical science, but in other sciences or cultural studies as well, that I am certain scholars, if provided with time and sufficient income, would not become indolent and lazy. Their habits of a lifetime will make them place their best efforts into research—they would not know what else to do. The result of their studies will be new discoveries and new devices which will be of credit to the scholars themselves as well as be the achievements of Japan's scholarship and the glory of the country.

Concerning publication of books, I notice that in recent years voluminous works have become rare, with only the number and variety of publications increasing. The more the publishing business thrives, the more popular and superficial books increase. The reason for this is that scholars do not have the time to ponder profound thoughts in the quietude of a secluded chamber. It is to be expected that a profound book will not find a large audience, and the profits from its sale will not cover its expenses. In comparison to popular books, this kind of book will require much more labor on the part of the author, and its return will be smaller, in negative proportion. From this it will be clear why great books are not published. These phenomena give cause for concern over the state of scholarship in this country, and the basic reason for this is that the scholars do not have time or money. Therefore, should the Imperial Household supply yearly stipends to the selected scholars of special ability and assure them security for life, scholarship in our country will take on a new dimension and soon reach the level in Western nations, and no doubt our scholars will begin to compete with scholars of the world.

From the point of view of national budget alone, it will appear uneconomical to divert funds to subsidize men who have no clear office or position. But it must be noted that even among those with offices, there are some who are not busy from day to day. These men hold what may be called "leisure offices" and among these leisure officials there are some fine scholars. Even among those who are not leisure officials, there are men with natural talent for scholarship. Such people are not able in administrative work; they will be efficient in supplying information in an emergency, but inefficient when assigned to daily office work.

If they earn the same salary, it would be better if they were spared a monotonous job for the peace of their life and spirit, rather than in a confining government organization and forced to wear an ill-fitting uniform. It will be very well to lose two or three scholars from the Elder Statesmen's Council [*Genrōin*], because the loss will not change the council's decisions, just as one or two cultured naval or army officers will not determine the outcome of a battle. Whenever the need for advice or information arises, the scholars can be easily summoned. Measured on the far-reaching scale of national economy, this proposition of yearly stipends for scholars is by no means an uneconomical one.

Installment Eight

The imperial sponsorship of private schools and special treatment of scholars will not only aid the progress of learning but it will be a great impetus for the cause of government and politics. In a broader definition, politics and government may be classified as fields of learning. The statesmen are always educated men, and political commentators are trained in schools. When students graduate and go out into society, they enter different fields: some into industry, some into commerce or into politics. And there are some who remain in school after graduation and spend their lives in research or in teaching. Such men are pure scholars. Therefore, those in industry, commerce, and politics are the ones who apply their learning to the practical operations of human life while scholars make learning their livelihood.

As was said before, the importance of politics and government to the nation is equal to the importance of learning. The science of politics must progress from day to day. All the citizens of a nation must have ideas on politics. They must always have intense political discussions. Citizens with no political awareness are fools, or a mob, as exemplified by people from ancient China and the Hsia, Shang, and Chou dynasties. They may be citizens in name, but in reality they are no better than sheep or pigs, unworthy to work for the nation in the company of true citizens.

Therefore, whoever possesses real love for their country must always be alert to the problems of government and politics. This importance of politics applies to general citizens. Statesmen or

[185]

politicians are different, for politics is their profession. They take part in politics and take responsibility which is much like men in industry or commerce who operate their family businesses or a scholar who devotes his whole life to learning. In short, my belief in the necessity of political awareness of all people is similar to my encouraging learning among all people.

Learning is necessary and important to all citizens, but it does not mean that all men should be scholars. In the same way, all men should be interested in politics, but this does not mean that they should be politicians. Many people do not understand this distinction, and as soon as they learn the importance of politics, they visualize entering politics and participating in government affairs themselves and making it their life work, just as when they learn the importance of learning, they think of becoming a great scholar and spending their whole lives among books. This sort of devotion is admirable, but people have natural gifts or talents of their own, and family obligations as well. Not everyone can elect a political life or a scholar's life, nor can they succeed in those professions. The histories of many countries since ancient times prove all this. Thus common people should be satisfied with general knowledge. And as soon as they acquire an average education, they should adopt whatever line of work they are talented in, go freely in this society in the work of their choice, for the benefit of their own families and also in the service of the country.

When politics and learning are recognized as separate and independent fields, it is important to remember that one must not interfere with the other, but that professionals must concentrate on their respective work, never meddling in the affairs of the other. A man in politics, when he has finished his education and has entered the profession, must abandon all thoughts of education as if he had forgotten it, even though as an individual he should continue to widen his knowledge and culture. A scholar, once he has chosen learning as his career, must abandon all ambition in politics though, of course, he must retain interest in it.

Yet, in recent days, politicians are often seen exploiting schools of education for their own purposes, and conversely teachers and students are discussing current politics, identifying themselves with this or that policy. This is the result of neglect on the part of politicians. When politics penetrates into schools and then to other sectors of society, all men will begin to form themselves into rival political parties. Even industry and commerce will become involved in party politics. In extreme cases, doctors taking in patients, temple priests, and even restaurant proprietors in offering rooms for meetings will begin to discriminate against customers according to political affiliations. Such a phenomenon runs against the principle of amity in community and mutual love.

Many scholars are abandoning their professions for the more lucrative political life because the whole society is leaning toward politics, and whoever talks politics is respected. Politics is an easier way to earn a living and rise in society, while the scholar's profession is far removed from profit. Even honest endeavors of many years in poverty are seldom respected because people pass them off as the usual lot of a scholar.

Under such circumstances, every youth and student would be tempted to trade in his books and fight his way toward a career in politics. This situation is not the fault of the individual; it is the natural result of the current trend. Critics often fail to look into the cause of a trend and simply blame the present young men as immodest, frivolous, and forgetful of their own place in the world. Granting that young men nowadays are out of their right minds, we must consider the cause of their madness as it is inconceivable that they should suddenly lose their minds at this particular time in the Meiji era. What is the cause?

I am sure it is the lack of security for those who aspire in the world of learning. We do not have to go far in finding proof for this. There are some people who have modified their views in order to protect the source of their living, or those who have changed the tone of their argument since acquiring a lucrative post. These men who have changed their views because of their new positions will change again when they lose them. Under these conditions, how can anyone take such people seriously? If one person is like this, the others must also be the same. As the Chinese classics [Shih-ching] say, "For cutting the proper length of wood for an ax handle, examples will not be hard to find" [i.e., the old, broken handle will serve as the measure]: One can surmise the other's mind with one's own.

[187]

The way to provide peace of mind is to assure security of livelihood—security of body is the key to security of mind. Therefore, should the Imperial Household give aid to the maintenance of private schools and also to the support of scholars, it will set an example for the nation. The public will come to respect learning, which, by extension, will result in a secure living for scholars. The next step will be for those who do not find careers in industry, agriculture, commerce, or politics to choose the academic world, assured of a secure livelihood, away from the turbulent but glorious world of politics.

I once said that any attempt to prohibit political discussion among scholars and students was like trying to extinguish a fire by throwing drops of water on it. To put out a large fire, it is far better to remove the fuel. Indeed, to enable scholarship to become a respected and secure profession, scholars should be kept from the temptation of politics, like removing the fuel from the fire.

23
Confucian Doctrine

Whenever a social change takes place, the young are the first to respond, and they are accused by men of the old school for their unruly behavior. In the early years of Meiji, older men declared, "As Western studies thrive, our youth grow insolent, particularly in political discussions." Voices were raised in favor of reviving Confucian teaching in schools to resuscitate some manners among young men. The present essay was written in refutation of such a view as *Jijishimpō* editorials between November 19 and 21, 1883.

Installment One

"The recent popularity of Western learning has made our youth insolent; to save them from their delusion, we must return to Confucianism and its doctrine of pure morality." This is an opinion I often come across. However, when one examines the true nature of Confucianism, one will find that it is not simply a moral philosophy; it is heavily imbued with political ideas.

Look at any one of the basic texts of Confucianism: In *Ching-shu*, any one of the opening chapters launches not into personal morality but politics: on how to govern a country or how to bring peace to the world. Large portions of the books are filled with political discussions, and morality occupies but a small portion inserted in between.

And so, this Confucianism is a school of thought of both politics

"Jukyō Shugi" (儒教主義), 1883. *Fukuzawa Yukichi Zenshū*, vol. 9, pp. 268–77.

[189]

and morality. Analysis shows that about 70 percent of the texts concern politics: how to govern a nation and how to bring peace to the world; and moral teaching occupies only the remaining 30 percent. This is a very straight fact, and there is no way to disguise it, however strongly some fanatics may insist that it is a school exclusively of moral teaching.

Some stubborn advocates may insist that what we need to utilize in modern times is confined to the sections on moral philosophy, therefore, one may simply refer to the relevant sections. But a doctrine cannot simply be split in two like some material object, using just the portion that suits one's purposes. Every chapter, every saying in the Four Books and the Five Classics, is an expression of one and the same doctrine, even if the wording may vary, and discusses both politics and morality.

To illustrate it using chemistry as a simile, politics and morality in Confucian doctrine are not simply a mixture; they constitute a compound. Mixing rice and sand or salt and water will not change the nature of these substances; they can be put together and separated, restored to their former states quite easily, either mechanically or by the use of heat. But when hydrochloric acid and soda combine, a chemical reaction turns them into a new substance which is not anything like the acid or the soda, rather something in between, ordinary table salt. And as this salt has been formed by a chemical combination, it cannot be restored to the former hydrochloric acid and soda unless tremendous power is applied.

Now, the relation between politics and morality in Confucianism is not a simple mixture like that of rice and sand; it is a combination like that of hydrochloric acid and soda. Their relationship is so close that the doctrine can be called neither political doctrine nor moral doctrine. The two change in nature to something in between which has come to be called Ju-chiao, Confucianism. The combination of hydrochloric acid and soda is called table salt; the combination of politics and morality is called Ju-chiao. Both are difficult to separate. Therefore, whoever converts to this doctrine cannot help referring to politics when discussing morality, and when studying politics, cannot help but touch on morality.

An important point in studying Chinese doctrine is not to give much attention to the implication of each word or phrase but to endeavor to understand the purpose of a whole chapter. And rather than understanding one chapter, it is more important to appreciate the thesis of the whole book and to study the interdependence of philosophical themes in different parts of the book. Unless one is capable of this approach in reading, one cannot be called a true student of the doctrine. In other words, the interdependence of political and moral philosophy is the true essence of Confucian doctrine: morality is inseparable from politics, politics is allied to morality, both being connected as links in an endless chain that cannot be broken at any point. When one appreciates this point, one will finally come to realize the true value of Confucianism.

For instance, take a word such as *jên* [*jin* in Japanese—benevolence, humanity, perfect virtue] and try to give it a complete Confucian annotation. Is this virtue a personal attribute of an individual? Or, is it something concerned with social or political affairs? It is a virtue neither solely of an individual nor of society at large. It is a human quality that is made manifest through public activity. Even when an individual does not take part in the government of the world, his mind should be alert to the problems of governing the nation and pacifying the world. Only when one attains such mental poise may he be called a man of true *jên*.

This definition of virtue is found not only in *Ching-shu* but in the histories and books by various scholars, or in the biographies of virtuous men and their words, or even in minor poems. If the writer is not a heretic, all the writings new and old are based on Confucian doctrine. For instance, the classic history books, such as *Tso-chuan, Kuo-yü, Shih-chi, Han-shu*, or the records of sayings and doings of famous men, the main points of the authors, or the annotations and criticisms of scholars in later years, both in China and in Japan, are all influenced by Confucian doctrine.

From this viewpoint, all the thousands and tens of thousands of Chinese books may be called books of Confucian doctrine. The condition is quite similar to calling all parts of the Tripitaka [the complete collection of Buddhist scriptures] the sutras of Buddhism. Therefore, one may regard the much revered *Ching-shu* as the trunk of the tree and the histories and other books by various scholars as the branches and the leaves making up the complete

[191]

tree of Chinese teaching in which moral teachings and political discussions of the sages are combined, the political discussions being the greater emphasis of the two.

Proof of this may be found in the actual histories of China and Japan. There has been a countless number of men who rose up with righteous indignation against the evil policies of government, some succeeding, some failing. But when one examines what kinds of men these revolutionaries were, without regard to the right or wrong of their motives, one will find that every one of them was a book-reading type. Rarely have there been any daredevils and crafty strategists without bookish knowledge who took over the reigns of power. But at those times when the nation was in turmoil and the people were hopefully anticipating a revolution, there was not a single instance in which a man who, inspite of being in the right position to lead a revolution, stayed back and let the world pass by. The greater a person's training in the doctrine, the more likely will he be to leap into political strife. Reading Confucian books does not keep a man from political heat; rather, it stimulates him.

Yet the youth of today are being blamed for their insolence, particularly for their political interests. The old school is endeavoring to correct these youths by means of Confucian teachings, which I consider to be the springhead of political consciousness. This is like throwing fuel on a fire when one wants to extinguish it. Those wanton advocates in the heat of their argument may have overlooked this inconsistency. They will certainly be enlightened if they would simply sit back and allow themselves some quiet introspection. Therefore, the idea to make use of only the moral portion from the Confucian literature for immediate application is simply the fantasy of unlearned men.

Installment Two

Confucian doctrine, as understood by contemporary people, is founded on four basic rules: discipline of self, management of the family, government of the nation, and the pacification of the world. Whoever seeks to be a man worthy of the name must first of all discipline himself and develop a fine personality; then with that personality, he must fulfill his family obligations and manage his family well; next he must seek good government for the nation, and, finally, endeavor to bring peace and security to the whole world. All this is clear, I must admit, and very reasonable. However, because some 70 percent of the doctrine consists of discussions on how to govern a nation and bring peace to the world, I consider that it is not proper to call Confucianism a purely moral doctrine.

I am not a specialist in Chinese studies, and I must confess I am not too intelligent, nor have I spent much time on Chinese studies. Yet, I have endeavored most carefully to understand its basic philosophy. I interpret its basic ideas on personal discipline and family obligation as moral doctrine and the teachings on government of the nation and the pacification of the world as political doctrine. Their proportion is about seven to three, and the two portions are combined as one substance. Such is Confucian doctrine, and the ideas of ancient sages, such as Chou Kung, Confucius, and Mencius, agree on this point.

In China of the Chou dynasty, there was a doctrine in four stages with the discipline of self as the first stage, the management of the family as the second stage, then the government of the nation and the pacification of the world as the last stages. There was good reason in that era for this code, and it is not fair for us to hastily dismiss it with scorn. The reason is this: In China of the Chou era, the insecurity of society had its origin always within the country and China's influence reached out toward the ends of the "world" like ripples of water. Naturally the ripples would grow fainter as they extended farther out and disappear as they approached barbarian countries untouched by civilization. Therefore, the fears never came from beyond the borders; the roots of unrest were always from within.

From the mythological, idealistic eras to the Chou dynasty, the Chinese did not fear barbarian invasions, but they knew that the solidarity of the society depended solely on the condition of the metropolitan area. If it was inhabited by good and loyal citizens who were the majority in that area, the government would be strong; if insolent and rebellious people held power among the majority, the emperor's household would suffer immediate decline. And so, the metropolitan area had to be governed more effectively than any other area.

In order to do so, the first requisite was to see that the inhabi-

[193]

tants there would discipline themselves and manage their families so that they would willingly stay in their positions in society. This was a social necessity of the times. For instance, even if they had a prime minister as illustrious as Bismarck, the present German premier, or as brave as Wellington, the British general of bygone days, if his personal behavior were questionable, he would be unfit to hold the people's respect and to govern the nation. In a way, the rulers in China of those days did not regard the nation as a nation. To them, a nation was a family, and this family had no neighbors around it. Therefore, it was natural that they did not see a clear line of demarcation between family management and national government.

The society of that era had as its central core the capital and its immediate suburbs, then surrounding it a circle of feudal fiefs closely allied to the emperor, and beyond this circle another circle of territories occupied by lesser people, and then outside of this last circle the belt of barbarians, and farther out the lands of extremely backward civilization. These were the five rankings of national territory. They were all supposed to be under the rule of the central government, but only those near the capital were important to the security of the nation while the outlying areas had less contact with the center. The two belts of barbarians in particular had very little to do with the progress of the nation, and the central government was not very concerned whether they truly belonged to it or not.

If the barbarians came to pay homage, it was customary for the central government to receive them graciously, but when they neglected to pay homage, the government would not question their insubordination, for their behavior little affected the fate of the nation. But when the people in the inner circles made an untoward movement, this was a matter that would directly affect the fate of the nation. In order to unify the inner circles, it was most expedient to have disciplined citizens and well-managed families to keep the people in order and prevent changes in society. Only when these two stages are satisfied can the nation be governed, and the nation being the center of the world, when it was well governed, its influence would extend to the barbarian areas and bring peace to the world.

As this was the priority in the policy, it would be unreasonable to consider subduing the barbarians of the outer areas before the inner territories had been pacified; such a move could very well threaten the very safety of the nation. Thus governing of the nation must come before pacification of the world; but even before that, its foundation must be solidified with the moral teaching of personal discipline and family management. In this way, the four stages of the Confucian moral doctrine, coupled with politics, was most appropriate in the ages of Chou Kung, Confucius, and Mencius. Indeed, in those days, it was a necessity, and with it, it was possible to rule the world. The reason why Chou Kung, Confucius, and Mencius adopted this doctrine wholeheartedly was because they were born in this era and their reasoning was geared to the society of that era.

There are men who belittle Confucianism and consider its doctrine of governing the nation and pacifying the world as idle talk. But during the Chou dynasty, it was a very appropriate political philosophy because it had its very simple but solid order in those four stages from morality to politics, and it must have been truly workable. And I have no objection to it in the least. However, there is one important factor which cannot be overlooked: the complete reversal of the structure of society in the present times from that in the ages of Chou Kung, Confucius, and Mencius. There is no reason to expect the theories of those days to apply in modern times.

During the Chou dynasty, the government's greatest concern was to solidify the central core of the nation, and there was really nothing to fear of the barbarians in the outer areas. The central government could very well afford to ignore the behavior of the barbarians, whether friendly or insubordinate. In contrast, today different circumstances have arisen, and our nation is obliged to hold intercourse on equal terms with foreign governments and foreign peoples. In times of peace, these relations seem to be very cordial, with much exchange of trade and transportation. Yet, behind the scene always lurks a streak of enmity, and among those rival countries there will be those with powerful armaments and evil ambitions. With such countries, there is no telling when even a trivial incident could cause them to usurp land and to confiscate the property of the inhabitants.

[195]

Therefore, in modern times, the security of a country does not depend on its central core but on its relations with foreign countries a thousand miles away. Also, because these foreign countries are not barbaric, they cannot be won over like children as Chou Kung and Shao Po did with their noble virtues. Equal relations with neighboring countries can only be maintained by the talents of a Bismarck and the bravery of a Wellington. Thus we may very well assert that the structure of modern society is the exact reverse of that in ancient times.

As the structure has changed, the method of governing society must also change accordingly. Because Chou Kung, Confucius, and Mencius were born in the ancient world, they decided to begin with personal morality and work toward pacification of the world. If it were possible to revive these ancient sages, and let them observe the circumstances of international intercourse today, they would certainly perceive that the security of a nation is not affected so much by its internal conditions as by its international relations. Then they would certainly add another article on foreign intercourse to the four stages of personal discipline, family management, national government, and world pacification. Rather, the sages would find it difficult to apply their doctrine to society without a fifth article.

Installment Three
Though there is much to be desired of my mental ability, I have tried my best to understand the true purport of Confucianism. I appreciate its system of progressing from personal discipline to national government and world peace as valuable in view of the conditions prevailing in the times of Chou Kung, Confucius, and Mencius, and I do not reject it lightly. However, what concerns me is not so much an antiquarian contemplation of how valuable it was in the Chou dynasty but the question of whether the doctrine can or cannot be applied to the world of this very year and this very month.

The new world of today has entered an era of very intense foreign relations, and the fate of a nation now depends on its ability to meet the competition of foreign countries. Will a doctrine of the Chou dynasty—when the best policy was to consolidate the center to the neglect of the outlying areas—apply to this world of turbulent vicissitudes? Foreign trade today is dozens of times more active than internal trade. Political intercourse with foreign countries is likewise many times more involved and difficult than domestic politics. On top of such intense and challenging competition in the foreign market and in foreign diplomacy, there is competition in the arts and learning. Unless we are on a constant alert and able to keep up with the times, like the adage of an inch of ease or a foot of evil, our very national security will be threatened. How should we cope with the challenges of this age? There is no telling when war may break out with a foreign country; the navy and the army must be prepared for any emergency. What kind of policy should be adopted for this military preparedness? These are the multitude of problems of the present day.

Therefore, even if Chou Kung and Confucius were to observe our world today, they would quickly perceive the impossibility of governing the present society by the old principles. And there is no doubt that they would create new principles, adding an item on foreign intercourse. This revised and enlarged version of the *Ching-shu* would probably include self-discipline, family management, national government, world pacification, plus foreign intercourse and extension of national rights. As a man, one must discipline himself and manage his family well. These are eternal moral duties for all people. I realize that national government and world pacification, too, are important concerns of our society today. But it is very doubtful that this old Confucian doctrine, whose code is founded on just the four stages, would be applicable.

Stretching the imagination, suppose this doctrine were to prevail in present Japan: our people, upon meeting a foreign visitor, would think that he had come in adoration of the virtues of this country ruled by the benevolent emperor; they would also assume that those countries under treaties of amity with our country are backward countries which come with tributes to pay homage to us. Such will be the sheer absurdity of the situation, but the ancient sages were not absurd thinkers by any means. Only when modern people examine their theories with modern minds do their theories seem absurd and the men who created them ridiculous. It was simply the misfortune of those sages that they were born 3000 years too early and that they were unaware

[197]

of the necessity of foreign relations in addition to the four stages they created. The times must be blamed, not the sages.

And yet, those scholars who today promote the preservation of the teachings of Confucius are simply convinced that a doctrine of 3000 years will be able to cope with the problems of today, in spite of the tumultuous foreign intercourse and bewildering social changes they live through. Indeed, everything that they witness is centered around this one point of foreign intercourse, and these scholars do not seem to realize the necessity of correcting the drawbacks in the old doctrine.

The Chou dynasty of Chou Kung, Confucius, and Mencius had no foreign intercourse, and circumstances required the sages to set down only the four stages of the doctrine. However, Japan of today is different in that its nationhood depends partly on foreign intercourse. Living in such a country and not sensing the need of something beyond the national government and world pacification, I must admit, is stupidity in the extreme.

Some people will still insist that because the Japanese today are lacking in morality, their morals must be corrected for times of emergency. But in their personal behavior, one must recognize that the Japanese are on the average quite disciplined. There are few criminals; the ways of Japanese swindlers are not particularly clever; bribery and such private crimes are not numerous in either official or private dealings; a sense of honor is great even among the people of lower strata, which is often a source of wonder for visiting foreigners. It might be appropriate to call Japan a moral country. Then in the public domain, the Japanese people have lived under one line of emperors since the birth of the country without a single instance of an attempt to break the line. And there shall be no such attempt in the future. Indeed, we may safely assert the solidarity of the public morality, for there is little that is wanting in Japanese morality, private or public.

Next, what about public security? There has been no instance of mutiny among the military men or among the common people. There sometimes have been some minor disturbances among the people and officials from time to time, but all in all the country has been well governed and order has been secure. The Confucian stages of self-discipline, family management, national

[198]

government, and general pacification have been fulfilled more or less to satisfaction. It is in foreign intercourse that our country still suffers: the manufacture of articles for export is insufficient, and our foreign market undeveloped; armaments for the navy and the army are insufficient; the efforts to extend national rights are not progressing satisfactorily; arts and learning are not progressing toward world competition. The whole nation is powerless.

To this sad state of the country, suppose Chou Kung, Confucius, and Mencius were to be brought back for their sound advice. Would they still hold to their old doctrine of self-discipline, family management, national government, and world pacification without alluding to the importance of foreign relations? I believe their advice would be different. And yet, the Confucian scholars of today, though they claim to have inherited the three-thousand-year-old school, do not attempt to fathom the true spirit of the sages in consideration of the changes in time and place. They simply continue reciting the old precepts and expect to apply them to the modern world. Can this be the attitude of true and faithful inheritors?

If these scholars claim to inherit the spirit of the sages who succeeded Chou Kung's line, they should seriously study foreign relations on top of the stages of national government and world pacification and thus expand on the doctrines. Such should be their duty and proof of being the true followers of the spirit of the ancient sages.

Granted that this is their duty, where would they place the new stage in the prescribed order? Before national government? After world pacification? Or, perhaps the scholars will decide that no further item is necessary besides national government and world pacification. They will then have to defend their position clearly, and state their stand as Confucianists of the present. I, being an outsider, do not have the right to dictate how the Confucian scholars should deal with this problem of foreign relations. But when they remain silent in the presence of others and yet murmur their discontent in private, I am forced to speak out and give them my advice.

In the years toward the end of the shogunate when Western studies were gaining popularity, there was a Confucian scholar named Ōhashi Totsuan who published a book entitled *Hekija Shōgen* [A Small Argument Against Evil] and viciously attacked the new ideas of the West. Aside from whether his reasoning was right or wrong, his wholehearted zeal in defending Confucianism with the free expression of his mind won my wonder and admiration. Why we do not hear any such arguments from the Confucian scholars today?

With Confucianism based on the moral principles of self-discipline and family management, and the political principles of national government and world pacification, is there not something missing for practical purposes? The Confucian scholars of profound learning must have much to say in defense of their belief and profession. I, for one, am ready to listen respectfully to their instructions.

24
Objectives of Education at Keiō Gijuku

This year again, the hot season has arrived and some of you students will be taking advantage of the month-long vacation to visit your homes. You will meet your parents and brothers and sisters and be happy to find them all in good health, and you will see old friends and exchange news of the city and the country Reunions are extremely joyous occasions in our lives.

You will certainly be talking about your life in Keiō Gijuku and your personal experiences, and your words will be heard with great interest. There is nothing extraordinary about Keiō Gijuku. What you observe and witness every morning and every evening is our school, and there is nothing to hide. However, there are certain ideals that our teaching staff always aspire to and apply in practice. I shall explain these ideals today so that you may remember them and carry them home as precious gifts.

Our school is the oldest among all the private and government schools in the country. It is a private institution and has not received an endowment since its establishment. For that reason, in all our educational activities, we have been frugal. We have always aimed at avoiding expenses and yet have sought the most useful and the most beautiful. The only reason why we offer no advanced courses in science and why we concentrate on cultural subjects[1] is to avoid expenses.

The expenses that are required for advanced physical sciences

Originally delivered to Keiō students before summer vacation. "Keiō Gijuku Shochū Kyūgyō ni Tsuki Enzetsu" (慶応義塾暑中休業につき演説), 1885. *Jijishimpō* editorial, July 31, 1885. *Fukuzawa Yukichi Zenshū*, vol. 10, pp. 353–57.
[1] Here Fukuzawa uses the word *bungaku* which implies both humanities and social sciences and for which there is no accurate translation.

are not minor: all the instruments and materials necessary in chemistry and the mechanical sciences are out of proportion to expenses required by other subjects. In this country where only a few people believe in the importance of learning, a private school cannot hope to obtain sufficient funds, and we are confined to cultural subjects, offering the sciences only at their elementary levels.

There is no difference in the importance of the sciences and cultural subjects. Those who are in the sciences, such as chemists, mechanical engineers, mining engineers, and civil engineers, work with material things, studying their theories, handling objects, and thus contributing to industry for the benefit of humankind. Scientists are obviously valuable and indispensable. However, cultural subjects must not be taken lightly.

Among the cultural subjects, to list those most necessary in our everyday lives, languages and the arts of communication come first, then history, economics, law, and commercial subjects dealing in business and trade; then at a higher level, psychology, sociology, and philosophy. There are countless subjects, some highly refined, others more practical. In short, cultural subjects pertain to the myriad aspects of human life. Therefore, for anyone who has the responsibility of managing a household or public affairs, the study of cultural subjects is indispensable.

Cultural subjects require no machinery for experimentation or any such paraphernalia. In this school, physical sciences are taught only at an elementary level, and when the students reach the level of cultural subjects, all they need are books. The expenses of learning will be minimal, and in contrast the extent of knowledge gained its application will be far-reaching. This is the actual reason for our emphasizing cultural subjects in Keiō Gijuku.

Whether one applies one's education for one's own benefit and for others depends on the person himself. Therefore, even when the subjects have been mastered, if the student is a fool, he will not benefit at all from his education. Or, at times, because of the many varieties of cultural subjects, a student will acquire only a superficial knowledge of them. Such abuse is very liable to occur in the study of cultural subjects; a long course of study will be unproductive, as if one had received no education at all.

Therefore, whoever wishes to put his knowledge to actual use must never regard any subject lightly but learn each one thorough-ly. At the same time a student must never be ignorant of the world around him; even if his body is in the school, his mind must be tuned to society, taking interest in everything—from the noble to vulgar, big to small, from extremely scholarly subjects to the most trivial incidents in life. One must always be aware of the "great school" called society outside of the classrooms, con-stantly training in this great school.

This point is where the civilized learning of the West differs from the old learnings of China and Japan, and this is where the value of civilized learning lies. If a student is able to study while learning from society, he will be prepared to serve in society or at home, in private enterprise or in an official capacity, in industry and in commerce. He will have the training to become a leader of men.

Academic activities, when they remain aloof from human affairs, will only be mental exercises, and the researcher, too, will become a playboy of society. Those inept Confucianists belong to this type. Or an example nearer at hand, even among those who pro-fess to be specialists in the new studies of civilization, there are some who shut themselves up within the small spheres of their own fields and are blind to the world beyond. Then they will be unable to use the knowledge they have gained in their specialized fields. Such scholars, at best, will be employed by other scholars who have a foothold in the actual world; or they will only shut themselves up in their own fields and their usefulness to society will not differ from professional chess players. Learning is a means for the benefit of a scholar himself, his household, and for the wider benefit to the society. One has not reached life's goal when a subject has been mastered. If a subject does not lead to benefits, it will be as if nothing had been learned at all.

According to my personal observation, Keiō Gijuku students can be divided into two types according to their backgrounds. One type comes from the former samurai families who once served in clans. These families are not very well off, and the sons hope to rise in society someday with the education they receive in the school. And the other type is the sons of wealthy families in the provinces.

For those who plan a career based solely on their own assets,

[203]

the only thing they possess will be knowledge and ability, and they have little to lose if they fail. Therefore, these men will be fearless of risks or hardships when they find a likely job, whether public or private. They will strive toward their goals without looking back once, and setbacks will not disappoint them as long as they live. These men seek many professional opportunities, whether good or bad, their prayers being only for many such occasions to arise. I can understand these honest thoughts of the young men, and I shall not discourage them by any means. Rather, I shall welcome any one of them to consult me on their trials.

However, I shall be disappointed if the sons of wealthy families become accustomed to life in Tokyo while studying in Keiō Gijuku and associating with many rough-living students. If they begin to dislike the quiet life of the countryside, and in spite of their having left home in tears three years ago, cease dreaming of the hills of home, or worse, plan to seek careers in the government and are willing to become petty officials despite their considerable property at home, then I will be extremely disappointed.

For, as I have been saying, the purpose of studying cultural subjects is to make life worthwhile in this society and to preserve the homes we live in. The daring risks of the former samurai are nothing more than for their homes and families. Their activities are quite understandable. But to bustle about with those wealthy students with a house and property already in their hands will be foolish behavior which could be described as a rich man's imitation of a poor man.

Some may claim that living in the countryside will be too restrictive. But transportation is improving daily. Today's 100 miles is closer than the 10 miles of 30 years ago. With only a little bit of energy and efficient use of transportation, there will be no difference between living in the city or in the country.

Again, there may be another argument that there is no end to learning; for serious learning, there is no place like Tokyo. But which will be more worthy for a man's life work: to study endlessly in Tokyo or to return home to establish one's own business? When we compare the levels of education and wealth in Japan with the countries in the West, Japan, of course, does not have many great scholars, but it is not by any means a country of illiterate people; we find some scholars fairly comparable with the scholars of the West. But when we compare rich people, there is little we can boast about. In all Japan, how many men are there with property over one million yen? How many with more than 50,000 or 100,000 yen? Compared with the rich world of gold in Europe and America, I regret that this "Great Japan" is a country devoid of gold.

Therefore, I say what we lack at present is not scholarship, but wealth! To work for what the country needs is the ultimate act of national service and that is where honor lies. Your returning home to the country upon your graduation from this school and engaging in your family business will lead to an accumulation of wealth on top of what you have inherited from your ancestors or a new start in acquiring wealth. Then, even if you should not be educated, your honor will be far greater than that of penniless scholars. However, in the administration of your business, unless you have knowledge and intelligence, you cannot expect to make any kind of progress in the present age. This is the reason, and the only reason, why I am encouraging you to be diligent in learning.

From this point of view, learning may be regarded merely as a means of increasing wealth. And this, again, is what we consider learning to be in this school, and this is my advice to our two types of students.

Twenty-odd years have passed since the foundation of this school, and the total number of students who have attended it is four thousand and several hundred. Among them, there are many whose careers after leaving the school are not known; but there are some men who absorbed the spirit of the school, and while braving risks and hardships, brought prosperity to their households; some have inherited their family businesses and greatly increased their wealth. Even when they did not increase the wealth, there must be many who made good use of the knowledge they acquired and successfully preserved the family property.

Among the numerous subjects in the cultural course, the present urgent need is skills in Western languages, both spoken and written, because foreign intercourse in both official and private capacities is growing more active by the day. Our school already has some teachers from England, but only one or two foreign instructors for the 400 students cannot provide satisfactory instruc-

[205]

tion by any means. Therefore, we have recently been discussing this and have plans to hire more foreign teachers. When you return to class in the autumn, you will find improvements in English instruction. This I am announcing here in passing.

25
Speech Delivered at the Inauguration of the English Law School

I am very happy and honored to be invited to this inaugural ceremony of the English Law School and celebrate this occasion with you. Indeed, there is no other word to express my sentiment at the opening of this school except "Congratulations."

The study of law as a subject of learning in Japan began only twenty years ago or less. Some law schools have already been established by the government or privately. Also, many of the schools in our country, if they are high-level schools, give courses in law even if they are not for advanced studies. And although the number of legal scholars is gradually increasing in our society, we are still unable to say that their number is plentiful. It is our wish to greatly increase their number so that there will be numerous legal scholars in the country. And so, for myself, the opening of this new school is a very happy occasion.

There are a variety of laws—French law, German law, English law, American law, and so forth. To a non-specialist like myself, there is no way to judge which of them is superior, but they all have their strengths and weaknesses. However, when taken together and averaged, all of them are efficient, as I understand. Personally, I am inclined to prefer English law. The reason is simply that since the opening of our country, the foreign language most commonly used has been English, and there is no question of its growing further in popularity. Therefore, if English law is adopted as our model, the advantages will be infinite as the English language is the most widely used foreign language. This is another

"Igirisu Hōritsu Gakkō Kaikōshiki no Enzetsu" (イギリス法律学校開校式の演説), 1885. *Jijishimpō* editorial, September 22, 1885. *Fukuzawa Yukichi Zenshū*, vol. 10, pp. 434–36.

reason for my expressing joy upon the opening of this new school.

Having thus expressed my congratulations and also my personal joy, allow me to say that the young men filling this room must be ready and eager to begin their study of law, and the faculty will be judicious and considerate in guiding students. And I am certain that you students will make good progress. But then, though the studies will advance daily, what are the prospects for your future careers? Should you expect to be appointed a judge or an official in a government department upon your graduation? I regret to say that your prospects are not realistic.

There is only a fixed number of seats for government officials, not enough to satisfy all applicants. There are already some 75,000 officials employed, a number by no means small. It is simply unthinkable to appoint more officials as students graduate from law schools in infinite numbers. One could consider becoming a lawyer, but again there is a limit as to how many lawyers society needs. The client in a lawsuit is like a sick person and the lawyer like a physician. When there are too many physicians and the sick few in proportion, the medical practice will not constitute a business.

For the present, very few officials and lawyers are needed, and the available openings will be filled by a small percentage of the legal scholars. To the question of where can the numerous legal scholars in our country be employed, I propose the following answer: The study of law should not be considered only as training for a man to become a judge in court or a lawyer to argue the rights and wrongs of a case. Law has a universal bearing on all things from big businesses in trade and industry to minor household affairs. Making contracts for business deals or selling a tract of land of only a few hundred square feet, or renting a house, or even purchasing one writing brush and one slab of inkstone—all is within the confines of the science of law. Therefore, one may regard law as an indispensable and essential discipline for a man's living. Those who study law only to prepare for a career as a judge or as a lawyer are simply ignorant of the wider uses of legal knowledge.

The same applies to medicine. The ones who study and practice it for curing patients are professional physicians, but anyone who realizes the value of his own body will have to have some medical knowledge even if he does not practice medicine for a living. To take an example near at hand, the cholera epidemic in Nagasaki is showing signs of spreading eastward. At this critical point, to declare that stemming epidemics is the concern of physicians and give no attention to personal hygiene and prevention of the disease will not be the attitude of an informed person. Hygiene and prevention are within the confines of medicine, and only those with medical knowledge are qualified to take proper measures.

Thus all people who realize the importance of their own rights must possess a general knowledge of law even if they are not judges or solicitors by profession. Those who are satisfied with superficial ideas on law are ignorant of their rights, rights that are more important than life itself and are carelessly approaching a cholera of human affairs and neglecting its prevention.

Without medical knowledge, we would not know how to describe our own illnesses. When we lack legal knowledge, we may fall victim to deceit and not know how to express our complaints. And in our society today, such mishaps due to ignorance are not rare. Physicians, judges, and lawyers often have difficulty in diagnosing exactly what the complaints are. Thus, the disadvantages of being ignorant of law are infinite, for law is indeed indispensable to human life. When you study law in this school, do not confine your dreams to a career as an official or lawyer. I pray that when you stand in the forefront of society someday, you will apply your legal knowledge to all your affairs and employ it in protecting yourselves, your households, and thus establish yourselves as respectable independent men.

I shall make one remark in closing: Study law in depth, but after you have mastered it, refrain from using it lightheartedly. In the era of samurai, those who drew their swords to kill dogs were always greenhorns who had just begun lessons in fencing. A skilled and mature samurai would not draw his sword once in his whole lifetime. Yet, if it were necessary, he would surely have cut down his opponent without error. Such was the true spirit of swordsmanship. Therefore, I advise you to follow the spirit of those swordsmen and never use your legal knowledge to cut down a dog. Do not boast of your knowledge of legal theories but when you speak you will be certain to defeat your opponent and defend your own rights and honor.

[209]

The difference between the possibility and impossibility of such an attitude depends on the depth of your learning. It is my wish that you will attain this profound level in your quest for knowledge.

26
Speech Delivered to Senior Alumni

Jijishimpō Editor's Note: The day before yesterday, the fifth, a meeting of senior alumni of Keiō Gijuku was held at Uehanrō in Mukōjima, Tokyo. Fukuzawa Sensei and his son were invited as guests, and Sensei gave a speech. In place of today's editorial, we are printing the gist of the speech, summarized from notes.

Looking into the beginnings of Western studies in our country, there is a remarkable account in the Hōei era of Arai Hakuseki's meeting with a man from Rome and his questioning the foreign guest about the geography and customs of foreign lands. That was in the year 1709 of the Western calendar. But a serious attempt by Japanese scholars at reading Western literature and translating it into our language did not begin until the 8th year of Meiwa [1771] when Maeno Ryōtaku, Sugita Gempaku, Katsuragawa Hoshū, Nakagawa Jun'an, and others met on March 5 at venerable Maeno's home on the estate of the Okudaira Clan in the area then called Teppōzu in Edo.

On that day, these men began their joint efforts to read a Dutch anatomy book titled *Ontleedkundige Tafelen*. This marks the beginning of an epoch of Western studies in Japan. That was 119 years ago. And the location of Maeno's home is across the canal

"Issaku Itsuka Uehanrō ni Hirakishi Keiō Gijuku Kyūyūkai ni okeru Fukuzawa Sensei Enzetsu no Hikki" (一昨五日植半楼に開きし慶応義塾旧友会に於ける福沢先生演説の筆記), 1889. *Jijishimpō* editorial, May 7, 1889. *Fukuzawa Yukichi Zenshū*, vol. 12, pp. 130–34.

from the area now called Tsukiji where the American Legation stands today. This is the birthplace of Western studies and the birthday is March 5, 119 years ago this year.

By coincidence, the place where we took up Western studies 30 years ago was also on the same estate of the Okudaira Clan. How strange that we chose the same place and same subject of study as our predecessors!

Our meeting today is to reminisce of the days past when our colleagues first studied in Teppōzu, then moved to Shinsenza in Shiba, up to the time of our move away from Shinsenza—which will mean between 20 and 30 years ago—those 10 years will be the subject of my speech. There will be many things that some of you know and I do not, also joys and worries that I alone experienced and you did not know.

Now, to reveal those memories usually unspoken: I recall that when I had just opened the school in the clan estate in Teppōzu, times were such that everybody simply hated things foreign. Our fellow clansmen living on the same estate also openly disapproved of our studies. For them, Chinese was the only subject worthy of attention. But we deliberately ignored Chinese, though we were well versed in it. We concentrated on Western culture first and foremost. Relations with our fellow clansmen grew bitter, which was natural, and there seemed no way to come to terms with them.

Even the children living on the estate would sing a rhyme with their games: "The Dutch school is fearful, the Dutch school is horrid! Big demons and small goblins are roaming inside!" Every day they would parade through the estate singing this at the top of their lungs. You will no doubt also recall this scene. Such were the times, lasting several years until the Imperial Restoration.

Antiforeign propaganda was rampant throughout the country, and we Western scholars constantly feared physical assaults or assassinations. Today this sounds like a curious tale, and it might even amuse some listeners. However, in those days the fear that filled us was something that defies description.

As scholars, the only way we could protect ourselves was by our swords. I even started fencing practice again, a martial art that I had learned in my youth. At night, in the dark, I secretly practiced my strokes, and I was ready to battle with anyone who might confront me. Those were depressing days indeed.

When our school was established, Dutch studies was naturally the subject taught, but after the opening of Yokohama port and the increase in contact with foreigners, we realized that Dutch alone would not fill the demand of the times. Consequently, we abandoned our Dutch studies entirely and switched to English studies.

The general trend in Western studies in our country at that point had been confined to the importation of technology. Beginning with medicine, there were military techniques along with the art of fortress building, casting cannons, shipbuilding, and training of soldiers. These subjects drew much attention from the general public. However, our group went a step further and included human and social studies in its curriculum. This was like building castles in the air, but our colleagues believed in it, and we all joined forces to work toward this common goal.

Because our goal was not confined to technology only, we planned to read the histories of Western countries. Also, we looked for books on politics and administration, and our efforts were rewarded with a book on world history published in the United States and also one on political economy.

The world history text was similar to history books in Japanese and Chinese, but the volume on political economy was interesting indeed. The fine points of its discussion often went beyond our usual reasoning, enough to challenge the old Chinese philosophy which had been the pillar of our minds. In considering the title of the translation of the book, after some deliberation we decided on *Keizairon*, although we were not entirely satisfied with it. And this was the beginning of the study of Western economics in our country.

If there are studies in economics in the West, there must also be ethics, counterparts to the *Lun-yü*, the Analects of Confucius, and *Ta-hsüeh*. While we were wondering about and discussing this, Obata Tokujirō found an old English book entitled *Moral Science* in a bookstore. We read it and discovered that it was indeed a discussion of ethics. We were delighted and ordered a number of copies from the United States. This was Wayland's *Moral Science*, which we translated as *Shūshinron*.

[213]

In our school, we had been studying a book on economics. We then acquired one on ethics, and another on law was to be added soon.[1] These findings were like obtaining proof of the learning which we had believed in, and now we felt that there was nothing in the nation to fear. Even if all the scholars of the old school in the whole of Japan should challenge us, we felt ready to confront and overcome them.

We were confident and we advanced straight toward our goal, but meanwhile the antiforeign movement had grown stronger. Finally, the wars and turmoils of the Restoration began. There was not a single person who could sit peacefully and read books. The great school of the shogunate, Kaisei Gakkō, too, was closed and its premises abandoned like a haunted lot. Western scholars in Edo, too, dispersed, their whereabouts unknown. For a period of about two years, Western studies came to a halt.

At that time, however, our school alone continued classes undisturbed. While the Imperial army was marching toward Edo and battles were being fought far and near, in the countryside and within the city, we built the schoolhouse, continued reading and discussing books, and we did not cease our studies for even a day. Our behavior under such circumstances may appear pretentious. But it was a natural expression of the seriousness with which we approached the new studies. It is thus an honor due to our school that it successfully assured the continuity of Western studies in our country without a single break for 119 years. And this honor is due those who are gathered together here tonight. Certainly no one in the country can argue this fact.

Holland lost all its territory during the wars of Napoleon I— both its homeland and overseas possessions. But there remained one place on the face of the earth where the flag of Holland waved proudly, proving that Holland still existed. And that was the Dutch concession of Dejima in Nagasaki. The Dutch remember this fact in history to this day. Keiō Gijuku is very much the Dejima of Western studies, an isolated island that persisted and survived external pressures.

[1]Fukuzawa gives the impression that he had obtained the books on economics, ethics, and law before the Restoration, but economics was the only Western subject he was acquainted with at the time. On the very day of the battle at Ueno, he was lecturing on Wayland's *The Elements of Political Economy*. *Moral Science* was acquired about two years later.

[214]

Two or three years after the Restoration, the disturbances in society subsided, and some schools of Western studies under private sponsorship were established in the city. The government also came to realize the importance of education and opened Tōkō and Nankō.[2] Later, the Ministry of Education was established, and it continues its activities to this day. A good number of men from our school were recruited at the establishment of the ministry. This is evidence of the important contributions private schools have made to government institutions.

Moral uprightness and informality in behavior are characteristics of our school atmosphere that have lasted since your time to the present. Looking back at the situation then, I now realize that in the beginning, we were promoting Western learning in the face of opposition from the old school, which comprised the whole of society. We naturally did away with old customs and preferred simplicity and convenience in all matters concerning our daily lives and social etiquette. Our attempts to free ourselves from the restrictions of others was a natural reaction of our basic stand. Moral behavior is determined by one's inborn nature and childhood influences, but in our case, it was partly out of the necessity of self-defense. When we promoted foreign and new ideas and lost public sympathy in the process, we would have certainly invited scorn if we had been irresponsible in our private behavior. Therefore, we took great care and tried to prove by our behavior that Western learning was a learning of honorable men, that Western scholars were respectable gentlemen.

We were prepared to say, "All members of the old school— whether Confucian or Buddhist or Christian, without regard to their doctrines—if you find the behavior of anyone in our group questionable, whether private or public behavior, do not hesitate to challenge us; we are ready with answers or counterarguments to defend our colleagues." It was as if we had formed a formal defense in preparation for an imminent attack. This, again, was a consequence of those hostile times.

What I have touched on thus far belongs to the past. Things have changed and time has passed since. And in these twenty years, education in this country has advanced to a much higher

---

[2] These schools together grew into the present University of Tokyo.

level, and our school is not the Keiō Gijuku it was. The progress that has been made is surprising indeed. But when we turn our eyes toward society in general, we still see that the moral behavior of some men has not improved along with the elevation of learning and many more changes are needed.

The gentlemen who are present today are no longer students. You are people occupying leading positions in society, and I am already quite old. In seeking improvement of moral behavior, let us not forget the spirit that has lasted 30 years since the beginning of our school. Even if we at times lose favor with the public, let it not hinder us. Let us be firm in our convictions, and in the end the whole society will join us in the way of civilization. We will all be thus blessed by the happiness heaven has prepared for us. Such is the ardent hope that I hold in my heart.

27
Do Not Lose Yourself
in Learning

Keiō Gijuku began as a school of general education
with special emphasis on Western languages and civilization. It soon came to be regarded as a superior
institution of learning, second only to the Imperial
University, which was then the only institution in
Japan worthy of being called a university. However,
the Imperial University's faculty at that time was made
up largely of foreign scholars.

In organizing the first private university in Japan,
Fukuzawa had the good fortune of having the cooperation of Arthur May Knapp, a scholar and missionary of the Unitarian Church, who was an alumnus of
Harvard University and close friend of Harvard President Charles W. Eliot. Fukuzawa asked Knapp to take
full responsibility in recruiting three professors from
the United States on an annual budget of 6600 yen. A
group of fine scholars chosen by President Eliot, including John Henry Wigmore, still very young at that
time, was thus hired by Keiō. Materials concerning
this aspect of Keiō's history have been found in
Harvard University's archives. (See *Birth of the University
Section in Keiō Gijuku*.)

Originally delivered at the inauguration of university departments in Keiō Gijuku.
"Gakumon ni Koru Nakare" (学問にこる勿れ), 1890. *Jijishimpō* editorial, January 30,
1890. *Fukuzawa Yukichi Zenshū*, vol. 12, pp. 361–63.

Our Keiō Gijuku is the oldest among all the public and private schools in Japan, and more than 30 years have passed since its inauguration. We are proud that classes were not interrupted for even a single day. During the battles preceding the Restoration, we were fortunate enough to escape destruction, and after the battles, our colleagues were able to demonstrate to the new Japan the proper direction of learning for the coming civilization and thus enlighten the people. Though all this was partly due to the times and fortunate circumstances, we are proud of our fine record, a claim that no outsider can contest.

Our beginning was brilliant, and we must continue to strive for the improvement of education and demonstrate to our people what direction should be taken to enjoy civilization. This is our duty in learning. All this has led to the opening of the university departments, which I hereby proclaim.

Through the generous donations of supporters, the university's financial base has been secured. Also, by the kind intercession of Mr. Knapp,[1] three fine teachers have been invited from America. For the Literature Department Professor Liscomb,[2] for the Economics Department Professor Droppers,[3] and for the Law Department Professor Wigmore[4]—these professors are to be the chairmen of their respective departments. For the instruction of Latin, Mr. Lloyd, who has been with us for many years, has accepted the duty.[5] The management of the whole school will be the responsibility of Obata Tokujirō, assisted by Hamano Sadashirō, Kadono Ikunoshin, and Masuda Eiji. Also, for the instruction of Japanese law, we have Messrs. Motoda Hajime and Sawada Shunzō in our service. Thus the faculty is ready, and I am delighted to attend the inauguration ceremony.

By nature I deeply enjoy learning, and my only happiness may be said to be learning. Despite this, I try not to place too much

[1] Arthur May Knapp (1844–1921). An American missionary who introduced Unitarianism to Japan in 1887. Author of *Feudal and Modern Japan* (Boston: L. C. Page & Co., 1897), 2 vols.
[2] William S. Liscomb. A Brown University graduate, extremely popular at Keiō.
[3] Garrett Droppers (1860–1927). A graduate of Harvard, taught at Keiō for nine years.
[4] John Henry Wigmore (1863–1943). A Harvard graduate, he became interested in the old laws of Japan in the three years he was at Keiō University, and returned to study in 1935.
[5] Arthur Lloyd. A missionary-scholar, graduate of St. Peter's College, England, who began teaching English at Keiō Gijuku in 1885.

emphasis on it. I regard learning as only one of the skills which we should acquire in our lives. If one acquires knowledge but learns nothing about human society, he is comparable to those eccentric chess players or poets. They may be gifted in their own fields, but they are by no means respectable people. I take every opportunity available to express this idea.

We are very fortunate among our group that the odd and eccentric scholar is rare, and we are proud of the large number of men prepared for any challenge. Their contributions are conspicuous in today's society; their application of their learning for practical uses in human life gives me an endless source of satisfaction.

From my point of view, of all the causes of misfortunes in human life, there is nothing more pathetic than lack of knowledge and lack of reasoning power. From the upper class of men, such as political leaders, men of wealth, and masters of great households, down to the lower classes, workers, and petti-officials, there are too many instances of people who lack education or the ability to make use of it. Their ignorance is not only their loss but it is to the disadvantage of the whole society as well. There are men who discuss their theories on the problems of the nation and the world or trade policies and profits and losses in the millions; yet when it comes to choosing the proper medical treatment for someone in the family, they betray their lack of common sense. They boast about the mysterious strengths of a patent medicine or supernatural powers of some deities, only to lose a family member prematurely, sinking into great sorrow as a result.

Such an instance may be passed over as a private family matter, but suppose such men extend their influence to the public domain or discuss law without knowing the law, supervise finances without a knowledge of economics, make decisions on education without having received an education, or start a business with only a cursory knowledge of trade practices. Even if such men should be successful with their limited experience, their success will be sheer luck, like hitting a target by accident. The dangers placed on society by such individuals will be like prescribing a patent medicine with no knowledge of physiology or pathology. The risks are beyond measure.

This danger is not confined to upper-class people. Lower-class

[219]

people, too, if they believe in superstition, will not be able to run profitable businesses. When they believe in divination, the magic of directions, or incantations, they are liable to bring disaster to their own family. If carpenters, masons, and such workers have no knowledge of physics and mechanical laws, they are liable to waste much labor; or, even worse, with a faulty calculation they could topple a whole building or for their ignorance of the transfer of heat could cause a fire. Take the stove in this room as an example near at hand: if an inexperienced workman installs its smoke pipe improperly, the heat from the pipe may transmit itself to the wooden pillar, causing the whole schoolhouse to burn down. And the disaster may not be confined to this school. Should the mishap occur on a night when the south wind is blowing strong, the fire may spread to Tokyo and the extent of damage it could cause would be immeasurable. It would be the doings of an ignoramus turning the whole city into ashes.

All these examples demonstrate misfortunes caused by ignorance. And the one and only way to correct it is education. Therefore, when I say that too much emphasis should not be placed on learning, I do not mean that it is useless. On the contrary, it is a necessity, a very important necessity in life. What I mean is that one must not see it as the only meaning to life and absorb oneself totally in its study to the neglect of life around us.

The new students entering our university, about 60 altogether, are healthy and vigorous young men with alert minds. When they graduate after a few years, they will apply their acquired knowledge to actual life situations, to their own benefit and at the same time contribute to the advancement of society and the whole nation. Their success will not only lift the reputation of their intellectual home—that is, this school—but they will regard themselves as sponsors of the school, rather than dependents thereof. This is what I ardently pray for.

Among these 60 students, there will be differences in their abilities, and due to an unexpected event, some may temporarily have to absent themselves from school. But with strong and healthy bodies, they can persevere and accomplish their goals. Therefore, first care for the body before seeking knowledge and care for the health according to the dictates of science.

My advice against total absorption in learning applies to your studies in this university also. The learning you acquire in university is a skill, after all. When you study and acquire an education, do not display your knowledge. And when you enter society, engage in business with vigor, associate with the masses and participate in their business. When you deal with these commoners, let them learn from your cultured ways and thus spread the influence of our learning.

The heroes of the past resorted to military power to extend their political influence. But we comrades in learning will use culture to lead the people. With the influence of culture, let all people share in the glory of civilization. This is the great field of your future. My aging soul will be praying for the vigor and health of both your bodies and minds. Never surrender to the many hardships you will meet.

28
When Educational
Policy Changes

The government has committed many blunders since 1881,[1] and those in its educational policy are among the most serious ones. A political error will have far-reaching influence. But once the administration becomes aware of and corrects it, the result will be like a stain on a mirror: wiped off easily and permanently. In the case of education, the matter is far more serious. Very much like opium, it will permeate deep into the body and will take many months or years before its effects are felt. Therefore, when the victim senses the effect and ceases his opium habit, it will be months or years again before he can actually feel an improvement. This is where an administrator must give special attention. The present government leaders ten years ago carelessly made a serious mistake in educational policy. They now see its effects before their very eyes. Yet, they do not seem prepared to correct it. Whether they are insensitive to their mistake or whether they want to correct it but do not know how, whichever the case may be, they cannot shirk their responsibility.

Since 1881, for some unknown reason the government made drastic changes in its educational policy. It revived the old school of thought which had been set back with some difficulty. Outmoded scholars of old Japan were recalled to teach in schools,

---

"Kyōiku no Hōshin Henka no Kekka" (教育の方針変化の結果), 1892. *Jijishimpō* editorial, November 30, 1892. *Fukuzawa Yukichi Zenshū*, vol. 13, pp. 575–77.
[1] In 1881, Ōkuma Shigenobu and his group of liberal and progressive men were ousted from government, and Itō Hirobumi took power. To reassure his opponents and the people in general, he announced that a constitution would be promulgated by 1889 and the Diet established in the following year. Also, as a means to control the people till then, Confucian teaching was encouraged.

and new ethics books were compiled as textbooks, and in extreme cases, Western-language courses were discontinued. The policy of bringing back the old moral education confined general education into a narrow, useless moral education: loyalty to one's lord, obedience to one's parents, and extreme patriotism. Furthermore, funds were provided to establish newspapers and to hold public lectures. The government did its best to hinder the progress of civilization. Some people must still remember these unpleasant policy changes of a few years ago.

Instilling loyalty, filial piety, and patriotism is not by any means objectionable. In making a home and in conducting oneself in society, one must follow proper rules as a man and as a citizen. Also, toward one's country, one must fulfill one's duty as a subject. These are acts of the patriotism which I expect of every citizen. And yet, this beautiful spirit can cause great harm when loyalty and filial piety are interpreted in their narrow senses as the old school leaders do. A man is labeled disloyal if he does not act according to traditional rules; in his conduct toward the country, he will be called a traitor if he does not follow the traditional way. This kind of reasoning can do great harm to one's sense of loyalty and patriotism.

Before the Restoration, members of the Mito Clan split into two rival factions, resulting in bitter feuds and assassinations. The split was caused by disagreement over the interpretation of patriotic and traitorous ideas, with no room for tolerance or coexistence. This should be noted as an example of extremism and intolerance.

My mentioning this example may sound ungracious, but it is clearly true that the number of men convicted of lese majesty has increased since the 1881 incident, which I personally suspect is attributable to the prevalence of extremism in our society. Having foreseen the outcome, I, along with others who shared my fears, warned that the ill effects of bad education could not be cured like those of alcohol. Alcohol shows its effects at once, but intoxication from education will not show for a long time, which means that the poison first permeates the body and, after some years, when it shows its effects does so prominently. This is the advice I often wrote in this *Jijishimpō*, and I am sure many people who read the paper will remember it. I suspect that the govern-

[224]

ment officials either failed to read it or they read it but did not understand its implications. They have let ten years pass without taking any effective measures, and thus our worst fears have come true and we now have a most regrettable state of affairs.

Anyone observing recent trends in society will note that the old-school advocates have become louder and more intolerant; they are accusing all those who oppose their own ideas as being rebels and enemies of the nation. They are seeking or rather endeavoring to make enemies where there are none, and the extremists seem to be returning to the spirit of 30 years ago [before the Restoration], reviving the anti-Western spirit that regarded all foreigners with enmity for no reason. This trend has manifested itself in real incidents, and they are disrupting the peace. Things having come this far, the officials in truth must be troubled with the question of how to deal with the situation. At times I even feel a private sense of pity for them.

The above statements will probably be criticized as mere conjecture with no tangible evidence. But I offer the following proof. Examine newspapers from before and after 1881 and 1882 and compare the wording in the papers of the two periods. One will find a good deal of strong expressions in the papers before those years, but the ideas in themselves are not extreme and few of them would offend us. However, in many of the papers published after those years, the use of words such as rebel, traitor, foreign barbarian, and beast are frequent, evidence of the old-school advocates complaining when there is no disease to torment them. And this change in the writing style of the papers before and after 1881 and 1882 is an indication of the sudden change in society. A newspaper is a leader and creator of social atmosphere, but at the same time it represents the social atmosphere as well. The government in a similar manner stands in a position to lead the minds of the people and represent them as well. Today's newspaper reporters are by no means influenced by the old school's obsessions. Indeed, many of them denounce it, but as members of society, they are obliged at times to change their own style along with current trends.

If all the cases I have listed above are true, it must be admitted that the negative effects of the change made ten years ago in the educational policy are gradually being felt and today are reaching

[225]

their peak. Therefore, even if a policy change is implemented today, it will be many months and years before any signs of recovery appear. There is nothing one can do about this as the matter depends upon the natural cycle of things, which no force can alter.

The men who organized the movement ten years ago and those who approved it and took part in it are still alive and holding high and powerful positions in the government. They must admit that there is now no way for them to escape their responsibility. They must reform their ways and do their best to correct their failures for the sake of the nation and the generations to follow.

29
Speech Delivered at
the Unveiling of His Statue

Jijishimpō Editor's Note: The following article is summarized from Fukuzawa Sensei's speech given at the
unveiling of his bronze statue on the campus of Keiō
Gijuku in Mita, Tokyo, on October 29. Although the
speech was given at a private school occasion, it
discusses moral affairs of society at large, and we have
decided to print it today in place of an editorial.

Today, I was graciously invited to attend the unveiling of the
bronze statue of my old self. The story of how this statue came to
be has been told in the speeches by Mr. Obata and Mr. Ōkuma.[1]
The efforts of Mr. Ōkuma in the past three years are beyond
description. How many times has the statue been made and
remade! There was infinite toil and disappointment. Particularly,
the model, this old man Fukuzawa, was often wayward: absent-
ing himself from modeling sessions and wasting the artist's time!
Still, we see the beautiful completion before us today. The reason
for all this I must attribute to Mr. Ōkuma's ardor in sculpturing
and his devotion to Keiō Gijuku. There are no adequate words to
thank him.

Now, at this splendid completion of the statue, to confess my

"Dōzō Kaihi ni Tsuite" (銅像開被について), 1893. *Jijishimpō* editorial, November 1,
1893. *Fukuzawa Yukichi Zenshū*, vol. 14, pp. 179–83.
[1] Ōkuma Ujihiro, recognized as the best sculptor in Japan at that time The statue is
a seated, life-size bronze, very minutely sculptured. People who knew Fukuzawa well
said it strongly resembled its model from the back but that the face showed no resem-
blance at all. The statue now stands in Keiō Gijuku Shiki High School.

honest feelings about it, I am naturally of a very boorish makeup, and I seldom give attention to my physical appearance. For instance, I care little about my reputation in the society or my fame after a century and other such things that some people in the world consider important. I seldom stop to think whether my lineage is high or low, or what people will think of me after my passing. And so, the bronze statue or any such copy of my likeness has been the farthest thing from my thoughts. It is something that would have never occurred to me.

This nature of mine, I believe, is well known to you all. Before the statue was commissioned, I said that it would be a sheer waste; if there was such money, it would better be used for the upkeep of this poor school. I said as much to Mr. Obata and others. And yet, all the school members were set on it, in spite of their knowing my disposition, and somehow today's celebration was brought about.

When I sit back and consider all this, I begin to see that my friends' wish to commission this statue was not exactly to duplicate my features; it was to leave a monument for Keiō Gijuku. Suppose you plant a pine tree in the year of a child's birth; the tree will remain a monument for the person while he is alive and also after his death. In the same way, because this school was begun on my initiative, my statue represents the school. And so, my friends must have commissioned the statue in place of a pine tree, so to speak. There will be no objection in saying that this bronze statue is Keiō Gijuku itself.

On this occasion I would like to tell you what pleases me most; 35 years have passed already since our school's founding; the number of students who have passed through its doors totals almost 10,000. It is the oldest and the largest of all the private schools in the country. It started as a poor private school with no property. It has managed to make ends meet from year to year without ever feeling secure.

We were very fortunate several years ago to have the Iji Shachū [Supporters' Association] established. Then, at the inauguration of our university departments, there was a very generous donation from the Ministry of the Imperial Household. Also, there were donations from other sources, and to this day we have managed to keep up the appearance of a school, and actually we have con-

[228]

tributed substantial results to education. Despite this record, we are still uncertain of the school's future. In short, we depend on outside aid from year to year. Therefore, when our existence is forgotten by those outside, that will spell our doom, and we and our 35 years of education will turn to naught.

I am 60 years old this year. The school has been run much like a Buddhist temple; that is, its finances have long been independent with no personal accounts involved.[2] The head priest for the present is Obata, and I am the old retired priest. But my involvement with the temple is so deep that I cannot detach myself from it. Suppose I am carried away from the convolution of this inconstant world and cease to live; I will leave children and grandchildren behind, and they will continue the Fukuzawa house, but they will not be able to contribute much to the continuation of the temple, that is, the school. This is the one torment that refuses to leave my mind.

My dear colleagues, this bronze memorial statue is proof of your lasting goodwill toward this school. This statue belongs to you alone, and it can never be owned by anyone else. Even if you should want to sell it, a buyer would be hard to find; even if you want to give it away, no one would want it. It should be preserved in Keiō Gijuku as a memorial. And as long as the statue exists, the school must also exist. My wish is for Keiō Gijuku to enjoy a long life with this bronze statue, and then I can die in peace when time comes for me to pass away.

I deeply appreciate your generosity and I congratulate the school for its good fortune in having such benefactors. When I address you in this way, it may sound as if the statue has brought the burden of the responsibility on you to continue the school. However, it will not be difficult to keep the school active. Its finances are not affluent by any means, but it owns property: it possesses a large school campus which I take pride in as the best and incomparable within the city of Tokyo, with an extensive area of more than 14,000 *tsubo* [404,000 sq. ft.]. Today it is worth about 200,000 yen.

---

[2] Up to this time, temples were the only institutions that stood as independent corporations with financial accounts of their own. The head priests would change, but the temples continued. In contrast, schools were always private enterprises run by scholars. Classes were usually held at a scholar's residence.

[229]

I am registered as the owner of the property, but I promised long ago to donate it to the school, and I never had any intention of personally owning it.[3] This property may be considered the school's first endowment, worth 200,000 yen. It can easily be sold and transformed into other forms of property. There also are buildings on the campus, several thousand *tsubo* in floor space. And the school owns many books and instruments. Furthermore, the funds donated by benefactors are substantial, though they are used up every year. There is still some 60,000 yen in our account today.

This school is poor if you regard it as poor, but it is not so impoverished as to have to scrape through from day to day. My concern is only that there is no real security for the future. If many people would join forces, this school should not be too difficult to carry on, for the foundations have been laid, and the work will rather be like filling in the gaps of what is already there. Your efforts will be rewarded greatly in proportion to the input you make. I trust in your goodwill for the future fortunes of this school.

When you gentlemen sit back and examine the general conditions of our society, you will easily see where the thoughts of the present-day people stand. The strong influence of foreign contact has overturned our social values and organization, and the people now have lost their bearings. They have not found a new set of values to replace what they have discarded. If they refrain from rushing forward blindly, they will have to either revert to their old ways or grope about aimlessly. Their actions will be either too free or erratic, with hardly an instance of truly responsible behavior.

The behavior and statements of social critics, the personal conduct and social etiquette of gentlemen, religious admonitions, or government orders—when these are examined carefully, we find they are not worthy to stand as exemplary models for the general populace to respect and follow. If there is no rule or model to follow, how will the people know what not to do or what not to say? The same goes for those who make hasty decisions, rushing

[3] The law to recognize a school as a corporation with the right to own property had not been passed, and it was necessary for a representative to act as the owner.

to extremes when the opportunity looks promising or taking some advice that only places the nation in jeopardy. With such light-footed people, it is impossible to preserve moral order. People today are so flippant and insecure, as light as dust with no weight to hold them down, that they could be blown away at a breath or charred by a flame. Even if they are rich and noble, they do not have the power of the rich or the dignity of a noble; even the poor are not pitiful and lowly, for both the rich and poor or noble and lowly are equal in being born by chance, living but a while, and dying. It is a pity not only because people have not understood the great doctrine of independence and self-government; it places us in the quandary of how to preserve the independence of the country. The responsibility is too great for such people to bear. It is like forcing a spineless animal to carry a heavy load. The mere thought of the present state of affairs leaves me in fear.

Keiō Gijuku is a school of learning, but the objective of our members is not confined to the study and analysis of books. We attach great importance to their personal independence, that of their households, and of the nation. They do not rashly involve themselves in political talk, but they maintain an interest in the administration of the nation and the morality of society. Our attitude is not by any means accidental. When you contribute to the continuation of this school, the school itself will become a model for people to look up to, and thus guide their activities and serve as the moral center of the whole of society. Our ideal will be of no comparison to the world of those small and big politicians of today acting nervously within the confines of the law with no long-range plans for progress of the society. They struggle within their confined world of politics, their interests and honor or shame as uncertain as drifting clouds. Even the religious sects who associate only with low-down commoners with no chance of ever expanding their sphere of activity will be of no comparison to our school.

In short, our objective is to find our sphere of thought and activity outside the world of law and politics. We shall obey the dictates of the law and government, never asking much of our fellow men. But we will secure the roots of our own independence and self-help, and, with the upper and middle classes of society, stand firm as the backbone of the nation. Our school is small, but its responsibility is great. Within this whole nation, there is no school besides Keiō Gijuku that carries such a responsibility. Whether the school can bear such a weight or not will depend upon the efforts and spirit of the friends of the school.

30
Speech Delivered
at His
Sixtieth Birthday Celebration

Fukuzawa's sixtieth birthday was actually in 1894, when Japan was in the midst of the Sino-Japanese War, the first major war that the country fought, and the festivities were postponed until after the war. The following is his speech at the celebration given by the entire student body of Keiō Gijuku.

The wonderful cele bration held for my sixtieth birthday—the happy gathering and all the kind wishes you offered me—all overflowed with your affection. I can only say thank you to express my feelings.

Normally, congratulating a long life implies a good life full of happiness, and I am not sure whether I deserve such felicitations. I have to confess that my life has had its share of good fortune and happiness, not of my own making but a sort of gift of the times which I gladly received. The health I have enjoyed and the security of my family are not uncommon today or in the past.

However, the tremendous changes in society and the great advancement of civilization in the past 40 years from my youth to this old age have been a veritable drama. And the fact that I was privileged to witness and also to have participated in the direction of the drama from the backstage, and that I have been

"Kanreki Juen no Enzetsu" (還暦寿莚の演説), 1895. *Jijishimpō* editorial, December 14, 1895. *Fukuzawa Yukichi Zenshū*, vol. 15, pp. 333–37.

fortunate to have a full house and applause from the nation—all this must be something no one in history could have ever dreamed of. Even people who are middle aged today have been able to observe only half of the drama. It is the special privilege reserved only to those around 60 to have enjoyed the whole from the introduction—the first act—through the 40 years. I am proud to have witnessed the drama.

Now to address the question of what part I played in this drama: the answer is that I simply expressed my ideas and made myself heard. In plain language, my contribution was only tall talk. That was 30 or 40 years ago when I was 20 or 30 years old. At the time Japan was a feudal country governed by 270 clan lords. Learning was dominated by Confucianism. In military science, several schools of martial arts vied for supremacy. The samurai, who took pride in their accomplishments in both martial arts and learning, served the lords and received stipends according to their inherited ranks. The rigid class system was even more sacred than the present constitution is to us. And the nation strictly observed a policy of isolationism and the exclusion of foreign influence.

We Western scholars were regarded as a gang of outlaws, but our determination was simply indomitable. In our private discussions we would boast: "Bows and arrows are no longer of any use; they would be better burned as fuel. The scarlet corded armor serves only as display, and the helmet fashioned by the famed Myōchin would be better turned into a flower vase. The shell-horns and the drums of the Kōetsu school of martial arts are too ludicrous to listen to; who do those generals want to lead with their duster-shaped batons? And who do they think they can cut down with the swords of the celebrated Masamune?"

I in fact brought out my ancestral swords—I had three sets—and, deciding they were of no use any more, sold them to a sword dealer, Tanaka Jūbei of Hikagechō in Shiba. That was in the Bunkyū era [1861–64] when the expel-the-foreigners movement was rampant and old swords were at the height of their vogue.

Our criticism of martial arts being as it was, we derided the old school of literature in the same way. Because the Chinese scholars were always discussing the square-looking characters and studying

[234]

the Chinese philosophy and history books with blue covers, we likened their studies to repetitious chanting of the Amida Sutra by Buddhist priests—nothing to them. As long as they were not contributing anything to *jitsugaku*, Confucian studies should be discarded along with Chinese writing.

[Western scholars in those days mockingly called Chinese scholars *kotatsu yagura* (footwarmer frame). This came from the Chinese characters which were square and looked like the frame of a charcoal brazier for foot warming. This was an extreme form of abuse. Collision of the new and the old was inevitable. It was partly of our own making that we Western scholars found ourselves often in physical danger during the years of national isolation, and we should not blame anyone.]

Our discontent was also directed toward the government, dominated by a hereditary system which dated back 300 years. The higher members of society, from the clan lords to the chancellors and the high officials under them, were all incompetent men, devoid of wisdom or courage, in contrast to their ancestors who had won their positions with courage and ability. We Western scholars were only interested in the abilities of men, not in meaningless pedigree and social ranks. We advised those dissatisfied with clan politics to leave their clans, for that would be a truly manly act. I secretly instigated such moves and helped some actually carry out their wishes.

Now to address the question of what were the real objectives of the vehement Western scholars: I must confess that we had no clear plans or even confidence of success. But we had read Western books and actually seen the material results, and also perceived the wealth and strength of Western countries; we contemplated over these and reached the conclusion that from both theoretical considerations and from actuality, adopting Western ways was the only way to enable our nation to preserve its independence. We gave a new name, *bummei kaika* [civilization], to these new ways, and we challenged all other ways which opposed civilization, regardless of their nature or importance, all to be swept clean from our society.

What impression did our reckless attitude give to honest citizens of those days? They must have thought we were raving drunkards who broke into the fairyland of Buryō's peach orchard,[1] or scholars turned ruffians calling for nonsensical changes. For instance, our theory on economics was that every man should earn his own living with the sweat of his brow, which is the law of nature. But here in Japan, how were the samurai with the hereditary stipends living? For the simple reason that their ancestors 300 years ago had performed some heroic deed on the battlefield, the descendants even to that day were receiving stipends to the amount of some hundred or thousand *koku* of rice per year! Is the price of one day's sweat worth 300 years of such stipends? The rest of the world would not regard this as a just reward!

As for the advantages of modern machinery, we called the people slow and as mindless as crawling worms, for they would trudge the 300 miles of the Tōkaidō highway from Edo to Osaka in fourteen or fifteen days. If the Ōi river was flooded, it would take seven or eight more days.[2] The Japanese were veritable worms. In civilized countries, there were railways. If only this railway was built, one could leave Edo in the morning, have lunch in Hamamatsu or Nagoya, and toward the evening reach Osaka. But such statements were not taken seriously and were considered the usual lofty dreams of scholars. And even among us scholars at that time, no one was thoroughly convinced that these dreams would ever be realized. It was, after all, idle talk for self-satisfaction with little further purpose.

The general condition 30 or 40 years ago was as I have described. And even the scholars themselves were quite unprepared for the various historical events and confusion that brought about the Imperial Restoration. The minds of all the people, high and low, without exception, were confused by the bewildering changes, as was the government itself, which switched from an extreme isolationism to an open-door policy. But our dreams, tall talk, and boasting were realized. The actual realization went beyond our earlier expectations, and even the scholars themselves were put to shame for not having boasted enough. Such was the happy turn of events, which has brought the civilization we enjoy today.

[1] A Chinese legendary paradise on earth.
[2] Travelers were obliged to ford or hire boats to cross the big rivers such as Ōi and Tenryū because the government, for the defense for Edo, did not permit bridges over them. Whenever there was continued rain and the river water rose, travelers had to wait until the flood subsided.

Since the Imperial Restoration, great advances in civilization have been made—the abolition of clans and organization of prefectures, the discarding of swords by samurai, permission for commoners to assume family names and to ride horses in public, revision of the law, organization of the army and navy, encouragement of learning, and the beginning of railways, telegraphy, and Western-style printing. Indeed, it is impossible to enumerate all the aspects of civilization that have been introduced. Particularly that great war we won last year which exalted our empire's glory is something that no Western scholar could have dreamed of 30 or 40 years ago. We did sometimes boast that our land would show its glory across the seas and even the five great continents would be thus and thus. However, all these were simply rhetoric, no more real or serious than the superlative adjectives in a poem. We did not expect such things to come true. But here we are witnessing these glorious events. It is a happiness miraculously bestowed upon us.

Recalling the past and observing the present, I feel that I am watching a dream. My happiness is so intense, there is nothing I can do but shed tears. Long life is a blessing; I am witnessing this wonderful turn of events because I have lived to celebrate my sixtieth birthday. The one sorrow I suffer is the loss of my old friends with whom I had shared the same ideals and hardships and longings but who unfortunately died early and were unable to see the realization of our dreams and share our joy today.

I admit that I am one of those who, 30 or 40 years ago, talked rather irresponsibly and used baseless arguments. But today we realize that those arguments were not unfounded after all; we were not simply talking off the tops of our heads, for all and more have come true. How should I describe this feeling? I am simply happy. I shall now turn myself to a sober subject and give you some advice.

I have been boasting that I have actually watched the 40-year drama from its very first act, but when you stop and consider the nature of civilization, it is obvious that it is a progressive thing which will not cease in a hundred or even a thousand years. This 40-year drama has not ended. It has simply reached a juncture between acts or the beginning of a new plot. What kind of program is to be revealed in the next 40 years and whether the new act will be exciting or boring will depend on the skills of those who will perform in the new drama. You must still be dissatisfied with our country, and you will certainly be enthusiastic about the daily progress that you will contribute to. For this, you must always be conscious of what is needed, and you must seek ways to fulfill it. I have no questions about your personal thoughts, and as long as you are conscientious students of the new learning, you will be eager to work for your country. I am depending on you to carry on the work and show me the results while I am still in this world or, if necessary, after I am gone.

You must delve deeply into your studies and also familiarize yourselves widely in all aspects of society, down to the minor details. Establish your personal independence and that of your households; then observe and contemplate the various facets of the society around you. Finally, at this point, plan with confidence an undertaking for the benefit of the nation; launch it at once and start a new enterprise. Or, if circumstances do not allow its undertaking, talk about it and write about it to circulate your idea to the public. Perhaps your idea will surprise the general public who will consider it an empty idea and a dreamer's wish. However, I assure you that the result of scholarly reasoning will always prove correct. Your "empty" ideas in time will prove true. This I will guarantee. And in 30 or 40 years when you are to celebrate your own sixtieth birthday, you will proudly announce that your former ideas which people thought absurd had been realized, and you will congratulate yourselves. I will forgo all modesty and predict that you will follow in my footsteps. However, this is not an occasion to discuss what should be studied and taken up in your future. That I shall leave entirely to your own judgment.

Today, I have spoken at great length. It was meant to be a speech in appreciation of your kind words on this happy day, and my speech has turned into an old man's self-indulgent ramblings. I am grateful for your tolerance.

31
One Hundred Discourses
of Fukuzawa

Two short pieces representing Fukuzawa's philosophical
and seldom revealed thoughts are presented here. In his
younger days, he was too occupied with the immediate
problems of life and society to discuss philosophy, except
in statements on his basic attitude toward life. In his
old age, society and his own life having settled down to
allow him some leisure, he decided to write on more
fundamental problems.

Fukuzawa was basically a scientist and his thought
pattern was always precise and clear-cut. He was also a
scientist of the nineteenth century. He believed that
because human nature was basically good, with the
newly acquired powerful tool of science, human life
was bound to improve toward a better order and
greater happiness.

"One Hundred Discourses of Fukuzawa" contains
short pieces on various subjects of human life from
philosophy to advice on social behavior and explanations of things people were often puzzled about. These
essays appeared in *Jijishimpō* every few days over a
period of abouto ne and half years, and were republished
in book form (1897). The book went into 70 to 80
printings and sold for many years after Fukuzawa's
death.

"Fukuō Hyakuwa" (福翁百話), 1896. *Jijishimpō*, March 1, 1896–July 4, 1897. *Fukuzawa*
Yukichi Zenshū, vol. 6, pp. 197, 207–9, 211–16.

Preface

Since the opening of the country 40 years ago, our civilization has advanced greatly, but true civilization will be attained only when the intellect and moral virtues of the entire population advance with it. Only then may we expect the consolidation of our nation.

By nature I enjoy receiving guests, and my friends are widespread. Our conversations have often strayed to various issues—how often, it is simply countless. After my guests left, these rambling conversations were quickly forgotten. However, I came to regret this, and since last year, I began to write down some of what I did remember of the conversations. I continued this, stealing a little time here and there, until the short pieces somehow accumulated to about one hundred.

I have called them "One Hundred Discourses of Fukuzawa" and have decided to publish them in *Jijishimpō* beginning this March. However, because of the time required to proofread the manuscript, it will probably appear two or three times a week.

My objectives will be realized if you readers will find in these simple essays ways to improve your lives at home and in society, leading to your independence and that of your households and making them the foundation of our nation.

Fukuzawa Yukichi

February 15, 1896

1. The Universe

Who created the universe? Or did it come to be of its own? This is the question that religious theorists have argued ceaselessly. Leaving those arguments aside, I prefer to simply observe the universe as it is and marvel at its beauty, its infinite greatness, the refinement and precision of its structure, and the permanence and regularity of its rules. When I seriously think about the universe, I never cease to wonder. The more I think, the more mystified I become, until I am simply lost in myself. In such a state of wonder, some will believe this infinite state to be the power of a god or the truth of the Buddha. Such beliefs are quite understandable.

I see and feel all the phenomena with my five senses, and they inspire my soul, but I am inconvenienced, for I have no name for these wonders. And not being acquainted with gods or the Buddha, I cannot call them by such names. Then, I remembered that there was a custom, which I was familiar with since my childhood, to call anything beyond human power "Heaven" [ten] or "Heaven's Way" [tendō]. Therefore, I will use this term to represent the wonders of the universe. This Heaven, Heaven's Way, Heaven's Wonders, Heaven's Will, and such terms are commonly used everyday, but this Heaven is not the blue sky above us or the sun. It is used here to represent the immeasurable, unfathomable something with no beginning or end, infinitely big while infinitely minute, extremely strong and extremely certain, mysterious beyond human comprehension. And we are to represent all these with the one word "Heaven." Therefore, if someone should think of a more appropriate term, he may freely use it in place of Heaven.

If we use this word "Heaven," we find ourselves at a loss to describe anything beyond its extent and its power that are simply beyond human comprehension or imagination. Human beings are wont to say that the mountains are high and the oceans are deep, but these are but objects on the surface of the earth, and the earth is nothing more than a small lump of rock and dirt belonging to the sun, and this sun, too, is but one star among the many in the universe. All the twinkling little stars in the sky are suns, the number of which is beyond our counting. The Milky Way is simply a crowd of those stars shining in many layers and appears to the eyes as a blurred, whitish wave, just like rows of pine trees appearing like a dark belt when seen from a distance. The Milky Way may appear to be the farthest object in the sky, but beyond it, there are what are called "specks," which appear like white dots. These dots are probably crowds of stars just like our Milky Way.

Leaving those specks aside, even ordinary stars are at distances measured by millions and billions and thousands of billions of miles. The most distant stars are so far that the light they emit will take millions of years to reach the earth. Therefore, there may be some stars which died a million years ago, but their light is still being seen by our eyes. Also, there may be a star that was formed a million years ago, and its light is not visible to us yet. So, their number is countless, their distances are infinite, and we cannot tell the time of their birth or disappearance. Thus the vastness of the universe is beyond our power of description, and at the same time its preciseness and minuteness are beyond us, and we are simply lost as to how to describe them.

The whales of the oceans are big and the little shrimps in the brooks appear to be small. But even these little shrimps are huge in comparison to other creatures, even more so than the whales against the shrimps. The bacteria swarming in a drop of water indeed exist in the millions, more numerous than the human population of the world. These microbes, when dissected and studied, will be found to have fibers, and various organs for digesting nourishment and for reproduction. And in the future when our microscope techniques advance, these bacteria may be discovered to be carrying even smaller microbes as parasites, and the bacteria we know may come to be regarded as comparatively large and coarse organisms. Thus advancing more and more to minuteness, there seems to be no end.

However, what really impresses us is not these extremes of largeness and minuteness. It is the mystery of the everlasting, infallible law that governs the universe with never an error. Our attempts to solve what cannot be solved will bring us only to the deeper realization of the limits of human intellect.

3. Heaven's Ways Are Kind to Man

The laws that govern all the phenomena of man and nature in this universe are basic and absolute. However, the question whether they are kind to man or not has been unanswered by those who have pondered this question since time immemorial. When the great historian T'ai-shih Kung exclaimed, "Is Heaven's will kind or unkind?" I interpret his query as a momentary and bitter complaint of an unhappy man, who expressed his disillusionment through historical narrations. The ways of Heaven or nature in infinite space and time cannot be judged by a few hundred or a few thousand misfortunes which occurred in a time span of a mere hundred or thousand years of history. One must conclude that T'ai-shih Kung failed to grasp the vastness of Heaven's ways. Such superficial views should be disregarded as worthless.

But another view will argue: "Heaven's ways are wonderful and generous. It ceaselessly provides the four seasons; all living things prosper, and men can till fields and produce food, weave and make clothing, and all conditions are favorable for human living. But the beauty is on the surface only. When the reverse side is examined, we find it is not necessarily so. For instance, in human life—we shall not discuss its briefness as we shall resign ourselves to Heaven's decree on this point—when one is born, the pain a mother suffers is excessive, and when one dies, again, the pain and suffering are severe. Even when an illness is not fatal, too often the pain becomes so severe that the suffering patient prays for death. Even more cruel are inherited disorders and communicative diseases. Year after year, countless innocent souls are lost as if nature were carrying out a plan to murder them all. If Heaven's ways are benevolent and charitable, it should prevent a mother who is prone to have a painful delivery from conceiving a child at all. Rather than killing a man after great suffering from illness, it would be much kinder not to have let him come into this world at all, for he was born to be murdered.

"The passage of the four seasons and the cycles of rains and winds may seem to be the usual state for our earth. But at times when the anger of Heaven visits us, strong winds and raging rains devastate cultivated fields and topple houses, and high waves sink ships and drown people. Such natural calamities are repeated year after year, or rather day after day, night after night, as we gather from news from other parts of the earth. The eruption of volcanoes and earthquakes are the extremes of disaster and the extent of the devastation they cause can be cruel and heartless, which is perhaps an understatement.

"Then turning our attention to society, great injustices will be found. If Heaven's ways are amicable and they intend to assure peace for mankind, the foremost condition would be to provide human hearts with a kind nature, but in reality there are many evil men in the world. Murderers, thieves, and prostitutes are nonhumans in the form of human beings. We may disregard them for the moment. But even those who are considered gentlemen

[243]

will often maneuver to their own advantage in politics, in financial transactions, or in their relations with others. When they establish a government, in the name of loyalty to the nation they place their personal interests first. When they establish a family, the family becomes a convenient device to justify placing one's own interest before others. The worst give no thought to inflicting pain to others and think only of their own interests.

"In the worst case, men will establish a government, proudly display their self-centered concerns, and when two nations quarrel over the differences in their interests, they might take up arms and declare war. The nation that kills the greater number and is the more deceiving wins the honor of becoming a "power," and among the leaders of that power, those who design the most ruthless strategy and succeed are called politicians and strategists, and are honored as great patriots. And the whole world does not wonder at such behavior. We might as well believe that Heaven's ways will not stop people from becoming evil but that it is inclined to urge people toward evil. The human being is said to be a piece of flesh wherein reside Heaven's ideals, but where is the idealism?"

These arguments have their own reasoning, backed by facts. However, from what I see, such arguments are too narrowly confined and their observations are limited to very short time spans. These theorists have not conceived the vastness of Heaven's ways.

Let us carefully consider human history since its beginning. There has been progress but never regression. Advancement and improvement are seen only in human beings. Of course, there are instances of suffering, such as difficult childbirth, painful diseases, and contagious diseases. However, the human body as bestowed by nature has no innate disease. When one becomes ill, it is from human doing. Because of lack of knowledge, human beings succumb to temptation and violate the laws of hygiene and thus harm their own health. The health of wild birds and beasts who follow the laws of nature is proof of this. Human beings possess lust and desire, but they are also provided with the unusual intelligence which is capable of conceiving eternal truths. Our intelligence will eventually overcome lust and desire to protect the body and by handing this practice down generation

[244]

after generation, some day we will doubtlessly return to the original state free of disease. The case of communicative diseases is more obvious. Infection by these diseases is caused by nothing but ignorance. As soon as medical knowledge spreads in society, people will discover that the prevention of contagious diseases is as easy as building houses or wearing overcoats to avoid rain and wind. Even at the elementary and superficial level of medicine today, some steps have been taken. Greater improvements can be expected in the future. (Bacteriology, though still a fledgling science, is a good example.)

Blaming Heaven's will for storms, earthquakes, and other natural disasters is the extreme of absurdity. Storms and earthquakes are necessary natural phenomena, but human beings are still ignorant of the necessity and foolishly fear their destructiveness. Human ignorance of this necessity may be tolerated, but Heaven always gives warnings for every movement without fail, and yet people are still too ignorant to interpret them to avoid disaster. This ignorance is like receiving a letter from a friend and being unable to read it. Even in the present state of ignorance, meteorological studies have made advancements in forecasting winds and rains, and ships, too, have begun to use steam to avoid disasters on the seas. When we compare this situation with what it was like a hundred years ago, our new-found ability to forecast natural phenomena does give hope of some day discovering ways to forecast and prepare for volcanic eruptions and earthquakes.

Then, in society, people's quarreling over personal profits and nations contending with each other with the use of arms may sound reasonable. But one must remember that, it has been only 5000 or 6000 years since the beginning of the history of mankind, which means that human intellect is still in its infancy—two or three years old if human history is to be considered one hundred. Because these "little children" are living in groups and acting at will throughout the world, their shameless or unruly behavior is not unexpected. The so-called financial wizards hoarding money and politicians making names for themselves are like greedy children fighting over a piece of cake or a toy. Some of them reign as boss over a gang of children, never conscious of embarrassment, obligation, or even of the value of things, or their personal

[245]

advantage in being leader, simply being proud and showing off. The difference is simply that these are infants of two or three years and the others are children of thirty or forty. The difference is only in their appearance. If these grown-up children are fond of fighting within their own gangs, by extension it will be natural for them to pick fights with other gangs. The nations of the world are formed by these groups of children who pick fights with other groups of children—what we call war. This is something unavoidable in children's psychology, and my only consolation is to place my hopes on the distant future in a thousand or ten thousand years and to leave all to the ways of Heaven and to wait for these children to mature.

Some may consider it unscholarly to dream of a thousand or ten thousand years in the future just for one's peace of mind. But my dreams are not necessarily empty dreams. I base my dreams for the future on facts of the past. Granting that Heaven's ways are true and that human beings are a progressing and improving species, forecasting the future in several thousand or several tens of thousand years with the examples of factual human progress of the past 5000 or 6000 years does not strike me as absurd. In comparison with the eternity of the universe, these 5000 or 6000 years are like only the first year of a century or perhaps even less than a day. Even then, in these brief spans of time, society has progressed constantly without an instance of regression. Ancient men were ignorant of hygiene, and many died young. The gradual disappearance of barbarians in modern times is proof of this. Civilized people are different. The extension of the human life span with the progress of science has been clearly proven by statistics.

Prehistoric men feared fire and water; they only sought to escape them. Today we would rather make use of them for our own convenience. Steam power and hydroelectric generation are good examples of this. Ancient man had little regard for human life and lacked compassion. In extreme cases, they boiled their fellow men to death, or, even worse, they devoured human flesh. In contrast, modern man is kinder and dislikes slaughter. A good example is the agreement to care for wounded soldiers on the battlefield. Ancient man lived like slaves if they were not actual slaves to one individual, a king or lord. Today we are

[246]

mostly able to live freely within the confines of law. Ancient man dealt with crime by resorting to torture and physical punishment. Modern man is working toward the abolition of such punishment. Ancient man wore coarse clothing and lived on coarse food. Food and clothing today are designed for comfort and beauty. Ancient society was threatened by many enemies, and people had to be on their guard at all times. Society today is safer, and we are able to enjoy leisure. There are countless instances of a better world. Whatever disagreements there may be, it will be difficult to prove that the barbarian conditions of a thousand years ago are superior to today's civilization. One need not say a thousand years—even a hundred years ago will show a great difference in the comforts enjoyed today.

But there still are people who think the present is declining and pine for the "good old days." These are the people whose minds are limited and do not realize the improvements of the whole or the happiness of a great proportion of the general populace. The ramblings of these men are not worth giving second thoughts to.

To summarize, we are now living on a new and primitive earth and our human society is still the haunt of ignorance and immorality, and nothing will satisfy our ideals, but these deficiencies are not to be blamed on Heaven. They should be blamed on mankind. Yet, our inner nature is good, and we have the intelligence to seek progress and improvement. When this inner nature is developed, people will advance and reach the state of harmony. With the experience of the past 5000 or 6000 years, human capacity for progress has been proved. We may look with full hope to the future in several million years. I need not make my prediction for such a distant future. Let us think of a mere 5000 or 6000 years in the future which is the length of the history of mankind. We can predict great improvements and happiness for our descendants. Suppose someone 5000 or 6000 years hence looks back to the present day; he will certainly pity our ignorance, vice, stupidity, and crudeness, much like our pity for the savages and cannibals of bygone days.

To conclude, the human beings who inhabit this earth today, even if they call themselves civilized, are in truth children still at the start of their growth—fledglings crowding this fresh planet, a young earth and childlike people. It is too much to expect perfection or maturity from them. However, looking on our past, I am convinced that we are increasing our state of happiness, proof of Heaven's kind ways for man. We do have a capacity for progress, although we have had our times of happiness and unhappiness. When we compare ourselves with our predecessors, we seem fortunate, but people in the future will probably find our present state quite backward. Still, the civilization we enjoy today is a precious legacy, the product of our ancestors' labors. And in turn, it is our duty as human beings to leave the results of our labors to posterity.

32
Fukuzawa's Last Testament

Fukuzawa was past 60 in 1896, an advanced age in those days. Many of his colleagues had already died, and Fukuzawa was beginning to think of his own death and the future of Keiō Gijuku. Therefore, when the old members of Keiō alumni and colleagues held a meeting on November 1, 1896, which was called Kaikyū Kai (Party for Reminiscing on the Past), Fukuzawa was naturally led to reminiscing on the past and the approaching day when he would have to bequeath the school to the next generation. His words spoken then befit a last will and testament.

I am going to speak on the genesis of Keiō Gijuku. This may turn into a good deal of boasting or self-flattery, but after all, my audience is composed entirely of men within my intimate circle who retain in their memory all that I am going to speak about; I do not feel obliged to be modest. I am sure that my reminiscences will stir particular sentiments within you all.

There is always happiness within hardship in this society. Thirty years ago when our colleagues left Okudaira estate in Teppōzu, moved into our new quarters in Shinsenza, and began a small school for the study of Western learning, we were in the midst of the wars of Imperial Restoration. Not a single person outside our group took interest in learning—least of all in Western

"Kihin no Sengen Chitoku no Mohan" (気品の泉源智徳の模範), 1896. *Jijishimpō* editorial, November 3, 1896. *Fukuzawa Yukichi Zenshū*, vol. 15, pp. 531–34.

learning, for it was at the height of the movement against foreigners. Scholars in Western learning were regarded as heretics and devils, and we were kept from associating with other circles, sometimes even exposed to physical danger.

But human nature is tough and stubborn. When people despised us so, we on our side were determined to outdo them. It would have been impossible to challenge them with force. In private we sneered at them for their ignorance and blindness; we purposely addressed topics they could not think of, did exactly what they hated to see done. We concentrated on the opposite of the usual ways of society. Our spirits were high, determined never to give an inch, ready to tackle the whole nation as our opponent. This was our singular determination at the time.

The reason for our firm stand was that the members of our group had early recognized the truth of Western civilization, and besides this cardinal philosophy of civilization we believed there was nothing to base our thoughts on—from our daily behavior and household management to the intricate problems of the national constitution. Thus we stood against all common beliefs and conventions or conservative doctrines.

Our public challenge to the whole generation—our promotion of the radical theories of the new civilization—was, after all, prompted in part by a recklessness or taste for conflict which resided in us. I am only beginning to realize this now as I recall the old days. But our recklessness was by no means without its merits. Our group at that time was not only opposing common ideas and conservative theories of the society in general; we sought to convert everyone to our way of thinking. In the pitch darkness that enveloped the nation, we were the only ones who held the one torchlight of civilization to indicate the true direction. For us there was only one direction to go: forward in spite of all the obstacles.

In the turmoil of warfare, all the schools of Western learning were closed: the school operated by the old shogunate was the first to go, followed by all the private schools which disappeared without a trace, and the new Imperial government could not be expected to do anything about education immediately. In all the provinces of Japan, there was only one place that continued to pursue Western studies: our Keiō Gijuku in Shinsenza.

[250]

People called our condition isolationism, but we regarded it as independence. And we likened it to Holland at the time of the Napoleonic wars when the whole country was occupied. But in faraway Dejima in Nagasaki, the national flag of Holland proudly flew, never lowered for even a day. Thus the Dutch proudly recall that the nationhood of Holland has never been broken since its establishment. The members of our group recalled this episode and likened Keiō Gijuku to Dejima which preserved the national flag of Holland, for Keiō Gijuku was preserving the lifeline of learning in Japan. They saw their role as a great mission and redoubled their pursuit of the importation of new knowledge.

Keiō Gijuku was able to add a new phase to the study of Western civilization. Books on world geography, history, law, political science, social sciences and economics, ethics, philosophy, and other subjects were obtained. The selection of Japanese words for some of the new terms in Western learning was actually made at Keiō Gijuku. For instance, *keizai* for political economy and *shūshingaku* for moral science were terms invented at Keiō. We also introduced the art of speech-making and holding of conferences, creating the word *enzetsu* for speech. In the face of strong opposition we began the new art of speech-making which has become common today. Steam was translated as *ki*, copyright was translated as *hanken*; if I begin to count all the contributions, there will be no end. Our group was united in its efforts, and we directed all our efforts to the promotion of civilization; we discarded the old and in its place promoted our innovations. Our energy was directed toward revolutionizing all phases of our society from the top to the bottom. But at the same time, we realized that our efforts were futile, considering our limited influence. After all, the innovations were no more than daydreams to us.

To our surprise we found that the Japanese people were both staunch and flexible. While retaining their own individuality they were quick to perceive where the advantages lay. Their minds had been redirected by the political revolution; they took to the new, and the development of civilization since has been stunning. Many of our daydreams have gone far beyond our dreams in reality, and our society is reaching toward a new Japan of the Meiji era.

This, indeed, is a miracle, a happiness beyond our simplest

wishes. Recalling the past and watching the present glory, I am touched, and only tears can express my feelings. I am fully aware that this is the trend of the times, but such results cannot be had without a cause. In enjoying these blessings, all I can do is to pay my respects to the great accomplishments of our forebears and be grateful for our heritage.

Since the time our school was in Teppōzu in the days of the old shogunate and then when it moved to Shinsenza and finally to its present location in Mita, the trials of our colleagues in their studies were true hardships, but looking around at society, we see that civilization is gradually gaining a hold, and society is steadily improving. This is a supreme happiness in life, incomparable with any other accomplishment, and this is a perfect example of the saying "There is happiness even in hardship."

However, our sentiments and greed have no limits. Keiō Gijuku today is functioning within the limits of its finances. Rather, it is doing what would be unthinkable in any other institution, whether public or private, with the limited financial means at its command. Yet, the times do not favor independent schools, and we are obliged to bear the limitations because of the financial restrictions.

Our lessons in the classrooms are more or less mechanical, and an increase in financial support will facilitate our activity. But what the members of our group value above all is noble character in men. This noble character is something beyond the usual definition in moral teaching—such as good and bad or right and wrong. It cannot be measured by law nor be controlled by it. It is something like a moral vigor and courage permeating the world [*kōzen no ki*] which Mencius discussed, difficult to define or to explain. However, unless one possesses this nobility in character, regardless of all the intelligence and skill one may have, the world will not recognize him as a gentleman.

Fortunately, Keiō Gijuku excels over other institutions on this point, and it has retained its peculiar character since its Teppōzu days, and we have never been accused of banality and vulgarity. This is something abstract that cannot be described in words nor pointed to with a finger. It is like that feeling which, in Buddhistic parlance, can only be communicated directly from mind to mind, without words. Or, when Keiō Gijuku is taken as a body, it is like the atmosphere that permeates this body. In short, it is the spirit or inspiration which is transmitted from senior members to junior members.

I notice that my hair has grown white, and so has that of the members assembled here. Human life is uncertain. We lost some years ago such colleagues as Obata Jinzaburō, Fujino Zenzō, Ashino Kenzō, Murao Shin'ichi, Kotani Shinobu, and Baba Tatsui. More recently, we lost much younger men such as Fujita Mokichi, Fujimoto Jukichi, Wada Yoshirō, Koizumi Nobukichi, Nomoto Teijirō, Nakamura Sadakichi, and Yoshikawa Taijirō. The death of a man may be likened to dying firewood. After one's death, one's influences is said to stay like the warmth that remains in embers, but still I fear that the warmth, too, will expire in time.

We have lost many fine men from our group, and now you and I are growing old as well. When, according to the laws of nature, we depart from this world one after another, what will become of those young men we leave behind? These active men with their inborn ability, I have no doubt, will maintain the legacy left by us senior colleagues. But to preserve the noble character of the whole institution and to guard its dignity is our special duty as senior members. We must attend to this till the end of our lives, and still I fear we will not be successful. Will it be possible for us to fulfill this duty within in our lifetime, and will we see the second generation succeed our positions? When I contemplate all this, I cannot help feeling deep pain and concern, despite the pleasures of watching today's wonderful developments.

I shall never be satisfied to leave Keiō Gijuku a mere institution of learning; I aspire to make it the springhead of noble character and a model of intellect and virtue for the whole nation. In practice, this spirit shall be the foundation of each member's household, as well as of society and the nation. I do not wish this to end up as a subject of mere talk. It should inspire everyone in his daily behavior and make our school a model and leader of society.

I am taking the opportunity of this gathering to express my thoughts. They are much like a last testament, and I entrust them with you.

[253]

33
Publication and Certification of Textbooks

In a recent editorial, I discussed why the adoption of elementary school textbooks should be the free choice of each school. I shall comment further on this subject today.

The idea of publishing all books for instructional purposes at national expenditure was brought up in the House of Peers some time ago, and it is said to be gaining support because of such shameful incidents as those in Niigata Prefecture. The basic argument behind the use of national funds is that school textbooks are directly related to the educational results of the citizenry and by extension to the rise and fall of national power. Also, the books used in schools today often have misprints, and some parts even use ambiguous expressions, and are often overpriced for families to purchase. Therefore, the government is to devise appropriate means for publishing perfect editions at national expense.[1]

What exactly is meant by "appropriate means" is not clear, but as long as national funds are to be used, the Ministry of Education is probably to be commissioned to compile and publish the books. If that is the case, we will be returning to a practice that was tried once in the past, and there is nothing new about it. I have no objection to who actually writes the books, but the officials of the Ministry of Education are of average intelligence

"Kyōkasho no Hensan Kentei" (教科書の編纂検定), *Jijishimpō* editorial, April 2, 1897. *Fukuzawa Yukichi Zenshū*, vol. 15, pp. 642–45.

[1] The government policy moved gradually toward absolute control, beginning with the inspection of all textbooks for prevention of inappropriate books (1886), then sanctioning for approval and recommendation of good quality books (1892), and finally compulsory use of government-compiled textbooks in all schools, including private schools (1903), which continued till 1948.

with no particular ability in scholarship or expanse of knowledge. It is very doubtful that they can produce ideal textbooks. In the present system, a good number of very unsatisfactory books is being used. But from past experience, the publications of the Ministry of Education were more or less of the same quality, and they were anything but perfect. We should not try to take the easy way out by entrusting all to the government, for one will be chided for idealizing past dreams.

What would happen if we turned to individual scholars and educators for the writing of textbooks? There certainly are some very appropriate works and translations among books already published. However, the ministry has established a rule to authorize publications. This authorization is harmless as long as the inspection is kept within bounds. But in actual practice, whenever an inspector, from personal prejudice, regards a book with distaste or some circumstance creates difficulties, the book is rejected without the least hesitation. In such a situation, none of the truly independent scholars will ever fall in their favor.

(For instance, Mr. Fukuzawa's books were all rejected several years ago when the Ministry of Education implemented its authorization policy. In fact, every one of his books, regardless of its subject matter, was rejected. He had never cared for the authorization of his books; he was only deeply saddened by the deteriorated condition of the ministry and the attitudes of the petty officials. The ones who took part in the inspection must still be living, and they probably remember the incident.)

At any rate, those men who are commissioned or hired by the ministry to write textbooks will be people below the ordinary officials, and as they are to write the books according to the will of the higher-ups, we cannot expect ideal results. An attempt at producing textbooks with government money will not result in anything worthwhile.

Financially, however, this way of textbook production will make the lowering of prices possible. But because the government cannot go into the retail business, the sale of the books will have to be consigned to professional booksellers. And because the shops which obtain the commission will monopolize the market and reap large profits, there will no doubt be another show of ugliness between the shopkeepers and the officials. The result simply will

be to concentrate the present unseemly practices of many outlying areas in the capital, and most likely the practices will grow
worse. This, in other words, is killing small worms and giving
comfort to the big worms—a ridiculous policy.

Therefore, I believe that this publishing and selling of textbooks
at government expense is entirely uncalled for; the production
and choice of textbooks should all be left free to each school,
with the Ministry of Education limiting its activity to an inspection to prevent truly objectionable books from being adopted.
And concerning this inspection, there is one more thing I must
point out: It is impossible to produce a perfect textbook. Even
if such a textbook existed, it would be impossible to guide pupils
solely by the power of the book. Therefore, the inspection of the
ministry should be limited to rejecting harmful books only, and
the harmless books should be left unrestricted. As a metaphor,
in lectures on hygiene, one will warn against unrestricted
eating and drinking, but to go beyond it and to recommend good
food and good clothing would be superfluous. The same goes for
the law for electing Diet members. The law will have to set
qualifications, but beyond that, all men have the right to vote
except when one is insane or an idiot or a criminal.

To look for higher standards of living, to improve the health
standards of the people, and to raise the standards of election
and have men of higher quality elected are desirable goals, but
all these will be impossible to realize in practice. In children's
education too, such impertinent activities as gambling games
and the reading of cheap love stories should not be permitted, but
at the same time, no effort should be wasted on endeavors such
as making every child a strict patriot and piously dutiful to his
parents or a national hero and champion fighter. Such excessive
expectations of all children is like trying to make a rice plant
blossom out with peony flowers—a wasteful attempt. Such being
the basic truth of education, in the inspection of textbooks, too,
elimination should be limited to those narrow-minded and
extreme statements of old-school scholars and those clearly mis-
leading materials for children even if by contemporary writers.
Let the others pass, and allow individual school administrators
to make their own choices.

Men of the world have a better sense of choice than one might expect. They know what they want and do not need coaching from the side. If the Ministry of Education were unreasonable and narrow-minded in its inspection and enforced its own prejudices mixed with personal foibles as they have in the past, it would only obstruct progress and education. They should reflect on their past and show penitence for their misdeeds.

34
Speech Delivered to the Students on the Reorganization of the Schools

In the reorganization referred to, all the sections of Keiō Gijuku from the university down to the high school and elementary school were brought together into one integral system which was called *ikkan kyōiku*. A vital reason for the integration was the very small number of students in the university section, causing a great financial burden on the entire Keiō system. Up to this time, Keiō high-school graduates earned a diploma, and it was regarded by the public as proof of the highest scholarship, second only to the Imperial University graduates. Keiō high-school graduates had little incentive to spend three more years in university, and there were very few applications from outside because of the proficiency in English required to study under American professors.

The reorganization encouraged a large number of Keiō high-school graduates to continue on to the university section. Also, the public gradually came to appreciate the advantage of higher education in general business. The number of students in the university section increased, and the financial burden was lightened. A new attempt at raising the endowment fund was successful, and from this time on Keiō Gijuku was

"Meiji 30 nen 9 gatsu 18 nichi Keiō Gijuku Enzetsukan ni te Gakuji Kaikaku no Mune o Honjuku no Gakusei ni Tsugu" (明治三十年九月十八日慶応義塾演説館にて学事改革の旨を本塾の学生に告ぐ), 1897. *Jijishimpō* editorial, September 21, 1897. *Fukuzawa Yukichi Zenshū*, vol. 16, pp. 105–12.

financially secure. However, all this must have been a heavy burden on Fukuzawa's health. About a year later in September, 1898, he suffered a stroke and though he recovered once, he was to suffer another attack and die on February 3, 1901.

While you students were away on summer vacation, this school underwent a major reorganization in its system of education and administration, and beginning this term, we will endeavor to carry out the changes as much as circumstances will allow. The details are what Mr. Hatano has just explained, but in brief, Keiō Gijuku University will be the top goal of education with the high school and intermediate school joined to it as much as possible. Under the new rule, graduation from Keiō Gijuku will require completion of the university course. Also, the new rule stipulates that Yōchisha is to be strictly for the education of children, and anyone beyond the stipulated age will continue in the intermediate school. This is the essence of the reorganization.

When these changes are enforced, those who expected to graduate at the end of their high-school course will have to go on through the university course before graduating from Keiō Gijuku. It will be a long wait causing impatience on your part, perhaps. But the progress of civilization is not confined to material matters. The rule is that the human spirit and intellect, too, must develop.

For instance, the use of machinery has increased remarkably in recent years, and the tedious operations which the people in bygone days had abandoned as hopeless have now become easy work for ordinary mechanics, thanks to the invention of machines. These wonders are well known to people, but how did all this happen? It came simply from the advancement of industrial designers' skills or the development of their brain power.

The same has happened to education as with machines. Western studies, which a hundred years ago our predecessors had struggled to learn and, nearer at hand, my colleagues and I grappled with in our youth, has become easier among present-day scholars. The problems which we had worked on for three days and three nights with no time for sleep or food until we grew thin with fatigue and yet were unable to solve, the students of today will solve and learn in five minutes of work in a classroom. This means a general rise in the level of Western learning as a whole as well as in scholars' abilities.

Your studying in the university and completing the course will not be such difficult labor. It will be comparable to the young men of bygone days taking lessons in the reading aloud (*sodoku*) of the Four Books and Five Classics of Confucianism and after some progress, studies of Chinese history and other books, gradually advancing to composing their own essays, thus somehow being admitted into the society of Chinese scholars. Such a process is not much to be called a scholar's life work.

Here is the reason why I place so much importance on the university departments. I pray that you will all be truly self-respecting, prudent, and conscious of exactly where you stand in society, or what position you will be working in when you grow to be an important figure in it, and exactly how you will assure your personal independence and that of your household and thus indirectly assure the independence and honor of the country. Think over all the possibilities carefully until you become conscious of the necessity of education and the development of intellect. Then think over your own physical capacity and the conditions and needs of your household and family business. After all these considerations, once you determine your course of action, absorb yourself in it even at the risk of making sacrifices. It is my great wish that you will make the days of your youth meaningful, for they will never return again.

Encouraging the study of English language and culture has been a special feature of this school from its start, and we have never changed this policy. Among the opinions in society, there are some who believe that a foreign language is not necessary for the instruction in the new civilization, for though its science and ideas must be imported, its instruction may better be done in Japanese. This naturally should be considered as one proposition, and I have no desire to contend with it. We shall leave the discussion to the disputants in that field, but on our part, we shall go our own way. It may seem that the same results will be obtained from reading translations and listening to the teacher's explanations of the original. But our experience over the years has proved to us the difficulty of transmitting the exact concepts in Japanese; it is like "scratching an itch from outside the shoe." Expressed in another way, one could say that teaching a foreign subject in Japanese does not give real nourishment. This is the reason why education in this school is provided in English with English books.

I do not consider the above as only an immediate concern. If you cast your view to the future world trend, you will see that in the past century the improvements in transportation and rise in trade has brought about the domination of the English language. In fact, there are Frenchmen, Germans, and people other than the English who travel widely in the world. But these people, when visiting the South Sea Islands or South America and in trading with the natives, depend on English for communication. This is a well-known fact.

Therefore, we Japanese, inhabiting a country on the east edge of Asia and now opening the country to the world and encouraging our own people to learn the art of navigation and to travel abroad, are acting out a drama to make the seas on four sides our brothers and the five continents our neighbors. What should the resolutions of our people be? The first necessity in intercourse is language, both spoken and written. And whether to take Japanese or English as the vehicle of communication is everybody's concern. It would be most convenient for us to have the Japanese language honored for use throughout the world, but that is a futile wish. The only way will be for us to go out, make friends, learn their ways, and with the use of English conduct our business. But English should not be confined to business alone. Excluding scholars specializing in particular subjects or in need of extensive knowledge, all students from their first to the highest grade should study all subjects in English. It will be most advantageous for us, and I do not hesitate in my belief in this.

As a parallel, let us recall those ancient days when Chinese civilization was first introduced to Japan. At that time, there was no comparison between Japan and T'ang China in the sizes of the countries and the levels of cultural advancement. Among our countrymen, the energetic ones would go to China, and at home, visiting Chinese scholars and missionary-priests were welcomed for the importation of their scholarship. The result had a remark-

[262]

able effect. Even to this day after more than a thousand years, Chinese learning has practically monopolized Japan's scholarly circles, and the word scholar has come to imply scholars in Chinese and nothing else; illiteracy was synonymous with ignorance in Chinese; there was no learning in Japan except Chinese learning. Japan was overwhelmed by the superior civilization of China, and as a natural development, we paid homage to it and assimilated it. Today we are regarded as a nation with the same language as China, an irrefutable fact.

Then, in the present century, some 40 years ago, Japan opened contact with various countries of the civilized world, and with the aid of modern transportation, we have been actively engaged in communications with many peoples, the ease and frequency of which is incomparable with the communication that our ancestors had with China. One may recall the repeated attempts that Kibi Daijin made before finally reaching China, and the fact that Abe no Nakamaro was never able to return home to Japan.[1]

In contrast to such ancient tales of difficulties, the students of today can go abroad and return home several times a year. Because of the freedom and frequency in transportation, I guarantee that foreign language and culture, particularly of the English-speaking peoples or the Anglo-Saxon language and culture, will prevail, and some day dominate our cultural circles, and people will say there is no learning in our country besides English learning.

Your relating to English-speaking peoples today does not entail the hardships that Kibi Daijin and Abe no Nakamaro had to endure. Besides, Chinese learning has come to its end with the opening of the country, and it has become obsolete. This is its fate dictated by the times, on which no one may hold a vestige of doubt. Therefore, the only learning that students today should take interest in is the English language and English civilization, which I call *jitsugaku*. There will be no way open to you but to master it and identify yourselves with it. Anywhere in this country, scholars like you who identify themselves with English civilization will be the only ones to gain the reputation of true scholars.

---

[1] Kibi Daijin, full name Kibi no Makibi (693–775). Reached China after several shipwrecks. Studied there and returned to Japan where he rose to the rank of Daijin (minister). Abe no Nakamaro (701–70). Shipwrecked on his return to Japan and was forced back to China were he became a T'ang official, never to return home.

The importance of English and English civilization in the world today is as explained above, and their benefit to individual students is also great. When a student first enters a school, he always comes with certain ambitions of what to study in the first year, what subjects to take in the second year; for every year he has an idea of what he wants to study until the fifth and seventh years. After graduation, he must find a position of his choice in order to fully make use of the ability he has cultivated in his many years of study. He may not reveal his ambitions to others, but they are clear in his mind. It must be the same with all young men.

However, in this transient world, one cannot predict in the morning what awaits at night. Even more unpredictable will be the future in five years or ten years. One's parents may become ill; the household business may have some ups and downs. Countless unforeseen events compel too many students to abandon their schooling halfway. But amid their misfortunes, the students are at least able to retain what they learned during the few years they were in school, which is exactly what the saying points out: Any skill will help in need. Therefore, it will be a wise policy to keep this in mind and choose one's subjects accordingly, preparing oneself for emergencies. At present the necessity for English is growing more acute daily in politics, in the military, in business, and in industry. And even those who are versed in new ideas with some education of the new school, unless they are able to read and converse in English, are regarded as useless, and no one will be interested in hiring them. For instance, in many of the commercial and manufacturing companies, when they consider a prospective employee, the first test they give to evaluate his ability and personality is in the English language. If his English is good, he is usually employed without further inquiries. Therefore, if a student must forfeit his education due to some personal reasons, if he has acquired skills in English, he will find it to his advantage when he seeks his way in the future. A skill will help one's living, as the saying goes, and English is the best and most powerful skill. This is the reason why I have been encouraging English for years, and you will never regret following my advice.

I shall next refer to the reorganization of the school administration. Supervising the dormitories on and off campus, the students in lodging houses, maintenance of the school buildings, overseeing the dining facilities, the food, ventilation, water, and general hygiene are most important. They are the responsibility of the administrative office. The staff attends to its duties day and night, but in a private school, the personnel are always insufficient. Even the teachers cannot confine their attention to classroom teaching alone. From the dean down to the faculty members, all have to keep their minds on order on the campus, aiding the administrative officers wherever their attention does not reach. And they will not overlook anything wrong on or off campus, however trivial it may seem.

I feel my age now, and the vigor of the past days is gone, but I am still blessed with good health. I at times make the rounds of the campus and personally meet the students and advise them on what should be pursued and what should be stopped. In short, we senior members of the school will give our best, but there is another, more important factor in raising the school spirit which you must not forget. That is the effort you students give in caring for yourselves and in governing your own behavior with the spirit of independence. Without it, whatever people around you may do, all our efforts will simply be lost.

There are worthless and servile men who depend on others and have no ideas of their own. They correct their behavior only when scolded by their superiors, and yet cheat on the side when no one is looking. This is a slavish attitude, deserving none of our attention. I trust there are no such people among our students. But at times there might be some among the new students who are not acquainted with our spirit. I want our senior students to give them proper guidance and show them the beauty of our school spirit through the self-government of the students so that we may all stand proud before the nation. This independence and self-governing spirit must not be confined to life at school. It should guide you through life, in your daily activities and family life.

For these reforms in the school order and in the administration, designed for the growth and expansion of our school, the immediate need is the funds to support them. A few years ago, at the inauguration of the university departments, many friends donated funds totaling 100,000 yen. But that amount was not large enough to earn a sufficient interest to pay off our annual

[265]

debts. We have been spending a part of the principal every year, and now only 30,000 yen or so remains of the original fund. And now that we are expanding our facilities and administration, that 30,000 yen will most likely disappear within a year's time. Our senior alumni have decided to launch a fund-raising campaign again, and as they are already making preparations, it will probably have some effect before long.

Fund-raising by a school is like donation-gathering at temples, and it cannot be judged by ordinary laws of economics. Under normal economic conditions, education may be considered a kind of business transaction. The educator builds a schoolhouse, purchases books and instruments, and offers to teach. The students pay tuition, making it a fair business deal. However, in the present age anywhere in the world, an education of a fairly high order cannot be offered based only on tuition. It thus becomes the general rule to have people with wealth and understanding donate funds to cover the deficit and thus enable the school to continue. The students are, in a way, having someone pay part of their tuition and receiving an education at a reduced price.

This may seem to be a strange arrangement, but when one raises oneself above the ordinary worldly way of thinking and places one's mind on a higher or nobler level, the reason is not difficult to comprehend. There is a great variety of enterprises in society, but there can be nothing nobler than developing the natural gifts of men and helping them reach the highest point possible for each to attain. When we see a plant in the field in spring, we hope that it will grow to bear blossoms. More so with human children. Children should receive a proper education to attain full manhood and womanhood. This process is like the blossoms blooming and bearing fruit. Who in the world would not wish to give a helping hand and pray for their safe growth? This is the natural reaction of men's true hearts, and it is not an accident that there are many charitable people.

In Western countries the wealthy who have satisfied their needs in living and yet possess a surplus of funds donate generously to the education of young people. And this is apparently a common practice. The saying that there is no heartless devil anywhere in the world was probably coined in appreciation of this practice. The actual practice of this charity varies according to circumstances. A man of great wealth might put down millions in a lump sum and found and finance a university. Others might be willing but lack time or experience to take part in education and thus choose schools of their liking and entrust money to them, quietly satisfying themselves. All other small capitalists have a custom of donating an amount regularly according to what they can afford. This practice is much like the donations to Buddhist temples in our country for building and maintaining the temples.

We are envious of the way the private schools prosper in the Western countries. When our committee members begin campaigning for funds for our school, I am sure they will have in mind the many precedents in Europe and America. From what I observe of the present condition of our country and the level of advancement in people's culture I am confident of the campaign's success.

But there is one word I feel I must say to the students gathered in this hall. As I have said, the donations of the generous members of society for the maintenance of the school is from a pure spirit of service, and there are no ulterior motives involved. For the private person, it is a manifestation of a virtuous heart; for the public person, it is service to society. It is an honor to the donor, and the students who receive the benefit will not receive a *sen* but the valuable education of civilization. Both the donor and the receiver are thus sharing the honor in an ideal state of circumstances.

Analyzing the backgrounds of all activities and clarifying the exact relations of things is what a scholar should always be mindful of. The students who study in a school supported by donations have, in the final analysis, a part of their tuition provided for through an indirect act of charity. Therefore, the donors must be regarded as benefactors, and the beneficiaries must repay the kindness. This should be a natural response and duty whether the donors expect to be repaid or not. The reason is clear-cut, with no need for elaboration. As you advance in your studies in this school and benefit from the instruction, you must remember that a part of what you have received is due to the benefactors. You should always be grateful. Even after you graduate and leave the school, recall the circumstances of your studies and whenever you have the opportunity, endeavor to repay the favors directly or indirectly.

In a public school or government school, the expenses are borne entirely by taxes which the students, too, partly paid, and, therefore, no one will be regarded as a benefactor. On the other hand, the situation in a private school is different. Simply put, government and public schools owe their existence to law, and private schools depend on voluntary benefactors. Personal bene-faction must be repaid with personal benefaction. I trust that you will understand the logic here easily.

35
Fukuzawa's Moral Code

In the late 1940s, in the years of turmoil following World War II, the administrators of Keiō Gijuku distributed copies of "Fukuzawa's Moral Code" among the university students. This was their endeavor to provide a guiding principle for the students. But the students were greatly offended, for the "Moral Code" contained passages approving armed forces and a declaration that it was the people's duty to serve in them. Also, the code recognized the Imperial Household as something hallowed or inviolable. Both ideas had already been abrogated by the new constitution. The students collected copies of the distributed "Moral Code" and returned them to the school in protest, an incident that turned the code into a historical document.

The translation which follows is by Hata Misao and Alfred William Playfair, both professors of English language and literature at Keiō University, made around 1907. This version of the "Moral Code" was used for ten years between 1923 and 1933 in Keiō high schools and in the preparatory department of Keiō University and served the double purpose of teaching students English and Fukuzawa's philosophy. For the circumstances surrounding the compilation of this code, see the Introduction.

"Shūshin Yōryō" (修身要領), 1900. *Fukuzawa Yukichi Zenshū*, vol. 21, pp. 353–56.

It is a point about which there is a perfect unanimity of opinion throughout the realm, that it is incumbent upon every native-born subject of the Japanese Empire, without regard to age or sex, to pay homage to the Imperial House that has reigned throughout the ages and to show gratitude for its gracious favour that has accrued to us from its many virtues.

But when we ask the question how, in these days, and in what manner, the men and women of today should order their conduct in society, we find that as a rule such conduct is regulated by various systems of moral teachings which have been handed down from past ages. It is fitting, however, that moral teachings should be modified from time to time to keep pace with the progress of civilization, and it is but natural that a highly advanced and ever advancing society, such as we find in the world today, should be provided with a system of morals better suited to its needs than the antiquated teachings already mentioned. It is for this reason, we venture to think, that it has become necessary to state anew the principles of morals and rules of conduct, individual as well as social.

1. It is the universal duty of Man to raise his personal dignity and to develop his moral and intellectual faculties to their utmost capacity, never to be contented with the degree of development already attained, but ever to press forward to higher attainments. We urge it, therefore, as a duty upon all those who hold the same convictions as ourselves to endeavour in all things to discharge their full duty as men, laying to heart the principles of Independence and Self-respect[1] as the leading tenets of moral life.

2. Whosoever perfectly realizes the principle of Independence, both of Mind and Body, and, paying due respect to his own person, preserves his dignity unblemished,—him we call a man of Independence and Self-respect.

3. The true source of independence of life is to eat one's bread in the sweat of one's brow. A man of Independence and Self-respect should be a self-helping and self-supporting man.

4. Strength of body and soundness of health are requisites of life. We should, therefore, always take care to keep mind and body

[1] It was at this time that Independence and Self-respect became the motto of Keiō Gijuku.

[270]

active and well, and refrain from any action or course of life likely to prove injurious to our health.

5. It is man's duty to live out the whole of his allotted span of life. To take one's own life, for whatever reason, or under whatever circumstances, is an unreasonable and cowardly act, altogether abominable and entirely unworthy of the Principle of Independence and Self-respect.

6. To realize the Principle of Independence and Self-respect demands nothing short of an audacious, active, and dauntless spirit. It requires a combination in a man's character of courage and fortitude.

7. A man of Independence and Self-respect should not be dependent upon others for the determination of his own conduct. He should be intelligent enough to think and judge for himself.

8. To treat women as though they were inferior to men is a barbarous custom. Men and women belonging to a civilized society should love and respect one another as equals, each sex realizing its own independence and self-respect.

9. Inasmuch as marriage is one of the most serious events in human life, great caution should be observed in the choice of a partner for life. All human relations have their origin in marriage, in the loving and respectful cohabitation, till death comes to separate them, of husband and wife, neither of whom should interfere with the Independence and Self-respect of the other.

10. Such husbands and wives maintain towards their offspring a relation which is both full of hope and natural, since there are no extraneous elements introduced into the family and since parents and children are wholly and exclusively each the other's own. The love that binds them together is sincere and pure, and the keeping of this love unimpaired is the foundation of domestic happiness.

11. Children, also, should be trained to become persons of Independence and Self-respect, it being the duty of parents to take charge of proper bringing-up of their children so long as they remain in infancy. Children, for their parts, should yield due obedience to their parents, and make every effort to fit themselves to become persons of Independence and Self-respect when the time comes for them to step out into the world.

12. The ideal person of Independence and Self-respect deems

it incumbent on himself to go on learning even to his old age, and never to allow either the development of the Intellect or the Cultivation of the Moral Character to slacken or cease.

13. Society having both individuals and families as its units, it should be borne in mind that the foundation of a healthy society is to be found in the independence and self-respect of the family as well as of the individuals.

14. The only way in which social life can continue is for each Individual to keep unimpaired his or her own Independence and Self-respect as well as that of others. This may be done by respecting the rights and happiness of others at the same time that we seek our own happiness and protect our own rights.

15. To harbour resentment and to seek revenge is another barbarous and cruel practice, a relic of the Dark Ages. We should employ only just and upright means for clearing ourselves from shame or vindicating our honour.

16. Every man should be faithful in the discharge of the duties of his vocation. He, who, regardless of the importance of the trusts committed to him, neglects his responsibilities, is unworthy to be called a man of Independence and Self-respect.

17. Treat others with trustfulness. If you trust others, they will trust you in return. It is this mutual confidence alone that can enable Independence and Self-respect to be realized in ourselves or in others.

18. Courtesy and etiquette are necessary to the continuance of social life. They should be observed strictly, and yet with moderation.

19. It is an act of humanity, and one of the human virtues, to strive to extend to others that love which we feel for ourselves, to lighten the burdens, and promote the happiness, of our fellowmen.

20. Humanity should not be limited towards human beings only. It should prevent men from treating animals with cruelty, and make them refrain from needlessly taking the lives of fellow-creatures.

21. Since a taste for art and literature elevates the character as well as delighting the mind, and since it contributes indirectly to the peace and happiness of mankind, its acquirement should be deemed an object of the greatest importance for human life.

22. Wherever there is a country, there is a government. It is

the duty of the Government to administer the country, to establish and maintain military power to protect the people of the land, and to guarantee to the individual citizen the inviolability of life, property, honour, and liberty. In return for these benefits, it is the duty of the citizens to give military service and to contribute to the expenses of the nation.

23. If citizens are under obligation to serve in the national army and to pay their share of the national expenses, it is also, naturally, their duty and privilege to have a voice in the legislation and a right to control the governmental expenditure.

24. Citizens of Japan, of either sex, should never forget their supreme duty to maintain their national Independence and Self-respect, against all foes, and at the sacrifice of even life and property.

25. It is the duty of every citizen, not only to obey the laws himself, but to see that others obey them likewise, for this is necessary for the maintenance of the peace and order of Society.

26. The number of nations in the world is by no means small, and they differ from us in religion, language, colour, and customs. Yet they are our brothers. In our intercourse with them there should be no partiality, and no attempt at swaggering or boastfulness. Such conduct only leads us to despise other people and is wholly at variance with the Principle of Independence and Self-respect.

27. It is the duty of the men living to-day to improve the civilization and happiness which they have received from their forefathers and so to hand them on unimpaired to their posterity.

28. It is natural that men should be born into the world with varying degrees of intellectual and physical strength. It is the Province of Education to increase the number of the wise and strong, and to diminish that of the weak and foolish. In short, Education instructs men in the Principle of Independence and Self-respect, and enables them to form plans for putting the principle into practice.

29. Those who share our convictions, whether men or women, will do well to lay these teachings to heart. They should also strive to spread them throughout Society at large and thus to advance, hand in hand with the whole people, towards the state of greatest happiness.

[273]

References

The Autobiography of Yukichi Fukuzawa, translated by Eiichi Kiyo-oka. New York: Columbia University Press, 1966. The same book is published by The Hokuseido Press, Tokyo, as *The Autobiography of Fukuzawa Yukichi*, 1960 and 1981.

Birth of the University Section in Keiō Gijuku, edited by Eiichi Kiyooka and Kazuyoshi Nakayama. Tokyo: Keiō University, 1983.

An Encouragement of Learning, Fukuzawa Yukichi, translated by David A. Dilworth and Umeyo Hirano Tokyo: Sophia University, 1969.

Fukuzawa Yukichi Zenshū (Complete Works of Fukuzawa Yukichi). 21 vols. Tokyo: Iwanami Shoten, 1958–64.

A History of Keiō Gijuku Through the Writings of Fukuzawa, by Eiichi Kiyooka. Tokyo: The Hokuseido Press, 1979.

The Japanese Enlightenment: A Study of the Writings of Fukuzawa Yukichi, by Carmen Blacker. Cambridge: Cambridge University Press. (University of Cambridge, Oriental Publications No. 10).

Keiō Gijuku Hyakunenshi (The One-Hundred-Year History of Keiō Gijuku). 5 vols. Tokyo: Keiō University, 1958–69.

An Outline of a Theory of Civilization, by Fukuzawa Yukichi, translated by David A. Dilworth and G. Cameron Hurst. Tokyo: Sophia University, 1973.

Preface to the Collected Works of Fukuzawa, translated by Eiichi Kiyooka. Tokyo: The Hokuseido Press, 1980.

The Speeches of Fukuzawa, Translation and Critical Study, by Wayne H. Oxford. Tokyo: The Hokuseido Press, 1973.

Index

INDEX

France, 13–14
freedom, vii, viii–ix, 36, 68, 69–70
Fujino Zenzō, 253
Fujita Mokichi, 253
Fujiwara Seika, 106
Fukuzawa Hyakusuke, vii, 115–16, 119–22
Fukuzawa Sannosuke, vii, viii
Fukuzawa Yukichi: career, viii, xv, 233–34; children, xv, 47, 119, 122; death, xv, 260; education, viii; family, vii, viii, 35, 116; last testament, 253; overseas travel, viii; philosophy, 35–41, 47–54, 66–72, 240–48, 260, 270–73; as reformer, 15, 43, 91–92; statue, 227–28, 229; youth, vii–viii
Fuyutsugu, Dainagon, 105

Gakumon no Susume. See *Encouragement of Learning*
Gotoba Jōō, 106
government, 39–40, 71, 86–92, 94, 95–99, 107, 108, 193–94, 272
government officials, xiii, 82, 98–99, 115, 129–30, 153–54, 165–66, 176, 178–79, 181–82, 208, 225–26. *See also* scholars, in government

Hamano Sadashirō, 218
Harvard University, 217
Hata Misao, 269
Hayashi Dōshun, 106
Hayashi family, 167, 168, 174
Heaven, 36, 66–67, 241–46
heredity, 150, 154
Hoashi Banri, 119
Hōjō Yasutoki, 106
Holland, 11, 16n, 17, 44, 214–15, 251

illiteracy, 86, 106
Imperial Household: budget, 146–47, 176–77; and education, 136–39, 173–74, 176–77, 182–84, 185, 228; honors and awards, 144–45, 179–82; and Japanese culture, 140–45; position of, 133–48, 269
Imperial Rescript on Education, xiv–xv, 111
Imperial Restoration. *See* Meiji Restoration

Imperial University of Tokyo. *See* University of Tokyo
independence: personal, viii, x, 36, 48–49, 68, 95–96, 122, 149, 151, 160–61, 231, 265, 270–73; national, ix, x, xii, 36, 68–69, 76, 85–86, 93, 94–95, 99, 231, 235
industry, 99
innovation, 98, 126, 184
Itō Jinsai, 121
Itō Tōgai, 121

Jijishimpō, vii, xiv, 119, 133, 149, 163, 189, 211, 224, 227, 239, 240
Jiji Shōgen, 124, 125
jitsugaku ("real" learning), ix, 45, 68, 80, 82, 235, 263

Kadono Ikunoshin, 218
Kaisei Gakkō (Kaisei School), 170–71, 214
Kangaku-in, 105
Katō Hiroyuki, xiii
Katsuragawa Hoshū, 16, 211
Keiō Gijuku: curriculum, ix–x, 24–26, 28–29, 126, 127, 131, 202, 205–6, 261–62; development, 27, 31–32, 37, 212, 216, 228–32, 250–52, 259–60, 265–66; faculty, 24–26, 205–6, 217–19; foundation, vii, 15–16, 18–19; funding, xi, 201–2, 228–30, 252, 259–60, 265–68; independence of, 99, 171n, 214–16, 250; motto, 270; philosophy of education, ix, xi, 32, 132, 213–15, 231–32, 253, 261–62; regulations, 21–26, 28–30, 32–33; students, 21, 28, 203–4; Supporters's Association (Iji Shachū), 228; textbooks, x, 24n–25n, 29–30, 43, 213–14; tuition, 24, 28, 29, 266
Keiō University, vii, viii, xi, 217, 218, 259–60, 269
Kibi no Makibi, 263
Kings College of London, 5
Knapp, Arthur May, 217, 218
Koizumi Nobukichi, 253
Kotani Shinobu, 253
kunren (training), ix
kyogaku ("false" learning), ix
kyōiku (education), ix

INDEX